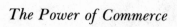

The Power of Commerce

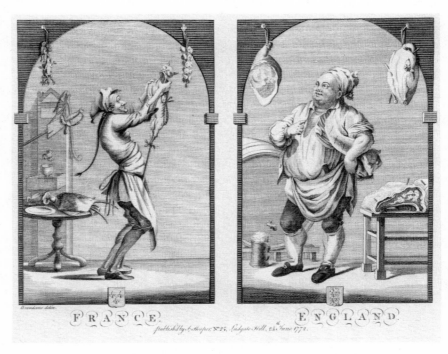

France and England, published 25 June 1772. British Museum Catalogue 5081.

❧❧❧THE POWER OF
COMMERCE

*Economy and Governance
in the First British Empire*

Nancy F. Koehn

CORNELL UNIVERSITY PRESS
Ithaca and London

First published 1994 by Cornell University Press.

Library of Congress Cataloging-in-Publication Data

Koehn, Nancy F. (Nancy Fowler), 1959–
    The power of commerce : economy and governance in the first
British Empire / Nancy F. Koehn.
        p.   cm.
    Includes bibliographical references and index.
    ISBN 0-8014-2699-5 (alk. paper)
    1. Great Britain—Commerce—History—18th century.   2. Great
Britain—Commercial policy—History—18th century.   3. Mercantile
system—Great Britain—History—18th century.   4. Great Britain—
Colonies—Commerce—History—18th century.   I. Title.
HF1533.K64   1994
382'.0941'009033—dc20   94-4314

Printed in the United States of America

⊗ The paper in this book meets the minimum requirements
of the American National Standard for Information Sciences—
Permanence of Paper for Printed Library Materials, ANSI Z39.48-1984.

For Colin, with all my love

Contents

The Triumph of Britannia, S. F. Ravenet after Francis Hayman, etching and engraving published by J. Boydell, 1765. Yale Center for British Art, Paul Mellon Collection. During the last years of the Seven Years War, Francis Hayman was commissioned to execute four huge canvases (each approximately twelve feet by eighteen feet, now all lost) depicting Britain's recent military history. Unveiled in May 1762, *The Triumph of Britannia* was originally hung in the Rotunda annex at Vauxhall Gardens. An allegory in celebration of Britain's naval mastery, the picture shows Neptune conducting a confident Britannia across a sea populated by sea nymphs. In her hands Britannia holds a medallion of George III, while the sea nymphs display medallions of victorious British commanders: Pocock, Boscawen, Hawke, Anson, Saunders, Howe, and Keppel. Describing Hayman's painting in May 1762, the *London Chronicle* summarized the accomplishments of these men: those "Admirals and Sea-commanders, who, during the late and present wars against France and Spain, have with a courage and conduct unstained by dishonour and inhumanity (and therefore peculiar to their country) extended the conquests, and raised the naval glory of Great Britain to a higher pitch than ever was known in this or any other age or nation."

Preface

THIS BOOK is about the relation between political power and the national economy during the first decade of a greatly expanded British Empire. It investigates how an industrializing and newly ascendant state, overwhelmingly victorious in the Seven Years War, grappled with the fiscal, economic, political, and perceptual imperatives of its triumph. I am interested in how, in the aftermath of an exhausting yet successful war, macroeconomic and political transitions shaped some of the most important problems, possibilities, and policies of dominion. The book is not a comprehensive reconstruction of the politics and economics of empire in the mid-eighteenth century. Rather, it is a rethinking of some of the central historiographic tenets of imperial decision making in the 1760s and 1770s.

The story opens in 1763, when Britain's victory in the Seven Years War gained it dominion over lands as vast and disparate as India and Canada, as tiny and scattered as Tobago and Senegal. It closes in 1773, when Parliament wrested primary control of the eastern subcontinent from the East India Company and, as compensation, allowed the great trading concern to consign 105,000 pounds of taxable tea to the port of Boston. In the ten years between the Peace of Paris and the Boston Tea Party, British ministers, members of Parliament, and the political nation faced a series of novel and urgent challenges.

As government officials and others apprehended them, these challenges were conditioned by the country's recent experience of international combat. Some dilemmas involved fiscal exigency: how, in the war's wake, to pay for victory and for the military and administrative responsibilities that accompanied the nation's newfound global position. Related problems concerned political economy: how to promote domestic economic growth, especially manufacturing capabilities, in an enlarged commercial empire. These problems were, as for other states at other times, closely intertwined. In 1763 Britons understood that the nation's global position was tightly bound to its transforming economy. This collective realization continued to influence imperial policymaking.

Broadly viewed, these imperatives of empire—with their attendant risks, responsibilities, and rewards—were not unlike those experienced by Americans and Russians in the wake of the Second World War or even by Japan in the aftermath of a different kind of global contest in the 1980s. Victory confronts individual states with the pressing geopolitical and economic demands of international authority. Founded on both power and plenty, global success also breeds political and perceptual transition at home. In each of these countries, governing elites and the larger citizenry struggle to decide who ultimately should superintend their nations' new strength. These societies have also tried to come to terms conceptually with their status and prosperity. In doing so, most have experienced an imperial schizophrenia, an often tempestuous blending·of ambition and angst regarding the future. In Britain after the Seven Years War—as in the United States after World War II— these collective and conflicted perspectives influenced national strategy.

My reconstruction of policymaking in the first British empire demands an integrated approach—one that reconstitutes imperial politics and economics as well as the dynamic between them. Oddly enough, this approach has few historiographic ancestors. Several scholars of military conflict have scrutinized Britain's involvement in the Seven Years War. A much larger group of historians has studied the war's colonial consequences. A few researchers have looked outward from Whitehall and Westminster to investigate the political rationale behind particular decisions involving the colonies. Students of eighteenth-century England have thus been left with an incomplete set of disaggregated analyses of the war and of specific decisions of empire made in the 1760s. Yet contemporary ministers, MPs, and journalists viewed these events not as discrete dilemmas but as interrelated parts of a general economic and political picture. It is from this interconnectedness that my book proceeds.

As important, the book resurrects the mid-eighteenth-century question of government objectives in the economy of empire in terms rather different from those that political and imperial historians have previously used. Many such scholars have employed mercantilism as the framework for analyzing eighteenth-century conceptions of dominion before 1776 and the publication of *Wealth of Nations*. A dense historiographic debate has grown up around the meaning of mercantilism in the seventeenth and eighteenth centuries.

This debate presents problems in several respects. First, scholarly sparring on narrow issues often precludes an overall reconstruction of contemporary attitudes toward state involvement in the economy—lots of mercantile trees, no fiscal forest. Second, much of the scholarly discussion has concentrated on the doctrine of mercantilism without reference to policy. Third, imperial scholars, hemmed in by the anachronisms of mercantilism, have paid insufficient attention to eighteenth-century political and economic writers *before* Adam Smith. The Scottish economist did not create the configurations of mercantilism or modern political economy. He was not even the first to use the term *political economy* in English; James Steuart had used it some eight years earlier. Smith built on a rich, complex, and at times precocious set of ideas rooted in the tracts of economic theorists working in the 1750s. Instead of directly engaging the historiographic controversy about mercantilism, I have concentrated on resurrecting the 1760s' dialogue about political economy and empire.

In examining the interconnections between imperial economics and politics, this book disturbs the apartheid that has tended to separate economic history from political, social, and cultural history. The economists who practice economic history are rarely concerned with the societal and political contexts in which all the hard numbers of capital formation, urbanization, and total factor productivity growth were generated. Historians of politics and society usually have not investigated how the surrounding economy shaped their subjects. For example, recent historians of British nationalism have been interested in the relation between popular politics and imperial ideology in the middle of the eighteenth century. This is fascinating stuff, but without an understanding of the economy in which these forces interacted, one's view of the connection is eclipsed. How many ships England had in 1716, in 1739, and in 1760 to fight imperial wars depended on how much tax revenue the state raised. This in turn was a function of how much wool and glass and Midlands cutlery the nation exported and how many casks of Madeira Britons drank. The state of the economy *mattered*; it shaped the politics, perspectives, and fate of the British Empire.

The book is divided into six chapters. The first examines how particular aspects of Britain's performance in the Seven Years War crystallized previously amorphous concerns about empire and pushed them into the center of a large public debate about imperial policymaking. The second chapter investigates macroeconomic transitions in the 1760s and how they shaped lobbying interests concerned with imperial governance. Chapter 3 reconstitutes the interconnections between ministerial objectives in the empire, the emerging field of political economy, and the policy choices that imperial experts confronted. Chapter 4 analyzes the elite political alignments that developed around the issue of imperial management and explores how these ministerial and parliamentary configurations were affected by economic and geopolitical change. Chapter 5 reconstructs Britons' views of their nation's new power and sketches the significance of these attitudes in legislative debates. The final chapter consists of two case studies of policymaking—the repeal of the Stamp Act and the enactment of West Indian free ports in 1766, and the First East India Regulating Act of 1773. Both exemplify the fiscal and commercial problems of governing a decentralized empire, and each illustrates the interaction of the economic and political factors that conditioned policy responses.

The new problems and opportunities that accompanied Britain's victory in the Seven Years War informed what went on at the peace negotiating tables in 1763, and the imperatives of empire formed a subtle, influential structure in which the more prominent constitutional battles of the next decade played themselves out. In India and North America, imperial experts sought divergent solutions to what kind of empire Britain was to have and how to govern and pay for it. Married to these considerations in 1763, in 1783, and beyond was the issue of how best to promote national power and plenty. Within a transforming economy and conditioned by the experience of war, Britons struggled to harness the power of commerce to the demands of international ascendancy.

I have lived with this work for some time, and as I prepare the manuscript for publication, I feel as parents must when they send a child to college. I'm sad to see a close relationship change. At the same time, it's gratifying to watch one's offspring assume a fuller existence.

I am hardly the first to use such an analogy. Charlotte Brontë thought all authors grew "tenderly indulgent, even blindly partial to their own." Writing, according to Annie Dillard, is working from one's love and knowledge to produce complex entities that endure. Like parenthood, the six years I have spent thinking about and writing this book have been filled with the joy and frustration of creation.

I have not been a single mother. More than a score of libraries, institutions, and colleagues have helped me see this work through to publication. I express my appreciation to the earl of Shelburne for permission to use his collections. I also thank the staffs of the British Library, the Houghton and Widener Libraries, the Kress Library at the Harvard Business School, the Clements Library, the Public Record Office, the Sheffield City Library, the John Rylands Library, the Scottish Public Record Office, the Bodleian Library, and the Bank of England Archives. These women and men showed me much kindness and courtesy.

I am grateful to the Division of Research at Harvard Business School, which provided financial support for research and writing, to the Whiting Foundation, which funded the writing of my doctoral dissertation, and to the Fulbright Fund, the Krupp Foundation, and the Frank Knox Fellowship, all of which helped finance my research in Britain.

I thank three historians, John Brewer, Franklin Ford, and Simon Schama; each brought distinct insights to bear on my work. I am especially grateful to John Brewer. Since 1984 he has turned keen attention to my ideas and their development, with humor and good advice. Franklin Ford offered historical insight and encouragement throughout my time in Harvard University's History Department. Simon Schama has been a constant source of inspiration, expanding my field of historical vision and my sense of literary reconstruction.

Several other scholars, at Harvard and elsewhere, read earlier versions of this work. I am indebted to them for their time and effort. Danny Goldhagen, John Hall, Peter Hall, and John Styles all offered useful suggestions. Philip Lawson read the work for Cornell University Press, giving generously of his time to make recommendations large and small. Several years before it became chapter 5, Linda Colley reviewed my analysis of perceptions of empire.

Other students of history and national strategy have influenced this book. I thank my Harvard Business School colleagues George Lodge, Cynthia Montgomery, Bruce Scott, Richard Tedlow, and Dick Vietor for their remarks on specific chapters. I am also grateful to the members of the Business History Seminar for advice and input on the first and third chapters. I owe special thanks to Tom McCraw, who read the entire work and offered valuable advice on style and substance. This book is more carefully and incisively crafted than it could possibly have been without him.

Other talented men and women helped me complete the project. At Cornell University Press, I've been exceptionally fortunate to work with Roger Haydon. For three years he has brought critical insight and literary grace to bear on all aspects of this book. I thank him as well for his wit and humanity. I could not have brought the work to publication without Catherine Reggio, who produced the final manuscript with intelligence and care. She assisted me with the last stages of research, chasing down eighteenth-century documents in Widener Library's labyrinthine stacks. I have profited also from her kindness and encouragement. With precision and organization, Becky Voorheis edited the footnotes and bibliography. Her understanding and support were equally important contributions to the manuscript.

My debts, intellectual and otherwise, to Margaret Talbot are large. For many years she has taken time from her own writing and editorial responsibilities to read my work. On a wide range of issues, her suggestions have improved this book. I am also grateful for the understanding and warmth she has so consistently offered. Judith Livingston helped me clarify my thoughts about the work; I owe her more than I can here say.

If this work is in many respects my child, it owes its development as much to Colin Davis as to me. On this side of the ocean and in England, he has given his time, energy, discernment, and support to me and my scholarly progeny. In a book about eighteenth-century economy and politics, I have not always found it easy to reflect his gentle wisdom and guidance. But they have been with me all along, and I am truly thankful.

NANCY F. KOEHN

Cambridge, Massachusetts

The Power of Commerce

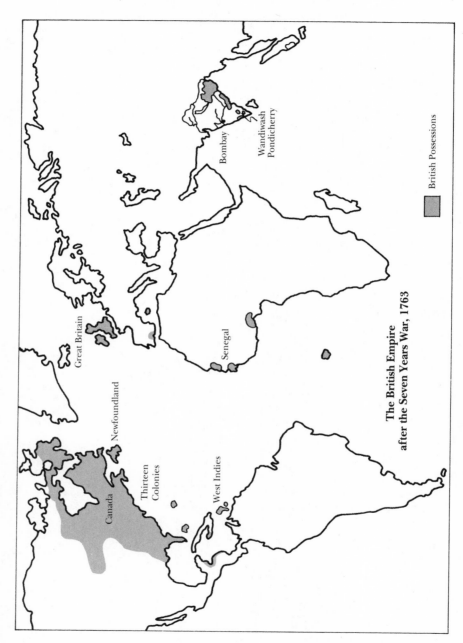

The British Empire after the Seven Years War.

 ONE

The Economics of War
and the Politics of Peace

IN FEBRUARY 1763, amid the splendor of Fontainebleau Palace, representatives of Britain, France, and Spain signed the treaty ending the Seven Years War. For all the major powers and their allies, this multicontinental conflict had been an exhausting and costly effort: most statesmen were glad to be done with it. Beginning in 1756 and continuing without interruption until the later months of 1762, Britain and Prussia had battled a coalition composed of France, Russia, Austria, and eventually Spain. On three continents, on the Mediterranean Sea and the Atlantic Ocean, the Anglo-Prussian alliance under the command of William Pitt and Frederick the Great fought the armies and navies of the French king Louis XV, the Austrian empress Maria Theresa, and the Russian empress Elizabeth.

In the evolving geopolitical order of eighteenth-century Europe, each of these powers had struggled to expand its territorial and economic authority. Austria had wanted Prussia out of Silesia. Frederick the Great had sought to preserve and expand his scattered, precarious frontiers. Initially, Russia had hoped to reduce Prussia to a minor German state. Britain and France had again taken up the contest for European ascendancy, begun some seventy years earlier during the wars of Louis XIV.

But this time Britain and its Bourbon enemy sought bigger stakes than in the previous wars. During the Seven Years War these two imperial powers also battled for the lion's share of territory and trade in North America and India. With the balance of European power at risk as well as economic and strategic control of much of the world beyond Europe, all the combatants marshaled large armies. France, with a population of 21 million, and Russia, with 20 million, each supported an army of over 300,000 men. Austria, with a population of 12 million, had 200,000 soldiers. Britain, with 6.5 million people, and Prussia, with 4.5 million, each put more than 150,000 men into combat.[1] In theaters as distant as Montreal and Madras, armies faced each other for seven years while the British and French navies struggled to rule the most important maritime routes and the leading ports in Europe.

Although for much of this conflict it was not clear which side was leading, by 1762 Russia had withdrawn from the war, Frederick the Great had beaten back the Austrians in Europe, and Britain had emerged victorious on land and sea in virtually all the other battle sites. The Peace of Paris, as the final treaty was known, symbolized the decisive military and economic might of Great Britain. By its terms, the nation gained dominion over all of Canada, most of India, East Florida, and significant islands in the Atlantic and the Caribbean—lands that, in conjunction with its existing territories in North America and the West Indies, constituted the territorial foundation of the first British empire.

As the other European powers nursed their wounds—military, economic, and fiscal—British ministers like George Grenville and Lord Shelburne faced the opportunities and problems raised by their victory. As statesmen, economic commentators, and others could see, this was an equivocal triumph for Britain. On one hand, the country's achievement heralded its new strategic and economic potential in an interdependent global system. The imperial accession of so many markets, the successful end of England's most expensive eighteenth-century war, and the quelling—however temporary—of significant threats from commercial and military rivals surpassed expectations and created new imperatives for government action. As Thomas Pownall, colonial governor of Massachusetts during the war, commented,

The several changes in interests and territories, which have taken place in the colonies of the European world on the event of Peace, have occa-

1. Population figures for France and Russia are from Paul Kennedy, *The Rise and Fall of the Great Powers: Economic Change and Military Conflict from 1500 to 2000* (London, 1988), 99; for Austria and Prussia, the figures are from Eric Robson, "The Seven Years War," in *The New Cambridge Modern History*, vol. 7, *The Old Regime, 1713–1763* (Cambridge, 1957), 467. The figures for British population are from R. D. Lee and R. S. Schofield, "British Population in the Eighteenth Century," in *The Economic History of Britain since 1700*, vol 1; *1700–1860* (Cambridge, 1981), 21. Army sizes are from Kennedy, 99. As all these sources

sioned a general idea of some new channel of business opening which may be applied to new powers; which ought to be guarded against, on one hand, or that is to be carried to advantage on the other. . . . [The ministers responsible] for the administration of these great and important [imperial] interests will certainly adopt the system which thus lies in nature, and which by natural means alone, if not perverted, must lead to a general dominion, founded in the general interest and prosperity of the commercial world, must build up this country to an extent of power, to a degree of glory and prosperity, beyond the example of any age that has yet passed.[2]

On the other hand, such a new and vastly enlarged dominion presented a series of unexampled economic, political, administrative, and fiscal problems to Edmund Burke, Charles Townshend, and other government officials. These dilemmas greatly affected imperial policymaking, domestic politics, and the fate of the empire in the 1760s, 1770s, and beyond. Some of these difficulties concerned finance and frontiers. Not only was the polity burdened with a huge national debt—further bloated by military expenditures—and thus with large and rising annual interest charges, but it had to find the funds to manage and defend the territories it fought for. And it had to do so while promoting economic growth at home and in its trade with other nations. British leaders and citizens thus confronted one overarching question: How could they pay the price of becoming and remaining a world power?

This book investigates how one country, caught up in a unique economic transformation, grappled with that issue. The work is thus a historical reconstruction of the making of national strategy in an industrializing state. My overriding premise is that the political management of the British Empire, as it was formulated by government officials and sanctioned by Parliament, was conditioned by several distinct but interrelated influences: the transforming national economy; contemporary knowledge of this economy, including the policy prescriptions that emerged from the field of later eighteenth-century political economy; particular extraparliamentary forces concerned with imperial policymaking; and the political alignments and perceptions of ministers and MPs.

---

caution, the statistics are often crude estimates and thus subject to large margins of error. See Lee and Schofield for a discussion of the difficulty of measuring eighteenth-century population.

2. Thomas Pownall, *The Administration of the Colonies* (London, 1766), 1, 10.

But this is not the whole story. The specific factors affecting imperial policy interacted within an evolving geopolitical order—an order characterized in the eighteenth century by almost regular warfare and keen economic competition between states. Within this system, European leaders and their citizens understood that global ascendancy was inexorably connected to economic performance. For Britons in 1763, including statesmen like Lord Rockingham and Charles Jenkinson and political economists like James Steuart and Arthur Young, this collective realization took on a particular form and importance in the aftermath of the nation's recent economic and military experience. Their conception of the relation between international authority and economic growth necessarily molded imperial objectives in the postwar decade. In this broad sense, the economics of war shaped the politics of peace.

Between 1689 and 1783, England fought five major wars with France. The two powers spent thirty-six of these ninety-four years in expensive combat. During the war years, the British government devoted an average of 67 percent of its total expenditures to military purposes. If we include debt service charges, the proportion of total public outlay committed to war costs rises to between 75 and 85 percent in each of the thirty-six years.[3] Clearly, being a world power in an evolving system of states entailed the political economy of waging frequent wars.

Britain, France, and their shifting coalition of allies fought not just for strategic control of parts of Europe and more distant eastern and western territories, but for economic sovereignty as well—for the power to rule the seas and thus control the bulk of the diverse international trade in agricultural and manufactured goods, for access to raw materials, and for expanding and manageable markets for each nation's output.

Why were the stakes of these armed contests so high? Why did William Pitt, other British officials, and their French counterparts want controllable markets and reliable inputs? There are geopolitical answers to these questions, responses rooted in the nature of eighteenth-century warfare.

Like World War I, the five conflicts fought between the Glorious Revolution and the Napoleonic Wars were, as historian Paul Kennedy has written, "struggles of endurance." Victory, Kennedy goes on,

therefore went to the Power—or better, since both Britain and France usually had allies, to the Great Power coalition—with the greater capacity

3. On the relation between patterns of military effort, fiscal politics, and the evolution of the British state, see John Brewer, *The Sinews of Power: War, Money and the English State, 1688–1783* (New York, 1989), 88–134.

to maintain credit and to keep on raising supplies. The mere fact that these were *coalition* wars increased their duration, since a belligerent whose resources were fading would look to a more powerful ally for loans and reinforcements in order to keep itself in the fight . . . What each side desperately required was . . . "money, money, and yet more money."[4]

This was especially true for the Seven Years War, Britain's most costly[5] and tactically sophisticated military effort to date. Fighting on three continents and two oceans, the nation spent over £160 million pursuing simultaneously a maritime strategy and a continental one.[6] This sum was more than twice Britain's gross national product in 1760. In twentieth-century calculations, it is analogous to the United States fighting a war with a $10 trillion price tag.

The greater part of military expenditures for this eighteenth-century conflict—as for the wars in our own time—was financed by state borrowing.[7] The British Treasury raised money by issuing government stock, usually long-term bonds with a guaranteed annual premium.[8] Each year the Treasury offered stock equal to the difference between military expenditures and taxes that were not earmarked for paying debt service and thus were available to meet running expenses. Department officials

4. Kennedy, 76.

5. Although in nominal terms the American War cost the British government more than the Seven Years War, it is important to adjust these costs for the general, sustained inflation that affected the British economy in the last quarter of the eighteenth century. As Elizabeth Schumpeter has noted, producer and consumer price indexes for this period are necessarily crude and subject, like so many of the economic statistics of this time, to significant margins of error: Elizabeth Boody Schumpeter, "English Prices and Public Finance, 1660–1822," *Review of Economic Statistics* 20 (1938): 21–35. Despite these measurement difficulties, it is useful to assess military expenditures in real terms. Using Schumpeter's price indexes and adjusting military outlays for inflation, we can see that the real costs of the Seven Years War rivaled those of the American War and swamped those of all previous eighteenth-century conflicts.

6. On the costs of eighteenth-century warfare, see Kennedy, 100–115, and Brewer, 88–134.

7. P. G. M. Dickson, *The Financial Revolution in England: A Study in the Development of Public Credit, 1688–1756* (London, 1967), explicates the mechanics of eighteenth-century debt financing in impressive detail. Alice Carter analyzes the eighteenth-century market for government stock along demographic and economic lines in *The English Public Debt in the Eighteenth Century* (London, 1968). On the specifics of government borrowing during the Seven Years War see Reed Browning, "The Duke of Newcastle and the Financing of the Seven Years War," *Journal of Economic History* 31 (1971): 344–77.

8. As Alice Carter notes, one of the incidental advantages of this kind of government loan "was that it stimulated the making of what became quite sophisticated actuarial calculations" (8).

such as the duke of Newcastle, who was head of the Treasury during the Seven Years War, coordinated the interest rates on the annual loans as well as the sale of these mass stock issues through a small group of wealthy London investors who underwrote the loan. Together, Newcastle and the financiers worked out an acceptable interest rate and other stock incentives.[9] The underwriters then guaranteed the entire loan, and government officials could be assured of continued funds. The underwriters disposed of much of what they had purchased in bulk to a variety of dealers, who then sold the stock to members of the investing public, to whom the state owed annual premiums.

The government's yearly borrowing needs increased at an unprecedented rate over the course of the Seven Years War, climbing from £2 million in 1756 to £12 million in 1762 without significant inflation. Newcastle and others in the finance ministry fretted continuously about the country's ability to float such large loans in the face of the nation's mounting debt. In each of the last two years of the war, the government was forced to borrow more than £12 million. In 1761, when Newcastle first went to the money markets to raise this sum, it represented the biggest single addition to government indebtedness to date—17 percent of GNP. To put these magnitudes in a more modern perspective, consider the president of the United States announcing a federal budget deficit of $850 billion.

These numbers seem impossibly high to our modern financial sensibilities, but over the course of the war the British state raised the funds it needed. How did it do this? Through trade, trade, and more trade, both at home and abroad. Unlike every other contest Britain was involved in during the eighteenth century, this war witnessed the *growth* of the nation's economic interchange with America, Europe, and Asia. With its navy firmly in control of the sea, Britannia ruled not only the waves, but the financial and commercial competition that underlay military success. Between 1756 and 1763, the country suffered none of the usual war-induced disruptions of its foreign trade. Stimulated by the exigencies of battle, demand for British manufactures and reexports in America, Prussia, India, and Ireland grew more than 33 percent, from £11.6 million at the onset of the fighting to £14.7 million in the last year of

9. When the market for government stock was "soft" and the government could not afford to offer a higher interest rate, the Treasury offered lottery chances, involving a gamble on an extra return, and discounted stock as inducements to underwriters.

the war. Imports also climbed substantially, from almost £8 million to £11.1 million over the course of the conflict, a 39 percent increase.[10] Customs receipts escalated in tandem—some 35 percent over the war years.[11] Activated in part by war-related increases in aggregate demand, domestic economic activity also accelerated,[12] and this pushed excise revenues up considerably. These receipts grew 31 percent, from £3.6 million in 1756 to £4.8 million at the close of the war.

Treasury officials needed this revenue to service wartime borrowing, and perhaps more important, to assure creditors—bond purchasers in London and Amsterdam—a competitive return on their investments. In the first decades of the eighteenth century, most of the income needed to service the national debt and guarantee lenders a profitable return on their investments had come from direct taxation in the form of the land tax. But beginning in the last years of the War of Spanish Succession (1702–13), indirect taxes, specifically excise and customs levies, became much more important sources of state revenue.[13] By 1760, the midpoint of the Seven Years War, excise and customs taxes accounted for 68 percent of the government's revenue.[14] Undoubtedly this growth in the importance of indirect levies as a proportion of the state's revenue was linked to the corresponding rise in the nation's indebtedness, which expanded with the frequency and scale of its military commitments. Practically as well as politically, the land tax could not support the financial burden imposed on Britain by the exigencies of eighteenth-century geopolitics. Other forms of economic enterprise, especially manufacturing and trade, had to finance most of the nation's borrowing. Burke and others recognized that this shifting pattern of fiscal imposition carried significant consequences for the politics of imperial decision making. As the relative contribution of duties on ale, candles, sugar, tobacco, and other goods to state revenue rose, so too did the demands of manufacturers and merchants for a voice in how their country's commercial empire was to be governed. Adam Smith bemoaned "the clamour and sophistry

10. Elizabeth B. Schumpeter, *English Overseas Trade Statistics, 1697–1808* (Oxford, 1960), 15–16.

11. B. R. Mitchell and Phyllis Deane, *Abstract of British Historical Statistics* (Cambridge, 1962), 387–88; Townshend Papers, Clements Library, 8/21/3.

12. A. H. John, "War and the English Economy, 1700–1763," *Economic History Review*, 2d ser., 7 (1955): 331–35.

13. On the changing significance of land, excise, and customs taxes in eighteenth-century Britain, see Brewer, 95–101.

14. Mitchell and Deane, 387–88.

of merchants and manufacturers"[15] in affecting regulation of the imperial economy. But he and his immediate predecessors—political economists, such as Josiah Tucker, writing in the 1750s and 1760s—could not
ignore the increased stakes and significance of the "trading interest of
England"[16] in policymaking.

If Cicero knew 1,700 years earlier that "the sinews of War are infinite
money,"[17] government ministers, stockholders, and commercial writers
during the Seven Years War saw just as clearly how profit was converted
into international influence. They understood that in large measure
Britain owed its military victory and its position in the global order to
the power of commerce and to the changing, growing economy that
undergirded it. This collective understanding shaped imperial policymaking after the war. Most of those who formulated and enacted
these policies agreed that the burgeoning economy of empire was to be
managed toward geopolitical ends—toward maintaining and expanding
the commercial and fiscal foundations of power.

In the grand sweep of diplomatic and military history, this was not an
altogether novel development. Some three centuries before the commencement of the Seven Years War, Renaissance rulers, early modern
merchants, and commercial commentators had been aware of how a
country's wealth influenced its strategic position within the international
order. Statesmen had been trying to harness economic resources to military power even before Ferdinand and Isabella financed Christopher
Columbus's venture in 1492.

What was novel about contemporary knowledge of the relation between commerce and national preeminence in the aftermath of the Great
War for Empire was the particular *form* this connection took in the
collective political consciousness of the British citizens—in and outside
government—who tried to influence government regulation of the empire. For men like William Dowdeswell, who advised Rockingham on
imperial issues, as for other colonial experts, two overreaching policy
objectives prevailed. First, the empire was to be governed with the end
of selling more manufactures at home and abroad than Britain's rivals.
Second, the nation's finances were to be administered to keep the mother

---

15. Adam Smith, *An Inquiry into the Nature and Causes of the Wealth of Nations*, ed. Edwin
Cannan, 2 vols. (Chicago, 1976), 1:143. See also 1:450–56, 2:128–30.

16. Edmund Burke, "Observations on a Late State of the Nation" (London, 1769), in
Writings and Speeches of Edmund Burke, vol. 2, *Party, Parliament and the American Crisis, 1766–
1774*, ed. Paul Langford (Oxford, 1981), 191.

17. Cicero, *Orationes Philippicae*.

country more consistently solvent—more able to raise men and money—than other states.

This is not to say that political concern with manufacturing and public solvency was born anew in the particular circumstances of the Seven Years War. Such British colonial ministers as the earl of Halifax (head of the Board of Trade in the 1750s) and Charles Townshend (a member of the board at the same time) had been interested in promoting domestic manufacturing before the war.[18] A few seventeenth-century writers on trade had emphasized manufacturing sales. Analogously, fiscal improvisation was hardly new. In the early 1750s Board of Trade members had tried extensively, if unsuccessfully, to increase the North American colonies' contribution to British administrative costs there.[19] Treasury officials had been tinkering with myriad proposals for excise taxes on luxury goods, such as carriages, and other products before the war broke out.

The Seven Years War did not *create* these political objectives, but it crystallized them. It sharpened and clarified them and strengthened their significance in the nation's consciousness. What had previously been scattered concerns for a few individual ministers and commercial observers became general political imperatives for the increasing number of people who affected the future of Britannia's empire. As important, the war publicized these priorities and brought them to the center of the informed and extensive debates surrounding imperial governance. In 1749 a half dozen Board of Trade members met twice a week to discuss colonial markets and various revenue proposals.[20] Seventeen years later during the parliamentary debates concerning the repeal of the Stamp Act, the entire administration led by First Lord Rockingham, more than three hundred legislators, scores of political pamphleteers, and a large group of commercial lobbyists from around the nation constantly discussed the significance of British manufacturing as well as the state's revenue needs. In the drafty chambers of government buildings, in crowded London coffeehouses, amid the bustle of trade fairs in Manches-

---

18. On metropolitan attempts to supervise more closely the commerce and public revenues of North America in the 1740s and 1750s, see Jack Greene, " 'A Posture of Hostility': A Reconsideration of Some Aspects of the Origins of the American Revolution," *Proceedings of the American Antiquarian Society* 87 (1977): 27–68, and idem, "An Uneasy Connection: An Analysis of the Preconditions of the American Revolution," in *Essays on the American Revolution*, ed. Stephen Kurtz and James Huston (Chapel Hill, N.C., 1973), 65–80.

19. Shelburne Papers, Clements Library, 50:1–15; Townshend Papers, Clements Library, 8/27.

20. Greene, "'Posture of Hostility,' " 45.

ter, Britons argued over how best to protect colonial markets for their expanding manufactures, and thus how to safeguard their livelihoods, while they considered how to pay the costs of maintaining an intercontinental empire. These imperatives and their public centrality in the postwar debates about what kind of imperium Britain was to have were legacies of the unique circumstances of the Seven Years War.

What was so special about this conflict? How did it transform political priorities, shape public debates, and influence policymaking? In geopolitical terms, the military alignments had assumed the general form of other eighteenth-century European contests. Britain and France faced each other on the battlefield and the ocean. The difference was in the unprecedented breadth and scope of the Seven Years War. Although it initially broke out over control of the Ohio and Mississippi valleys, the range of disputed territory immediately widened to include Canada, various Caribbean islands, and much of India. The number of combatants also quickly escalated as Prussia, under Frederick the Great, prepared for French attacks through Germany on the British province of Hanover. Austria and Russia, eager to punish the ambitious Frederick, allied themselves with France.

It was a formidable alliance that the Anglo-Prussian combination confronted, and for much of the first three years of war the Franco-Austro-Russian coalition appeared to be winning. Prussian and British troops suffered significant defeats on the Continent, in India, and in North America until mid-1759. But then, seemingly in all the varied theaters of combat, the tide began to turn in favor of Britain and Prussia. Frederick the Great recaptured Minden; the English general James Wolfe took Quebec; and British naval vessels defeated the French fleet in Quiberon Bay, ending Britons' fears of an enemy invasion. The year 1759 was a kind of military inflection point in the progress of the war, an annus mirabilis—like 1943 during the Second World War. From 1759 Britain had the strategic advantage and, as important, the economic resources, in the form of the efficient fiscal machinery of the English state and the nation's expanding economy, to exploit its superior position.[21]

Throughout 1760 and 1761, Britain's two-pronged approach to military conflict—coupling a maritime strategy with significant continental engagements—in combination with French and Austrian financial ex-

---

21. On financing the British naval effort during the Seven Years War, see Larry Neal, "Interpreting Power and Profit in Economic History: A Case Study of the Seven Years War," *Journal of Economic History* 37 (1977): 20–35.

haustion, continued to pay off. By 1762 much of India, several Caribbean islands, and most of Canada were under British control. Spain's late entry into the war on the side of France worried large numbers of Britons, especially those officials and financiers concerned with floating the £12 million loan required to fund much of that year's military costs. But the Treasury sold all the necessary securities, and the country financed successful attacks against several Spanish strongholds.

Nevertheless, by late 1762 the leaders of Britain, like the leaders of all the other major powers, were worried about men and money. From the hindsight afforded by historical reconstruction, the earl of Bute, Newcastle, and other British officials had much less to be anxious about than did Prussian and French statesmen. The British economy had prospered during the war as overseas trade and manufacturing output increased. Despite the collective worries of creditors in the City, the state had consistently raised the loans it needed, and it did so without having to pay high and escalating interest rates. Throughout the war, the return on government securities hovered between 4 and 5 percent,[22] rates comparable to those that prevailed in the less developed, often informal and localized private markets for debt.[23] The stability of the return on government debt in the face of unprecedented increases in the demand for loanable funds suggests that the supply of capital was much greater and the market for government stock less volatile than contemporary statesmen and underwriters took them to be.[24]

It is difficult to measure objectively the upper bounds on the state's borrowing capacity, but it is clear that Britain did not come up against these limits in financing the Seven Years War. Ceteris paribus, the nation's economy had the funds, in the form of surplus wealth and income, to support several additional large loans. But twentieth-century economic theory did not affect eighteenth-century ministerial decisions. Contemporary perceptions did; and in 1762 a majority of government officials, financiers, and commercial commentators were significantly concerned about the country's continued ability to raise the loans the war effort demanded.

22. Interest rates on short-term navy bills fluctuated more significantly—between 3 and 12 percent over the war.

23. Usury laws, coupled with the progressive availability of savings relative to investment opportunities, maintained interest rates for private lending at close to 5 percent for most of the century.

24. On the supply of loanable funds and savings behavior in the eighteenth century, see N. F. R. Crafts, *British Economic Growth during the Industrial Revolution* (Oxford, 1985),

Related to these widespread concerns was the issue of debt service. Between 1756 and 1762, Britain's national debt had grown almost 70 percent to an unparalleled £126 million. Even at lower levels, government borrowing throughout the eighteenth century had inevitably bred more taxes. By earmarking the revenues from a new levy or hikes in an existing tax for debt service, finance ministers had assured government bond purchasers of a reasonable return on their investments. Now, during the enormously expensive Seven Years War, Treasury officials were forced to seek parliamentary approval for a series of tax increases. In 1756 the legislature had doubled the land tax to four shillings in the pound—a fairly standard wartime revenue-raising measure at that time. Four years later, Parliament approved a significant rise in the excise taxes on beer and malt. By 1762 these revenues, in combination with existing excise levies and growing customs revenues, totaled £9.4 million, or 12 percent of national product.

Some of these revenues were needed to help defray the immediate costs of combat. They were used to buy soldiers, ships, and more. The remaining funds were spent on servicing the debt. In the penultimate year of the war, the annual interest charges on the cumulative total of the nation's borrowing were £4.5 million, almost half the government's net income that year. To throw these fiscal circumstances forward into our own time, imagine interest charges on the United States national debt that consumed fifty cents of every federal tax dollar. This is a financing burden more than three times that currently facing the American government. Like their counterparts 230 years later, many statesmen believed in 1762 that Britain could bear no additional fiscal burdens. As Thomas Whately, junior minister in the Treasury, commented, "*Great Britain,* strained to the utmost of her Strength, sinks under the [fiscal] Exertion and will hardly recover by Rest alone."[25]

Economic historians have corroborated the heavy taxation borne by eighteenth-century Britons. Throughout this period, but especially toward the later decades of the century, the English paid significantly more taxes per capita than did French citizens: in the 1760s, annual taxes cost each Englishman twice what a Frenchman paid.[26] There has been much

72–78, 123–25, and Peter Mathias, "Capital, Credit and Enterprise in the Industrial Revolution," in *The Transformation of England: Essays in the Economic and Social History of England in the Eighteenth Century* (London, 1979), 88–115.

25. Thomas Whately, *The Regulations Lately Made concerning the Colonies and the Taxes Imposed upon Them, Considered* (London, 1765), 56.

26. Michel Morineau, "Les budgets d'état et gestion des finances royales en France aux dix-huitième siècle," *Revue Historique* 536 (1980): 320; Peter Mathias and Patrick O'Brien,

less reconstructive agreement on the net effect of these impositions on the British economy.[27] Historians have seen beneficial, inhibiting, and offsetting influences on macroeconomic performance. What is not ambiguous is that this increase in the government's claims on financial and other resources occurred within a changing economy that simultaneously sustained rising population growth, unprecedented increases in urbanization, faster rates of output growth, accelerating integration of goods and credit markets, rising rates of investment, and significant sectoral transition. Britain in the eighteenth century did not have to choose between guns and butter. Historians may debate whether without military conflict the country would have had more butter (and churns) than it did during this period, but the fact remains that Britain waged frequent wars while the national economy grew at a revolutionary rate.

Contemporary economic historians, with scores of regressions, can see this retrospectively. But government officials, commercial writers, and other British citizens suspected as much at the end of the Seven Years War. They had fewer numbers than twentieth-century economists and no computers to manipulate what figures they possessed, but they understood that during this war their nation had made both muskets and millinery. In 1762 and beyond, they argued about the relation between the fiscal demands of the state and the commercial and manufacturing potential of their nation's economy. They worried about how to balance musket and hat production and about the government's role in managing this equilibrium. Yet they knew that their nation's victory was a unique military and economic accomplishment.

Certainly the Prussian and French economies fared significantly worse than Britain's during the war. Frederick the Great described the repercussions of the conflict in his country, one of the major theaters of battle:

Prussia's population had diminished by 500,000 during the Seven Years War. On a population of 4,500,000 that decrease was considerable. The nobility and the peasants had been pillaged and ransomed by so many armies that they had nothing left except the miserable rags which covered

"Taxation in England and France, 1715–1810: A Comparison of the Social and Economic Incidence of Taxes Collected for the Central Governments," *Journal of European Economic History* 5 (1976), 601–50.

27. John, 329–44; Peter Mathias, "Taxation and Industrialization in Britain, 1700–1780," in *Transformation of England*, 116–30; Jeffrey G. Williamson, "Why Was British Growth So Slow during the Industrial Revolution?" *Journal of Economic History* 44 (1984): 687–712; Brewer, 178–90; J. V. Beckett and Michael Turner, "Taxation and Economic Growth in Eighteenth-Century England," *Economic History Review*, 2d ser., 43 (1990): 377–403.

their nudity. They had not credit enough to satisfy their daily needs. The towns possessed no longer a police. The spirit of fairness and order had been replaced by anarchy and self-interest. The judges and the revenue authorities had given up their work owing to the frequency of invasions. In the absence of laws a spirit of recklessness and of rapacity arose. The nobility and the merchants, the farmers, the working man and the manufacturers had raised the price of their labour and products to the utmost. All seemed intent upon ruining each other by their exactions. That was the terrible spectacle which the formerly so flourishing provinces offered after the conclusion of the war. The appearance of the provinces resembled Brandenburg after the end of the Thirty Years War.[28]

In France the most important effects of the war were financial. French trade declined 50 percent over the course of the hostilities.[29] Customs receipts dropped off markedly, exacerbating the fiscal woes of Louis XV and his financial administrators, who all consistently refused to fund military expenditures through any means besides debt issuance. Faced with a populace and parlements loath to countenance any tax increase and intractable in their decision to preserve the sanctity of the national debt, the French king and his ministers realized by 1762 that the country faced both an immediate and a longer-term financial crisis. The nation's indebtedness had doubled over the war; French interest rates were among the highest in Europe and were still climbing. Most pressing, financial authorities had no means to continue funding the war effort.

Throughout the war, according to historian James Riley, these same ministers made a series of short-sighted decisions concerning debt management. Fiscal incompetence, he contends, not the condition of the French wartime economy, was primarily responsible for the financial crisis in which the Bourbon nation found itself at the end of the war.[30] Regardless of the causes of France's fiscal problems, the interruption of

28. Quoted in H. A. L. Fisher, *A History of Europe* (Boston, 1939), 785.

29. François Crouzet, "England and France in the Eighteenth Century: A Comparative Analysis of Two Economic Growths," in *Britain Ascendant: Comparative Studies in Franco-British Economic History* (Cambridge, 1990), 19, 36. James C. Riley is less pessimistic than many historians about the war's shorter-term macroeconomic effects. He contends that fiscal decisions concerning French financing of the war effort significantly constrained the nation's economic and political possibilities in the last three decades of the ancien régime. See his careful revision of the traditional historiography surrounding these issues, *The Seven Years War and the Old Regime in France: The Economic and Financial Toll* (Princeton, N.J., 1986).

30. Riley, 162–91, 223–36.

the country's international trade, the loss of customs revenues, and the erosion of much of the commercial fleet's capital stock did not augur well for the nation's economic or geopolitical future. Government officials in France knew this in 1762. They also knew that their enemy's ability to manage the financial sinews of power—its debt and taxes—was bound up with Britain's buoyant imperial trade during the war and thus with its naval superiority.[31] Even the French minister in charge of negotiating the peace, the duc de Choiseul, had to admit that "in the present state of Europe it is colonies, trade and in consequence sea power, which must determine the balance of power upon the continent."[32] Statesmen on both sides of the conflict recognized in 1762 that Britain was the only nation that controlled these indispensable supports to international authority. Only Britannia had successfully converted profit into power. The significance of the achievement was not lost on European leaders or on Britons in the aftermath of the war.

Confronted by severe financial exigency and a string of military defeats, in the early spring of 1762 French emissaries began active discussion of settlement terms with British officials. In the autumn, after much negotiation, diplomatic officials from both countries signed a preliminary treaty to end the conflict. By the terms of the Peace of Paris, Great Britain gained dominion over Canada and its dependencies, India, East Florida, Senegal, and the West Indian islands of St. Vincent, Dominica, and Tobago. These prizes were lands of enormous commercial and geopolitical potential. They represented expanding and controllable markets as well as important strategic strongholds. The sheer weight of territory ceded to the British Empire was unheard of in the context of previous eighteenth-century conflicts. A laconic George III said Great Britain had never before concluded such a peace.[33]

It was a big, complex, and expensive peace treaty to end a big, complex, and expensive conflict. Describing the scale and scope of the Seven Years War two centuries later, Winston Churchill pronounced it "the First World War."[34] But in reconstructing the influence of this eighteenth-

31. This is not to suggest that other aspects of fiscal management were not significant in influencing the outcome of the Seven Years War. Institutionally and individually, Britain had a significant comparative advantage in government finance. For a thorough analysis of these factors, see Brewer, 13–22, 64–134.

32. Quoted in H. Rosinski, "The Role of Sea Power in the Global Warfare of the Future," *Brassey's Naval Annual* 58 (1947): 103.

33. Quoted in Zena Rashed, *The Peace of Paris, 1763* (Liverpool, 1951), 201.

34. Winston Churchill, *A History of the English Speaking Peoples*, vol. 3, *The Age of Revolution* (New York, 1956–58), 124.

century conflict on postwar British perspectives and policies, it is perhaps more useful to think about the United States at the end of World War II. Without drawing the historical analogy too closely, there are striking similarities in the ways these conflicts affected the victorious countries. For Britain in 1763, as for America in 1945, the successful conclusion to an incomparable war helped shape its citizens' perceptions of national potential. This victory clarified older, somewhat amorphous assumptions about economic and geopolitical power, and it gave these conceptions new focus and importance in national policymaking.

The strength of the British victory in 1763, the financial and strategic demands of the hostilities, and the country's uniquely strong commercial performance in the midst of war combined to affect the perceptions and priorities of ministers, MPs, manufacturers, and others toward the postwar empire. These citizens reasoned that if their country had managed to fight *and* trade profitably during a contest that devastated its enemies militarily and economically, then Britain must "control a general kind of *lead in commerce* distinct from any of the governments of Europe . . . [that] will become the basis of a [great] commercial dominion."[35] This collective conception of governance in a newly enlarged empire depended, as ministers and businessmen recognized, on Britain's ability to sell large and increasing quantities of manufactures in international markets. It also rested on its capacity—financial as well as military—to protect these outlets in an unstable order. Never before had so many persons so clearly conceived and articulated the rewards and risks of international authority and its relation to economic change.

But exactly how was Great Britain to develop its manufacturing capabilities, preserve its markets, man its recently acquired territories, and pay the rising costs of maintaining its newfound international status? In an imperial economy expanding in novel ways, how was it to balance the need to sustain its strength abroad with the demands of promoting prosperity at home? And ultimately who—institutionally and individually—was responsible for the choice and execution of these national strategies? Given effective focus in the specific circumstances of the Seven Years War, the broad, newly manifest policy objectives for the British Empire presented a host of challenges.

In confronting the challenges, government officials also frequently faced a significant policy trade-off between furthering British manufacturing at home and abroad and raising the revenues the state needed.

35. Pownall, 4–6.

Although ministers and MPs wanted both markets and revenues in the decade after the Peace of Paris, they usually believed they had to choose between them, and this perception had important implications for government action from Boston to Bengal. Where did this perceived incompatibility between policy goals come from? The genesis of the trade-off and the relative weight that various ministers assigned the objectives of imperial policy grew out of the interrelations between the various influences on imperial policymaking. The changing economy shaped the power of manufacturers and other commercial lobbyists as well as the doctrines of political economy. The theories of the emerging social sciences and these extraparliamentary forces, in turn, effectively circumscribed the spectrum of policy choices acceptable to government officials charged with managing the newly enlarged empire. Constrained by the changing balance of power in an industrializing polity, by accepted economic wisdom, and by their own often contrasting perspectives, they debated how to control the power of commerce.

Underlying and affecting each of these interrelated influences on imperial policymaking was the powerful presence of macroeconomic transition. The transforming British economy increased the opportunities, demands, focus, and perceived importance of specific lobbyists who came to Westminster and Whitehall to try to mold government policy. It undergirded and shaped the theory and practice of political economy, and it colored the priorities, actions, and outlook of political elites.

To understand the story of government action toward the nation's extensive and disparate dominions, it is essential to reconstitute the British economy in the 1760s. What did this changing and significant economy look like? What were its most important sectors? How did the nation's trading patterns change during the war? A synthetic cast of the most vital aspects of the British economy—one that encompasses the numbers *and* the sociology of England's economic evolution—is needed. This model will help us examine how the state of the economy affected the balance of power, the structure, and the policy outcomes of the political debates over government action toward the country's dominions.

The reconstruction of the British economy will illustrate how specific macroeconomic (and fiscal) developments increased the effectiveness of various commercial lobbyists in the policymaking process. The growing importance of smaller and medium-scale manufacturing in the nation's output and occupational structure and the accelerating integration of goods and credit markets created new incentives and opportunities for political organization and action by the country's *nonlanded* interests. The unparalleled growth in numerous provincial cities, the changing pattern of Britain's international trade, and the increasing importance of indirect taxes as a fraction of government revenues expanded the political prospects of these interests. In the 1760s and 1770s the "men of moveable property"[36]—as historian John Brewer has called these merchants, manufacturers, and financiers—were more and more dependent on transatlantic and Indian interchange. Not surprisingly, in London and beyond such men as Samuel Garbett, a Birmingham ironmaster who throughout the 1760s was active in organizing Midlands manufacturers, and William Reeve, a merchant from Bristol who helped mobilize business opposition to the Stamp Act, sought greater control over the thriving economy of empire.

In the decades after the Seven Years War, the men of movable property, specifically those representing *manufacturing* concerns, gained greater influence in government decision making. The factors that pushed the extraparliamentary forces into positions of sporadic significance in the making of high-level national strategy were not political, *tout court*. The lobbyists were given effective focus and form by the changing British economy. This same economy increased the numbers, confidence, and tax contribution of manufacturing interests. It affected the perceived importance of the political demands the men of movable property made as well as the issues with which they concerned themselves. The changing economy gave them a score of novel reasons to invest their energy, time, and money in national policymaking. One of the most compelling issues around which they chose to do this was what kind of empire Britannia would have and how the government would manage the "great trading interest" that permeated it.

What did the men of movable property—iron manufacturers from Wolverhampton, textile makers from Bradford, London merchants—want from the government ministers and MPs? Like their counterparts in the late twentieth century, these commercial leaders and lobbyists sought a stable and hospitable environment for conducting business. In the 1760s and 1770s—formative decades in Britain's industrial transformation—such a business environment meant greater (freer) access to inexpensive raw materials and to large and growing colonial markets. Commercial leaders knew that their livelihood and that of their communi-

---

36. John Brewer, "Commercialization and Politics," in *The Birth of a Consumer Society: The Commercialization of Eighteenth Century England*, ed. Neil McKendrick, John Brewer, and J. H. Plumb (Bloomington, Ind., 1982), 201.

ties depended on the burgeoning imperial economy. In 1763 Sheffield steelmakers successfully lobbied George Grenville for bounties on American iron imports. Three years later, during the parliamentary debates surrounding the repeal of the Stamp Tax, Robert Dawson, a worsted manufacturer from Leeds, testified that he had dismissed almost a thousand laborers as a result of a slowdown in American demand for British manufactures.[37] Dawson and many other business lobbyists believed the slump in North American trade was a result of colonial boycotts staged to protest the Stamp Tax. In 1773, during legislative discussions on how to administer the lands, commerce, and people under the control of the East India Company, business representatives were less united in their recommendations than lobbyists had been in 1766. But commercial interests were no less significant in affecting political debate.

As important in shaping imperial policy was the emerging field of political economy. This evolving social science, practiced by men who observed rather than engaged in commercial activity, was informed at a variety of junctures by the British economy. For political economists working in the two decades before Adam Smith published *The Wealth of Nations* (1776), the transforming English economy was the "laboratory" in which they usually gathered observations, formulated theories, and put forward proposals for government action. In the late 1750s and 1760s, for example, such thinkers as Josiah Tucker, who wrote his first economic tracts in the busy trading port of Bristol, became very interested in the relation between domestic employment and colonial markets. Responding to the expanded importance of England's manufacturing sector and its growing colonial connections, he and other political economists suggested a variety of policies to improve trade within the empire and thus increase the number of Britons employed in manufacturing enterprises. Interested in and knowledgeable about this new field, numerous government ministers took up the recommendations of the political economists. In this way macroeconomic transition—sectoral change, the increasing integration of credit and goods markets, the expanding network of Britain's international trade, even technological change—acted as midwife to specific imperial policy priorities championed by statesmen like Rockingham and Lord North.

But the field of eighteenth-century political economy, though new in its self-proclaimed objectivity, was not some kind of Scholastic tabula rasa absorbing the facts and figures of the industrializing British economy

37. Commons debate, 12 February 1766. Add. MSS 33,030, fols. 141–42.

as they were generated and priming itself for Adam Smith. In many respects, political economy in the 1760s and 1770s was Janus-faced. Its practitioners anticipated the late eighteenth- and early nineteenth-century genesis of classical economic theory, articulating doctrines that were to prove significant to Smith and Ricardo. But they also looked back to commercial ideas of the preceding century. Older conceptions of government action in the economy commingled with the new—with important repercussions on imperial governance.

Government officials in the Treasury, the Board of Trade, and other departments took their policy cues from commercial writers. Like their seventeenth-century predecessors, Josiah Tucker, Arthur Young, and other political economists writing in the decade after the Peace of Paris believed that excise taxes on necessities—bread, beer, salt, candles—slowed the "great machine of trade," as they dubbed the nation's economy. They reasoned that such levies raised wages and thus increased the cost of British manufactured goods, making them less competitive in colonial and other international markets. Throughout the postwar decade—ten years of significant fiscal exigency—ministers consistently refused to levy duties on essential English goods. Officials were forced to turn to North America and India for the revenues they believed they could not raise at home. These policies and the reaction they occasioned in the outlying parts of the empire rebounded on London and the seat of imperial authority, molding political argument and action.

In the corridors of power, imperial officials responded to the theories of political economy, the increased importance of manufacturing lobbyists, and the changing configurations of elite politics. In a political landscape cleaved by fiscal transition, parliamentary instability, a realignment in ideologies, and the growth of organized activity "out of doors," ministers and MPs struggled to define and buttress their positions in a changing order. They used several important issues, including how Britain was to rule the "body of the empire" and its territorial "appendages" salubriously.[38] In the aftermath of the war, most government officials and much of the larger political nation agreed that this commercial imperium was to be administered so as to sell as many of the mother country's manufactures as possible and to maintain the fiscal sinews that sustained its military might. There was much less concurrence on how these objectives were to be accomplished. For several important elite factions, the policies

38. Maurice Morgann, "On the Right and Expediency of Taxing America," Shelburne Papers, Clements Library, 85/71.

by which the ends of empire were to be achieved became weapons to define and secure their own positions in the contest for parliamentary influence and political legitimacy.

Macroeconomic change affected this contest for power. In later years the statesman Edmund Burke dubbed the unstable order of high politics that emerged after the accession of George III and the war a "tessellated pavement."[39] On this checkered, often uneven surface the leaders of various factions knew that political success on imperial issues depended on convincing MPs that their groups' policies, by securing colonial markets for British manufactures or by raising revenues outside the mother country, best promoted the nation's commercial health. To do this, each faction often needed extraparliamentary assistance. For Lord Rockingham, George Grenville, and other heads of elite groups, this support was to be sought from the men of movable property—the manufacturers, merchants, and financiers—who owed their prosperity to the expanding economy of empire and who paid a progressively larger proportion of the state's taxes. Macroeconomic transition thus legitimated and reinforced the significance of commercial support from "out of doors" for various competing factions. Perhaps at no time in the decade after the war was commercial backing more important in policymaking than during the repeal of the Stamp Act in 1765 and 1766. It was with pride and a sense of accomplishment that Burke in 1769 celebrated the part the opinion of the "whole trading body of England" had played in the repeal of the stamp tax: "The universal desire of that body will always have the greatest weight with [ministers] in every consideration connected with commerce."[40]

As a political strategy, this collective realization was a product of economic and fiscal transition. A shifting output and occupational structure, from agricultural to secondary and tertiary sector production and employment, heightened the perceived political importance in a commercial empire of these progressively more numerous men of trade. As important, the growing significance of excise and customs revenues—themselves a product of increasing economic activity—in funding the state's military obligations strengthened the political power of the nation's commercial interests. Conditioned by Britain's experience during the Seven Years War and well aware of contemporary economic theories and political realities, elite politicians knew that the "whole trading body of En-

39. Edmund Burke, quoted in John Brewer, *Party Ideology and Popular Politics at the Accession of George III* (Cambridge, 1976), 44.

40. Burke, "Observations on a Late State of the Nation," 191.

gland" as well as their manufactures, including cutlery, calicoes, and more, mattered to the empire's power and prosperity.

The economics of war increased the importance of new actors on the stage of elite politics. It also helped shape official and popular perceptions of empire in the 1760s and early 1770s. Government ministers and the political nation as a whole experienced significant imperial ambivalence— ambivalence that became increasingly apparent as the 1760s became the 1770s and that had important consequences for policymaking. Heady anticipation of the unprecedented power and wealth that fueled the newfound empire's potential coexisted, often tempestuously, with collective anxiety about England's ability to manage and finance its newly acquired lands and govern the people who lived in these dominions.

These contrasting but simultaneously sustained perspectives served as powerful lenses on ministerial visions of empire. They colored how imperial experts saw certain problems, circumscribing specific policy options and creating at times very strong incentives to ease this ambivalence. Most officials agreed that the imperium was to be governed as an integrated commercial system with open, regulated colonial markets and well-ordered public finances. How these objectives were to be pursued, which policy tools were to be used, and how much intervention and regulation were to be exercised by the mother country owed much to this pervasive indecision, as did the timing and specific geographical focus of imperial policymaking. In 1763 and 1764, George Grenville wanted both colonial markets and revenues, and he and his junior ministers undertook an extensive reform of imperial trade legislation and of revenue collection in North America. Parliament strongly supported this broad program, enacting the stamp tax in 1765. A year later officials in Westminster and the larger political nation were much less sanguine about Grenville's obejctives. In the wake of North American boycotts of British manufactures, the mother country's commerce, and thus its prosperity and power, seemed precarious. By almost two to one, MPs revoked the Stamp Act they had so recently championed.

Where did these bifurcated and influential perspectives come from? As many twentieth-century analysts of American power and prestige have commented, there is a lengthy history of interest in geopolitical rise and decline in Western thought.[41] Certainly Britons living in the later eighteenth century, during the time of Edward Gibbon, whose

41. Joseph S. Nye Jr., *Bound to Lead: The Changing Nature of American Power* (New York, 1990), 12.

Decline and Fall of the Roman Empire was a smash hit, soaked up their share of historical examples of imperial ascendancy and fall: ancient Rome, sixteenth-century Spain, Holland in the seventeenth century. Undoubtedly this collective knowledge of imperial history reinforced ambitions and anxieties about England's international and commercial ascendancy after the war. But the ubiquity of contrasting perspectives of empire and their importance in affecting the parliamentary enactment of various policies before the American Revolution cannot be attributed to a largely literate and history-crazed polity.

Rather these perspectives, like the political imperatives of managing Britain's new empire, crystallized in the specific and ambiguous circumstances of the nation's recent experience. On the one hand, these circumstances included a decisive victory and a huge accession of territory, a significant increase in England's wartime commerce, coupled with control of the Atlantic and the Mediterranean, and the consistent ability of the national government to finance this costly war effort. But on the other hand, the conditions of this war and its peace also entailed a long and expensive multicontinent commitment and the initial specter of defeat, unparalleled imperial obligations, and a huge, growing national debt. These equivocal circumstances sharpened older, once nebulous and politically dormant aspirations (as well as fears) of international ascendancy, pushing them into the arena of public debate.

For Britons after the Peace of Paris, the making of national strategy in the aftermath of a victorious but expensive war—a conflict undergirded by an increasingly prosperous economy—had significant implications for their nation's future. English citizens in 1763 were certain of their dominion's economic and military potential in an increasingly interdependent global order. They knew their imperium had to be fiscally sound and committed to selling as many as possible of the country's manufactures in international markets. As Lord Shelburne said after the war, the "Interest of Commerce" was the "great object of ambition" of imperial policy.[42] But ministers, manufacturers, and others were less sure of how to govern and pay for this kind of empire. As the next chapter evinces, the formulation of metropolitan action toward the empire owed much to the changing British economy and its accompanying political transformation.

42. Shelburne Papers, Clements Library, vol. 165.

❦❦❦ TWO

The Landscape
of Economic Change

ALTHOUGH they argued vehemently over imperial policy in the mid-1760s, George Grenville and Edmund Burke agreed it made little sense to analyze the politics or economics of empire in isolation. For those who debated colonial issues after the Seven Years War, the great machine of imperial trade was a *political economy*, a dynamic commercial system inextricably related to the exercise of state power. In the aftermath of the war, wrote former Massachusetts governor Thomas Pownall, it represented a "new concatenation of powers . . . [that should] be activated by a system of politics adequate and proportionate to its operations."[1]

Adequate and proportionate politics demanded an understanding of economic transition, as many eighteenth-century statesmen and commercial writers knew. They realized that the growing national economy underpinned a host of social, material, and perceptual transformations. Henry Fielding, never one to mince words, commented on Britain's commercialization: "Nothing has wrought such an Alteration in this Order of People, as the Introduction of Trade. This hath indeed given a new Face to the whole Nation, hath in great measure subverted the former State of Affairs, and hath almost totally changed the Manners, Customs and Habits of the People."[2]

1. Thomas Pownall, *The Administration of the Colonies* (London, 1766), 16.
2. Henry Fielding, *An Enquiry into the Causes of the Late Increase of Robbers, with Some Proposals for Remedying this Growing Evil* (London, 1751), xi.

Economic success and imperial success were interdependent. Officials and manufacturing lobbyists knew that the nation's prosperity and global stature rested on the state's ability to exploit economic transition. Imperial policy was the government's most important tool of national strategy. Even Adam Smith, who fretted and fumed about the condition of imperial governance, acknowledged the connections between the politics of dominion and the British economy:

It is the object of that [colonial] system to enrich a great nation rather by trade and manufactures than by the improvement and cultivation of land, rather by the industry of the towns than by that of the country. But in consequence of these discoveries, the commercial towns of Europe, instead of being the manufacturers and carriers for but a very small part of the world (that part of Europe which is washed by the Atlantic ocean, and the countries which lie round the Baltic and Mediterranean seas), have now become the manufacturers for the numerous and thriving cultivators of America, and the carriers, and in some respects the manufacturers too, for almost all the different nations of Asia, Africa, and America.[3]

In the spirit of Smith and his often astute predecessors, this chapter analyzes the landscape of eighteenth-century economic change—transformation that conditioned and in turn, was affected by imperial policymaking.

How can the British economy of the 1760s and early 1770s be reconstructed? What were its most important sectors, and where were they situated? What kinds of regionalized economies grew up around them? What happened to the country's international trade during and after the Seven Years War? Most important, how did these changes affect the politics of empire in the postwar decade?

To answer these questions, we need a model of the eighteenth-century economy—one that traces the most important aspects of Britain's economic evolution. Such a model will help us analyze how specific macroeconomic changes influenced the structure, the balance of power, and the parliamentary results of the debates surrounding government action toward the empire.

In the middle decades of the century, a series of significant macroeconomic transitions occurred. Small and medium-scale manufacturing be-

---

3. Adam Smith, *An Inquiry into the Nature and Causes of the Wealth of Nations*, ed. Edwin Cannan, 2 vols. (Chicago, 1976), 2:142.

came noticeably more important in the nation's output and its occupational structure. Goods and credit markets integrated. Provincial cities experienced unprecedented growth, and Britain's patterns of international trade shifted. These changes created new incentives and opportunities for political action by the country's nonlanded interests. The "men of moveable property"[4] became progressively more reliant on transatlantic and Far Eastern interchange to sell their growing number and variety of manufactures. Accordingly, they sought imperial policies that promoted commercial and industrial expansion.[5] In London and in a host of provincial cities, they wanted greater access to and protection of the burgeoning economy of empire.[6]

Who were these men who clamored—ever more loudly in the 1770s and 1780s—for a say in imperial policymaking? They were metropolitan and provincial manufacturers, men who made or supervised the making of a wide range of metalwares, beer, candles, leather goods, and above all cloth—wool, silk, linen, fustians, and cotton. In eighteenth-century parlance, "manufacturer" was used not only in its twentieth-century sense of "industrialist" but also to designate a workman or master.[7] Writers like Samuel Johnson and Arthur Young used the word in both these senses. Taking its cue from them, this chapter is concerned with manufacturers in both eighteenth-century meanings. It deals with the men (and women), who worked in shops, in factories, or at home as part of a putting-out system, and with the men who owned and supervised these places of production. These people were of the middling sort; they composed a subset of the increasingly heterogeneous and significant commercial classes.

That this social group wanted a larger voice in government in the 1760s is not a new historical discovery. Several scholars of eighteenth-century Britain have scrutinized mercantile and to a lesser extent manufacturing demands for greater representation and influence in parlia-

---

4. John Brewer, "Commercialization and Politics," in *The Birth of a Consumer Society: The Commercialization of Eighteenth Century England*, ed. Neil McKendrick, John Brewer, and J. H. Plumb (Bloomington, Ind., 1982), 201.

5. Nicholas Rogers, *Whigs and Cities: Popular Politics in the Age of Walpole and Pitt* (Oxford, 1989), 5.

6. Ibid., 403.

7. P. Mantoux, *The Industrial Revolution in the Eighteenth Century: An Outline of the Beginnings of the Modern Factory System* (London, 1928), 375, quoted in François Crouzet, *The First Industrialists: The Problem of Origins* (Cambridge, 1985), 2. As Crouzet points out, "The meaning which came to prevail is one which is documented as early as 1752: 'One who employes workmen for manufacture' " (2).

mentary decisionmaking.[8] These demands often took on older rhetorical forms. The organized radical groups in the 1760s that attempted to confer power on the men of movable property used country party arguments to legitimate their positions.[9] These arguments were oratorical legacies of the Tory party and other disfranchised metropolitan groups of the 1730s and 1740s.[10]

Less frequently studied has been the role of the domestic economy and the enlarged empire in the urbanization of country party ideology and its employment by the commercial classes. In a changing and often unstable order, the factors that propelled extraparliamentary forces into positions of influence in Whitehall and Westminster were not simply political. As Nicholas Rogers and others have pointed out, British lobbyists and radicals of the 1760s owed much to the history of popular politics in London *and* in provincial cities. In the 1740s and 1750s these men and groups frequently lacked organization and unity, but after the Seven Years War the accelerated pace of economic change strengthened their hand. Macroeconomic transition and the increasing stakes of dominion gave the men of movable property effective political focus. It also increased their numbers, altered the significance of their demands, and provided them with a host of novel reasons to invest time and energy in national policymaking.

In the 1760s these men chose to organize around the issue of imperial management. As the economy of empire expanded in size and scope, as markets within Britain became more integrated, and as information about colonial markets proliferated, the means and ends of political action became clearer and more accessible to the growing number of Britons dependent on imperial interchange. At the same time in the nation's capital, the forces of high politics were reconfiguring. Various factions struggled for parliamentary influence, using the issues of empire and commercial constituencies as weapons. Economic change and Britain's experience in the Seven Years War stimulated elite politicians' interest in the men and the issues of imperial commerce. In the postwar

8. See especially John Brewer, *Party Ideology and Popular Politics on the Accession of George III* (Cambridge, 1976); Linda Colley, *In Defiance of Oligarchy: The Tory Party, 1714–1760* (Cambridge, 1982); Paul Langford, *The First Rockingham Administration, 1765–1766* (London, 1973); John Money, *Experience and Identity: Birmingham and the West Midlands, 1760–1800* (Manchester, 1977); Rogers; Kathleen Wilson, *"Sense of the People": Urban Political Culture in England, 1715–1815* (Cambridge, forthcoming).

9. Brewer, "Commercialization and Politics," 201; Brewer, *Party Ideology*, 206–7.

10. Colley makes a similar argument in reference to the rhetorical legacy of the Tory party.

decade, the balance of political power surrounding governance of the empire was shifting.

Cain and Hopkins, two historians interested in the "connexions between the slow and uncertain development of British industry and the pace and direction of British overseas expansion,"[11] disagree. They contend that although eighteenth-century imperial policymaking can be related to macroeconomic transition, manufacturers were not a significant political force before the 1780s brought the accelerated growth of the cotton industry.[12] It is true that in relative terms the political clout of various manufacturing men and associations in Parliament and in Whitehall was less consistently significant in the 1760s and 1770s than that of the older, larger trading and financial interests. But throughout the middle of the century, and especially during the postwar decade, small and medium-scale manufacturers became increasingly influential in affecting executive and legislative policy.

As the returns and risks of dominion mounted, the middling sort came more frequently to Parliament and to Whitehall to try to influence imperial governance. They often came, as later chapters of this book will make clear, under the auspices of Rockingham, Shelburne, or likeminded ministers. But this in itself underlines the perceived political importance of manufacturers. Ministers and MPs claimed these men—whose prosperity and public stature owed much to the economic changes of the mid-eighteenth century—as their own constituents and provided them with a parliamentary forum. Well aware of the shifting balance of power in the first empire, elite politicians could not afford to do otherwise. Armed with information, petitions, and perceived legitimacy, the men of movable property came to the corridors of national power, and they mattered. When, how much, and to whom depended heavily on the macroeconomic context in which decisions were made.

This is not to suggest that in the decade before the American Revolution the middle class appeared de novo as a major force in imperial politics, blazing a developed and unmistakably liberal trail. It did not.[13]

11. P. J. Cain and A. G. Hopkins, "Gentlemanly Capitalism and British Expansion Overseas: The Old Colonial System, 1688–1850," *Economic History Review* 39 (1986): 501. See also P. J. Cain and A. G. Hopkins, "The Political Economy of British Expansion Overseas, 1750–1914," *Economic History Review* 33 (1980): 463–92. For a broad-ranging critique of their arguments, see Andrew Porter, " 'Gentlemanly Capitalism' and Empire: The British Experience since 1750?" *Journal of Imperial and Commonwealth History* 18 (1990): 265–95.

12. Cain and Hopkins, "Gentlemanly Capitalism," 513.

13. This new assertiveness by commercial men was also not part of a larger challenge to the *social* parameters of power. As Cain, Hopkins, and Rogers note, throughout the

The nineteenth-century emergence of middle-class politics was the product of the struggle over corn and cash—a battle between agrarian capitalism and industry, concerning economic expansion and state protection.[14] But this does not diminish the importance of the argument. The *eighteenth-century* entrance of commercial interests onto the national stage was significant. The roles these men played in the 1760s debates surrounding imperial management were rehearsals for the expanded parts and louder voices they would have in the next century.

What did the British economy look like in the 1760s? To answer this question, we must plunge into the dense thicket of economic historiography surrounding the Industrial Revolution. Few economies have been researched as intensively as that of eighteenth-century Britain. There are debates about the timing and origins of the Industrial Revolution as well as statistical investigations of sectoral, regional, and national growth. Economists argue about the relative contribution of labor, capital, and technological change in industrialization and the significance of agriculture and international trade in accounting for England's rising national product. No other eighteenth-century European economy has received so much attention.[15] The historiographic complexion of this literature has changed noticeably over the past century.[16] In reconstructing the eighteenth-century economy, this chapter relies primarily on the most recent research, but I have tried not to ignore the significance of older observations or to allow the numbers that currently reign supreme in economic historiography a solitary and final say.[17]

---

eighteenth century "there was no fundamental questioning of aristocratic power and privilege, save perhaps among a minority of crypto-republicans in the metropolis" (Rogers, 405).

14. Rogers, 403–4.

15. John Brewer, *Sinews of Power: War, Money and the English State, 1688–1783* (New York, 1989), 179.

16. See David Cannadine's insightful article, "The Present and the Past in the English Industrial Revolution, 1880–1980," *Past and Present* 103 (1984): 131–72.

17. As Cannadine writes, "Whether they intend to or not, whether they know it or not, and whether they like it or not, economic historians write tracts *of* their times and often *for* their times. Rightly or wrongly, contemporaries discerned four readily identifiable phases in the evolution of the British (and latterly, world) economy since the 1880s; and during the same hundred years, the four generations of economic historians writing on the Industrial Revolution have each evolved a dominant interpretation sufficiently akin to these contemporary perceptions of the economy for it to be more than mere coincidence. The fit is close enough to be remarkable" (167). "[This] suggests that the dominant interpretation which prevails (albeit not completely) in any given generation is never more than a partial view of that very complex process we inadequately refer to as the Industrial Revolution" (171). "Ironically, one of the greatest weaknesses of present-day economic

Before turning explicitly to the statistics, it is useful to place them in a broader context. Britain in the eighteenth century was perhaps the richest country in Europe. When the century opened, its relative prosperity was of a traditional form, flowing from "productive if unscientific agriculture, busy if unmechanized industry, and vigorous if narrow commerce."[18] One hundred years later, a smaller farming sector fed more Britons more efficiently; a growing number of men, women, and children made an expanding variety and quantity of goods in familiar and novel ways; and a broader range of exports and imports traveled to and from a more distant set of ports. As Maxine Berg has written, "The British economy in the eighteenth century contained all the contrasts of youth's inclinations, at once the backward and the forward, its gaucheness as well as its quickness of perception and response."[19] It was an age of improvement, set within an age of manufactures. Artisans' skills and traditions mingled with new goods, markets, labor relations, and mechanical contrivances.[20]

Until recently, the most distinctive aspect of the British economy historiographically was its accelerating two-stage growth—one stage in the middle of the century and then a "takeoff," to use Rostow's phrase, in the final two decades.[21] In the past fifteen years, however, this vivid picture of the eighteenth-century economy, one in which a "Prometheus unbound" characterized technological change, has been significantly redrawn. Revisions of earlier estimates of growth suggest a more gradual and steady improvement in economic output across the entire century, with a less momentous acceleration in 1780 than previously thought. Economic indicators from the early part of the century have been revised upward, and those at the end downward. The curve of economic growth has been redrawn with a shallower slope.[22]

---

history is that its practitioners may forget (or may, indeed, never have known) what their professional forbears said, and so unwittingly resurrect old heresies in the mistaken belief that they are new insights produced by new methodologies" (172).

18. N. F. R. Crafts, "The Eighteenth Century: A Survey," in *The Economic History of Britain since 1700*, 1, *1700–1860*, ed. Roderick Floud and Donald McCloskey (Cambridge, 1981), 1.

19. Maxine Berg, *An Age of Manufactures: Industry, Innovation and Work in Britain, 1700–1820* (Oxford, 1985), 23.

20. Ibid.

21. The pioneering work on eighteenth-century economic growth is that of P. Deane and W. A. Cole. See *British Economic Growth, 1688–1959* (Cambridge, 1962). See also W. W. Rostow, "The Take-off into Self-Sustained Growth," *Economic Journal* 66 (1956): 25–48.

22. Brewer, *Sinews of Power*, 179. See N. C. R. Crafts, "The Eighteenth Century"; idem, *British Economic Growth during the Industrial Revolution* (Oxford, 1985); and idem, "English Economic Growth in the Eighteenth Century: A Reexamination of Deane and Cole's

How fast did output increase? Through a series of cost-reducing innovations, the most significant being the introduction of fodder crops into the rotations, agricultural output expanded an average of 0.7 percent per year in the first four decades of the century. The rate of increase slowed between 1760 and 1800 to an average of 0.44 percent.[23] Cumulatively, these figures mean farming sector output grew by about 50 percent over the first half of the century, 28 percent over the latter half. In commerce and in the manufacturing industries—wool, iron, linen, silk, cotton, beer, leather, soap—output increased by 0.7 percent each year before 1760, accelerating to annual growth rates of 1.05 percent from 1760 to 1780 and 1.81 percent in the last twenty years of the century. These growth rates suggest that real output in industry and commerce almost doubled between 1760 and the turn of the century. As many economists have recently noted, these rates of increase and their acceleration are considerably lower than previously believed and are not particularly high by twentieth-century standards.[24] The reconstructed road to industrialization was smoother and slower than was once thought.

All this sustained and steady growth may diminish the drama of the Industrial Revolution, but it underscores both the widespread nature of improvement and the variety of commercial and manufacturing enterprises that defined the eighteenth-century economy. Economic breadth and diversity had significant repercussions for imperial politics. Although growth rates were highest among the "big three" industries—cotton, iron, and engineering—industries that rose to significance after 1760, these sectors did not produce the lion's share of output over the course of the century. The "big three" produced less than 25 percent of British manufactures even into the 1840s. Older agricultural processing—baking, milling, brewing, and distilling—the textile industries, and leather processing generated more income than the technology leaders.[25] These

Estimates," *Economic History Review*, 2d ser., 29 (1976): 226–35; C. K. Harley, "British Industrialization before 1841: Evidence of Slower Growth during the Industrial Revolution," *Journal of Economic History* 42 (1982): 267–89.

23. Crafts, "Eighteenth Century," 2–3; N. F. R. Crafts, "British Economic Growth, 1700–1831: A Review of the Evidence" (working paper, Oxford University, 1982), 15; Crafts, *British Economic Growth during the Industrial Revolution*, 40. On the difficulties of measuring agricultural output in this period, see Crafts, "British Economic Growth, 1700–1831," 16–17. On eighteenth-century English agriculture, see A. H. John, "The Course of Agricultural Change, 1660–1760," in *Studies in the Industrial Revolution*, ed. L. S. Pressnell (London, 1960), 125–55, and E. L. Jones, "Agriculture, 1700–80," in Floud and McCloskey, 66–86.

24. Crafts, "Eighteenth Century," 2.

25. Berg, 26.

Table 1. Sectoral growth of real output (percent per annum)

	1700–1760	1760–70	1770–80	1780–90	1790–1801	1801–11	1811–21
Cotton	1.37	4.59	6.20	12.76	6.73	4.49	5.59
Wool	0.97	1.30	—	0.54	—	1.64	—
Linen	1.25	2.68	3.42	− 0.34	0.00	1.07	3.40
Silk	0.67	3.40	−0.03	1.13	−0.67	1.65	6.04
Building	0.74	0.34	4.24	3.22	2.01	2.05	3.61
Iron	0.60	1.65	4.47	3.79	6.48	7.45	−0.28
Copper	2.62	5.61	2.40	4.14	−0.85	−0.88	3.22
Beer	0.21	−0.10	1.10	0.82	1.54	0.79	−0.47
Leather	0.25	−0.10	0.82	0.95	0.63	2.13	−0.94
Soap	0.28	0.62	1.32	1.34	2.19	2.63	2.42
Candles	0.49	0.71	1.15	0.43	2.19	1.34	1.80
Coal	0.64	2.19	2.48	2.36	3.21	2.53	2.76
Paper	1.51	2.09	0.00	5.62	1.02	3.34	1.73

Source: Adapted from Crafts, *British Economic Growth during the Industrial Revolution,* 23.

older industries demonstrated significant innovation and important, though discontinuous, productivity gains.[26] In the decade after the Seven Years War and indeed well into the nineteenth century, real output growth was significant across many manufacturing industries, including many traditional sectors (see table 1).

In all the traditional sectors except brewing and leather processing, output growth in the 1760s was significantly higher—as much as 300 percent higher—than in the century's first half. That economic historians of our time have revised productivity numbers downward from previous calculations in no way undermines the *eighteenth-century* importance of extensive improvement. Economic commentators, ministers, and manufacturers—men working in the 1750s, 1760s, and 1770s—saw a burgeoning economy with newly obvious productive potential. As the prolific political economist Josiah Tucker observed in 1774, "No Man can pretend to set Bounds to the Progress that may yet be made in Agriculture and Manufacture; . . . is it not much more natural and reasonable to suppose, that we are rather at the Beginning only, and just got within the Threshold, than that we are arrived at the *ne plus ultra* of useful Discoveries?"[27]

26. On the importance of the "traditional economy" in the eighteenth century and its treatment in the current historiography, see Pat Hudson, "The Regional Perspective," in *Regions and Industries: A Perspective on the Industrial Revolution in Britain,* ed. Pat Hudson (Cambridge, 1989), 5–38.

27. Josiah Tucker, *Four Tracts Together with Two Sermons on Political and Commercial Subjects* (London, 1774), 23.

Throughout the eighteenth century, but especially after 1760, contemporaries knew they were living in an age of economic improvement. Daniel Defoe had been impressed with the pace of economic growth in 1720. As he noted in his *Tour Through the Whole Island of Great Britain*,

New Foundations are always laying, new Buildings always raising, Highways repairing, Churches and publick Buildings erecting, Fires and other Calamities happening, Fortunes of Families taking different Turns, new Trades are every Day erected, new Projects enterpriz'd, new Designs laid; so that as long as *England* is a trading, improving Nation, no perfect Description either of the Place, the People, or the Conditions and State of Things can be given.[28]

Other commercial writers, working in the late seventeenth and early eighteenth centuries, analyzed the quickening of the economy, the growth of colonial markets, and the emergence of new manufacturing industries.[29]

But beginning in the late 1750s, political economy as articulated by men like Josiah Tucker, Thomas Mortimer, and Malachy Postlethwayt took on a new urgency. These men understood that a combination of geopolitical circumstances and economic transitions had brought the nation as well as their discipline to an important juncture. The next chapter will introduce these midcentury political economists in some detail, examining the significance of their work to the imperial policy debates. Here it is important to note that some of the urgency in the works of Tucker, James Steuart, and other immediate predecessors of Adam Smith derived from contemporary assessments of the speed and extent of economic transition in the 1760s. The transformations that had concerned Defoe and earlier writers had not always been salient to the untrained observer. By the end of the Seven Years War, according to writers such as Tucker, economic change had become so extensive and so quick relative to what past generations had known as to be *publicly*

---

28. Daniel Defoe, *A Tour Through the Whole Island of Great Britain, Divided into Circuits or Journies*, 3 vols. (London, 1724), vol. 2, preface.

29. On the evolution of economic thought in the seventeenth and early eighteenth centuries, see Joyce Oldham Appleby, *Economic Thought and Ideology in Seventeenth-Century England* (Princeton, N.J., 1978); Berg, 48–68; Klaus Knorr, *British Colonial Theories, 1570–1850* (London, 1963).

manifest in most parts of the country. There was no turning back; the consequences of economic transition were irrevocable.[30]

Manufacturing in the developing economy was widespread and diverse. As the political economists of the time realized, the British economy in the middle decades of the century was significantly industrialized. In 1759 almost half of the workingmen of England labored in manufacturing or commercial enterprises. Almost a quarter of the country's families farmed, and most of the rest were laborers or in the military.[31] Even in the shires that were predominantly rural, 25 to 30 percent of the labor force worked outside the farming sector.[32] This was hardly the stereotypical preindustrial economy, completely dominated by agriculture and its downstream smaller-scale manufacturing processes.

Although agricultural employment continued to be very important after 1750, the economy and its labor force were increasingly dependent on more complex, less traditional medium-scale manufacturing such as textile and metal production and shipbuilding. The stability of Britain's occupational structure eroded progressively faster after the century's midpoint. Peter Lindert elaborates: "The pattern of these changes seems to reflect the classic mixture of technological change, population growth, and war associated with the Industrial Revolution era . . . [T]he number of men labelled by a textile trade name more than tripled across the second half of the eighteenth century. The number of weavers apparently more than doubled."[33] As workingmen and workingwomen moved from farming into manufacturing and service sectors, the economic countenance of various regions evolved.[34] Anthony Wrigley sketches these changes:

30. In 1764 the political economist Adam Anderson organized his *Historical and Chronological Deduction of the Origin of Commerce from the Earliest Accounts to the Present Time*, 2 vols. (London, 1764) as a catalog of new manufacturing industries and the novel machinery being introduced into specific industries.

31. Peter H. Lindert, "English Occupations, 1670–1811," *Journal of Economic History* 40 (1980): 685–712; Peter Mathias, "The Social Structure in the Eighteenth Century: A Calculation by Joseph Massie," *Economic History Review* 2d ser., 10 (1957): 30–45; Crafts, *British Economic Growth during the Industrial Revolution*, 12–14. As Lindert and Crafts note, these estimates—econometric revisions of Joseph Massie's eighteenth-century calculations—come with significant margins of error. On the close fit between Massie's estimates and current, more quantitatively sophisticated assessments, see Lindert, 707–8.

32. Brewer, *Sinews of Power*, 181.

33. Lindert, 709. Arthur Young, writing in 1772, also observed similar transformations in the nation's social structure. See his *Political Essays concerning the Present State of the British Empire* (London, 1772), 194.

34. Lindert, 702.

In certain rural areas in the eighteenth century the growth in non-agricultural employment was so great as to dwarf the remaining agricultural population. Framework knitting became the dominant source of employment in Leicestershire villages. In parts of Warwickshire and Staffordshire there was very rapid growth in the manufacture of small metal wares—nails, chains, buckets, etc. In much of south Lancashire and the West Riding of Yorkshire, the textile industry, whether cotton or wool, provided income for many more men and women than did agriculture. . . .

Moreover, in areas which attracted little industry, there was often a growth in employment in service industries. In the rare cases where parish registers provide data on occupation over long periods of time, it is a commonplace to note a growth of specialist employments not previously encountered, especially during the eighteenth century. A small town like Colyton, for instance, even provided a living for a peruke [wig] maker in the 1760s.[35]

Occupationally, after midcentury the economy experienced a profound structural transformation. As contemporary political economists and others recognized, the 1760s and 1770s were on the cusp of this transition.

The country's income and output ratios mirrored the changes in its occupational organization. That is, the share of income accruing to farm families fell during the second half of the century, from almost 25 percent in 1759 to 19 percent in 1801, while the proportion of total income earned by families engaged in industry or commerce rose from 38 percent to 55 percent.[36] In 1750 industrial output, in constant 1700 prices, accounted for 38 percent of the national product of England and Wales; in 1770 it composed 45 percent.[37] In the first ten years of its expanded empire, Britain was well on its way to becoming a nation of manufactur-

35. E. Anthony Wrigley, "Urban Growth and Agricultural Change: England and the Continent in the Early Modern Period," in *Population and History from the Traditional to the Modern World*, ed. Robert I. Rotberg and Theodore Rabb (Cambridge, 1986), 136–37. On the significance of economic transition from a variety of regional perspectives, see Hudson, *Regions and Industries*.

36. Peter H. Lindert and Jeffrey G. Williamson, "Revising England's Social Tables, 1688–1812," *Explorations in Economic History* 19 (1982): 385–408. That as much as 45 percent of England's national product was agricultural in 1770—a time when labor force contribution to this sector was declining—is testimony to the significant productivity gains agriculture experienced throughout the eighteenth century. Crafts attributes these efficiency gains primarily to total factor productivity growth (Crafts, *British Economic Growth during the Industrial Revolution*, 84).

37. W. A. Cole, "Factors in Demand, 1700–80," in Flood and McCloskey, 40, 64.

ers. And these increasingly numerous and prosperous men of movable property wanted a voice in how the imperial economy was governed.

Much of the national political activity of these manufacturers grew out of regional organizations and associations. Such political clustering was itself a function of economic development, a product of the geographic concentration of most manufacturing. Even within regions there was often some specialization by area. In Lancashire one could distinguish three manufacturing clusters: the first to the east concerned with making woolens, a second to the west and south occupied with linens, and a third lying between the two concentrating on fustians, mixes of cotton and linen.[38] Analogously in the West Riding of Yorkshire, woolens were made in and around Leeds and Wakefield. Worsteds—strong woolen textiles without a nap—were manufactured in Halifax and Bradford.

Woolens were generally produced by independent artisan households, whereas worsteds were made in a sophisticated putting-out system based on a division of labor between various households.[39] There were thus important social and economic distinctions between the two industries. Berg explains:

The worsted manufacture, based on combed rather than carded long-fibred wool, was organized in Yorkshire on a much more capitalistic basis right from the outset. There the small independent clothier never existed; instead there were merchant-manufacturers who resembled the large West of England clothiers. They bought large quantities of wool at big fairs and put it out over a wide area to be spun and woven. The open marketing at the Leeds cloth hall with over 1,000 stallholders was in sharp contrast to the concentrated industrial structure indicated by the worsted hall at Bradford with its 250 stallholders. The Yorkshire worsted manufacturers ran extensive putting-out networks, commonly distributing wool within a radius of twenty to thirty miles. Woolpacks were often consigned to shopkeepers or small farmers who received a sum for delivering

38. T. S. Ashton, *An Economic History of England: The Eighteenth Century* (London, 1966), 95. On industrialization in Lancashire, see John K. Walton, "Proto-industrialization and the First Industrial Revolution: The Case of Lancashire," in Hudson, *Regions and Industries,* 41–68.

39. On the West Riding's eighteenth-century economic transformation, see Pat Hudson, "Capital and Credit in the West Riding Wool Textile Industry, c. 1750–1850," in Hudson, *Regions and Industries,* 69–99, and idem, "From Manor to Mill: The West Riding in Transition," in *Manufacture in Town and Country before the Factory,* ed. Maxine Berg, Pat Hudson, and Michael Sonenscher (Cambridge, 1983), 124–44.

and receiving wool and spun hanks of yarn. "The mother or head of the family then plucked the tops into pieces the length of the wool, and gave it to the different branches of the family to spin about nine or ten hanks a day."[40]

Complementing the wool and worsted industries was framework knitting, which was centered in the Midlands and in London. Like worsteds, this industry was organized in complicated putting-out networks. Beginning in the early decades of the century, this sector began to be characterized by medium-scale workshops as well. In Nottingham, the center for a variety of knitting enterprises, a leading hosier, Samuel Fellows, constructed a large manufactory in 1763 to make imitation Spanish lace gloves.[41]

The geographical distribution of textile manufacturing in the second half of the century reflected a remarkable change from earlier periods. In 1700 the geography of the industry was centered, as it had been since the Middle Ages, in East Anglia, the West Country, and Yorkshire. But the swift growth of the Yorkshire worsted industry from the 1680s on was represented in the eighteenth-century expansion of Leeds, Bradford, Huddersfield, Wakefield, and Halifax. The West Riding grew while the woolen industries of Suffolk, Essex, and the West Country declined.[42] Some of the most organized and effective demands for input into state regulation of the imperial economy came from these young textile cities. These were areas that owed their new growth and prosperity to the thriving economy of empire.

Textile production was not the only regionally concentrated industry. In the West Midlands, metal and metalworking provided families and communities with their chief source of income. Throughout the century, pig and bar iron were produced in Shropshire and Worcestershire. In Birmingham, Sheffield, Wolverhampton, and other Black Country regions, skilled artisans working in workshops and factories turned iron into guns, cutlery, nails, brooches, tools, toys, candlesticks, and a world of other finished goods. As much as any of the transforming industries of the later eighteenth century, the metal trades were export oriented, especially dependent on colonial markets for consumption of their goods. In 1759 some 20,000 Britons were employed in the manufacture of small

40. Berg, 209–10.
41. Ibid., 212.
42. Ibid., 31.

metal goods in Birmingham. The value of the ornamental part of the trade—buckles, buttons, bracelets, boxes, watch chains, and more—was estimated at £600,000, of which £500,000 was derived from exports.[43]

Contemporary commercial writers, concerned with the demand side of the economy and thus with expanding old markets for British manufacturers, and creating new ones were impressed with the variety of exportable metalwares made in the Midlands. Postlethwayt argued in 1757 that promoting economic growth and nurturing "the general perfection of the manufactures of a state consists in obtaining the preference of every class of consumers." A large variety of inexpensive goods, such as those produced in Staffordshire, was essential to the country's economic health. "That choice of various kinds of goods multiplies the desires of other nations," Postlethwayt continued.[44]

Political economists were not alone in their interest in the Black Country. Government ministers admired the rapid growth of manufacturing in this region. As Shelburne commented in 1766,

Birmingham originally had no manufacture except a small one of linen thread, which continues there to this day, though now to the amount of ten or twelve thousand pounds. It is not fifty years since the hardware began to make a figure, from thence begun by people not worth above three or four hundred pounds a-piece, some of which are now worth three or four hundred thousand, particularly a Mr. [John] Taylor, the most established manufacturer and trader; some, however, are beginning to rival him in the extent of his trade.[45]

Other eighteenth-century industries were localized. Tied by geology to specific areas, mining gave rise to a series of regional economies. Tin was mined in Cornwall in the seventeenth century, and before 1700 miners had penetrated below the tin-bearing rock to reach copper, which by 1750 had become the foundation of the Cornish economy.[46] Lead was mined in Derbyshire, Cumberland, and West Durham. Rock salt

43. Marie Rowlands, *Masters and Men in the West Midlands Metalware Trades before the Industrial Revolution* (Manchester, 1975), 135. See also Marie Rowlands, "Continuity and Change in an Industrialising Society: The Case of the West Midlands Industries," in Hudson, *Regions and Industries*, 103–31.

44. Malachy Postlethwayt, *Britain's Commercial Interest Explained and Improved*, 2 vols. (London, 1757), 2:400.

45. Lord Shelburne to Lady Shelburne, 19 May 1766, quoted in Lord Fitzmaurice, ed., *Life of William Earl of Shelburne*, vol. 1, *1737–1766* (London, 1912), 276.

46. Ashton, 92.

was worked in Cheshire. Slate was quarried in the stark hills of North Wales. But the most important mining industry was, of course, coal. Coal was essential to a score of manufacturing processes, including the smelting of iron and the development of the glass and sugar industries. Concentrated in Shropshire, Worcestershire, Yorkshire, South Wales, and Staffordshire, the rapidly expanding coal mining industry fed the growth of manufactures in London, the Midlands, Yorkshire, and other areas.

In coal mining and in tool, ship, and cloth production, a wider local economy grew up around a given industry. Subsidiary trades developed to serve the principal occupation. Thus the making of spindles, reeds, combs, and cards became important enterprises in the textile areas. Similarly, the production of grindstones and crucibles—capital equipment in metalware manufacture—drew skilled artisans to Sheffield. In Kendal, a leather-making center, a half dozen smithies made shoemakers' knives and awls to supply the town's primary business.[47]

The commercial connections between members of regionalized economies spilled over into social and political relations. As T. S. Ashton noted, "Manufacturers, who competed in the market, co-operated for common ends. '[P]ublic mills' for scribbling and fulling were common in the West Riding, and societies to encourage invention and improve technique arose in many parts of the country."[48] The Society for the Encouragement of Arts, Manufactures and Commerce, established in 1754, and the Manchester Committee for the Protection and Encouragement of Trade, founded in 1774, recognized and rewarded applied ingenuity and inventions. The members of regional manufacturing associations, such as the Midland Association of Ironmasters, the London Merchants Trading to North America, or the West Riding Committee of Worsted Manufacturers, also had social and political reasons for coming together. Much of the conviviality in such societies had a businesslike purpose. Being a member of a club or society enabled the tradesman or manufacturer to broaden the range of his acquaintances, to meet new customers, creditors, or partners in an amicable atmosphere, and to exchange commercial

47. Ibid., 96.
48. Ibid., 97. One eighteenth-century observer was much less optimistic about the economic consequences of industrial cooperation. Adam Smith bemoaned this interaction: "People of the same trade seldom meet together, even for merriment or diversion, but the conversation ends in a conspiracy against the public, or in some contrivance to raise prices" (*Wealth of Nations*, 1:144). It is important to note that Smith's predecessors, political economists like Tucker and Steuart working in the 1760s and 1770s, were much less critical of manufacturing societies and industrial cooperation than was Smith.

gossip and information.[49] Often these associations acted as guilds, regulating prices, product quality, and wages.

As transport services improved and the scope of manufacturing markets expanded in the second half of the century, interregional trade increased. So did the responsibilities of trade associations. When the reputation of a particular manufacturer became nationally known, these business groups, such as the Cutlers Company of Hallamshire, controlled trade and hallmarks. The same developments that knitted the nation together commercially also extended its international economic activity. Economic transformation created novel incentives for commercial societies, which were accustomed to collective action, albeit on a regional scale, to try to influence regulation of imperial trade.

As regional economies developed, they became more integrated. Whereas France, Austria, and the German states retained internal customs duties through much of the eighteenth century and in some cases well into the nineteenth, Britain abolished all of its own in 1707. People and goods could move across England, Scotland, and Wales duty free— and they did, in increasing numbers. By the second half of the century Parliament responded to the movement, allowing hundreds of miles of turnpikes to be constructed through Britain.[50] The abolition of internal customs taxes alone did not nurture the mushrooming linkages between traders and regions. Upgraded transportation, by road, river, and canal, promoted interregional and national distribution of goods. In 1751 a journalist could describe some of Britain's primitive roads as being "what God left them after the Flood."[51] But in the middle decades of the century a series of local and parliamentary turnpike acts constructed scores of new roads and improved existing ones. It became possible to move goods and livestock to market towns and cities at all times of the year. Trade quickened. "As to new Markets at home," Josiah Tucker remarked in 1758, "every Road well mended produces that Effect in one Degree or other."[52]

River transportation also expanded, most rapidly after 1760 when England entered the canal era. From 1760 to 1800 some 165 canal acts

49. Brewer, "Commercialization and Politics," 222.

50. Linda Colley, "Britannia's Children: Images and Identities" (unpublished paper, Davis Center Colloquium, Princeton University, October, 1989), 15. On the difficulties of reconstructing markets and the distribution of goods and service in eighteenth-century England, see Julian Hoppit, "Understanding the Industrial Revolution," *Historical Journal* 30 (1987): 218.

51. *Gentleman's Magazine*, 21 May 1751, 208.

52. Josiah Tucker, *Instructions for Travellers* (London, 1758), 13.

were passed, with subsequent construction costs of approximately £113 million.[53] Canal building during this period added more than a thousand miles of navigable waterway to the nation's total.[54] Although many canals were constructed by individuals, most were the product of corporate enterprise.[55] The bulk of the money to build a given canal was raised locally. For example, 71 percent of the shareholders in the Leeds and Liverpool Canal lived in Lancashire or Yorkshire.[56]

These kinds of collective economic initiatives undertaken by men of the middling ranks represented the emerging political significance of the trading classes. Successful promotion of a proposed canal navigation, like that put forward by Josiah Wedgwood in 1765, involved extensive political activity by regional businessmen. Wedgwood, Garbett, and other Midlands manufacturers spearheaded the effort to link their region with other parts of the country by a Liverpool-Hull waterway. Wedgwood understood the importance of public opinion—locally as well as in Parliament—in approving the proposed canal. " 'A *bustle*, popular bustle must carry' the navigation 'through all difficultys at last,' " he told his partner, Thomas Bentley.[57] Wedgwood therefore asked his associate to "draw up one plain Pamphlett upon the subject."[58] Printed in 1766, Bentley's *A View to the Advantages of Inland Navigation with a Plan of a Navigable Canal*, extolled the local and national economic benefits of the projected waterway:

To have the means of conveyance so greatly facilitated; the price of carriage so much diminished; old manufactures encouraged; new ones established; estates greatly improved; plenty widely diffused; and the country, in general, rendered still more affluent, populous, and secure; are consid-

---

53. Ashton, 74–75. For more recent research on eighteenth-century canal expenditures, see G. R. Hawke and J. P. P. Higgins, "Transport and Social Overhead Capital," in Floud and McCloskey, 227–52, esp. 229. See also Paul Langford, *A Polite and Commercial People: England 1727–1783* (Oxford, 1989), 410–17.

54. Langford, *Polite and Commercial People*, 410.

55. In 1759 the second duke of Bridgewater constructed a canal from Worsley to Manchester, complete with subterranean waterways and an aqueduct over the Irwell River at Barton.

56. Ashton, 75. On the socioeconomic composition of canal investment, see Hawke and Higgins, 233. They calculate that men of commerce—manufacturers, traders, merchants—supplied 54 percent of the capital invested in canals between 1755 and 1815.

57. Josiah Wedgwood to Thomas Bentley, 26 August 1765, Wedgwood MSS, Barlaston, quoted in Money, 26.

58. Josiah Wedgwood to Thomas Bentley, 20 April 1765, manuscript copies of Wedgwood Correspondence, John Rylands Library, Manchester, 1101, 63–68.

erations of such weight as cannot fail to interest all benevolent and public-spirited persons, in the success of this *important undertaking.*[59]

On transportation issues, as in those concerning the imperial economy, provincial manufacturers in the 1760s displayed a sophisticated awareness of the importance of public opinion in parliamentary policymaking. Like Wedgwood, other spokesmen and lobbyists for business groups understood as early as 1765[60] how to marshal public consensus along commercial lines. It was the knowledge and organizational capabilities evident in such episodes as Wedgwood's canal-building efforts that helped tilt the balance of political power—local and national—in the century's second half.[61]

What did all this corporate construction do for the British economy? Thomas Bentley was correct: canals lowered the cost of transporting many commodities, most significantly those with a high ratio of bulk to value.[62] All the raw materials and finished products of the growing industries, as well as agricultural products, were carried along canals. By far the largest freight tonnage was coal.[63] Over the second half of the eighteenth century, the transport costs of coal fell approximately 50 percent,[64] and as Bentley had predicted, these reductions lowered the prices of a wide range of manufactures for which coal was an intermediate good. As the duke of Bridgewater said, "A navigation should have coals at the heel of it."[65]

Improvements in river and road transport speeded goods distribution

59. Thomas Bentley, *A View of the Advantages of Inland Navigation with a Plan of a Navigable Canal* (London, 1766), 42.

60. With reference to much of the historiography, John Money has judged precocious this eighteenth-century political awareness on the part of West Midlands manufacturers concerned to affect canal activity: "Though canal navigation was not a matter of national politics—at least, not in the eighteenth century's conventional understanding of the term— it was becoming a subject of wide concern, and in the strategy adopted by the navigators can be seen the genesis of a relationship between politics and public opinion more characteristic of nineteenth century England than of the age of oligarchy" (Money, 25). I agree, although as the rest of the chapter makes clear, I would extend this assessment to the political activity of manufacturers outside the Midlands and concerned with affecting public opinion *nationally.*

61. Paul Langford, paper presented to the Eighteenth-Century Seminar, Institute of Historical Research, University of London, summer 1988.

62. Hawke and Higgins, 234.

63. Ibid.

64. W. T. Jackman, *The Development of Transportation in Modern England* (Cambridge, 1916).

65. Quoted in Ashton, 74.

and augmented the volume of commercial traffic. Seasonal variations in prices owing to road haulage were significantly reduced. After 1760, coal was transported to London year round at prices consistent across seasons. The demand for transportation services met and nourished the growing supply as manufacturers, wholesalers, and retailers rapidly absorbed the augmented capacity of the road and canal systems.[66] From Anglesey to Edinburgh, commerce pulled Britons closer together in national (and international) economic networks. By 1760 it was not unusual for a shopkeeper like Abraham Dent of Kirby Lonsdale in Westmorland to buy primary and finished products from 190 suppliers in 51 locations.[67]

One of the most common bonds in this growing economy was that between lender and borrower. Contemporary observers estimated that two-thirds of all transactions involved credit rather than cash.[68] As goods and services markets became wider and more integrated, so too did the credit markets, formal and informal. A Leicester shopkeeper purchased silk from a Spitalfields wholesaler and paid for it with a bill of exchange. An exchequer bill—a form of government bond—settled an account between a City merchant and his solicitor. A widow in Bedford Square bought Bank of England stock with her husband's legacy. A Norwich day laborer was paid with a promissory note. In Scarborough, local tradesmen extended credit to one another. Artisans, small masters, and farmers raised funds by mortgaging their property or by signing what amounted to short-term bonds.[69] For businesses, this short-term borrowing and lending was extremely important. Peter Mathias has noted that business assets "requiring short-term credit were usually at least four or five times greater—sometimes much more than this—than the fixed assets in large-plant industry."[70] In short and longer-lived forms, credit became increasingly important as the century wore on, feeding on the expanding British economy.

66. Brewer, *Sinews of Power*, 183.

67. Ibid., 184. For another example of the diversity and breadth of retailing in the mid-eighteenth century and the underlying economy that supported it, see the diary of the Sussex shopkeeper Thomas Turner, *The Diary of Thomas Turner, 1754–1765*, ed. David Vaisey (Oxford, 1984).

68. Brewer, *Sinews of Power*, 186. See Julian Hoppit's thoughtful article on contemporary perspectives toward the explosion of credit in the eighteenth century, "Attitudes to Credit, 1680–1790," *Historical Journal* 33 (1990): 305–322.

69. Brewer, *Sinews of Power*, 186.

70. Peter Mathias, "Capital, Credit and Enterprise in the Industrial Revolution," in *The Transformation of England: Essays in the Economic and Social History of England in the Eighteenth Century* (London, 1979), 94.

By making transactions easier, all this credit certainly greased the wheels of England's inland and international commerce, but there were other macroeconomic benefits as well. The existence and flexibility of credit in a wide variety of forms helped ensure that savings did not lie idle but were channeled into productive arenas with relatively high rates of return.[71] As important, the ubiquity of trade credit went a long way toward compensating for the frequent shortage of specie in the eighteenth-century economy. And finally, all this borrowing and lending kept the developing markets for financial capital functioning even in the face of slow communications and returns on investment where the speed of realization was uncertain and unpredictable. "Credit was vital," Julian Hoppit has observed, "in allowing businessmen to cope with this, enabling them to balance income with expenditure."[72]

As trade and personal credit spun a wide web over the British economy,[73] it entangled ever more people in the potential problems of such a system. An economy in which as many transactions were conducted on credit as in cash made, as Hoppit notes, "any individual's chances at least partially dependent on the success of those both within and without his immediate circle of trading contacts. Interdependence is of course a timeless fact of business life, but it was particularly damaging in the eighteenth century because of the articulation of many loans by bills of exchange."[74] Many contemporary observers were frightened by the speed with which the new network of borrowing and lending bound together individuals' economic fates. Men and women who had to extend credit, commented one commercial writer in 1756, were "certainly in a constant hazardous Situation, and though perfectly circumspect and parsimonious themselves, as their Effects are in so many different Hands, may chance to be hurried in an Instant to the most distressful Ebb, by the failure of a Customer or Correspondent."[75] During the middle decades of the eighteenth century, growing numbers of people became involved in inter-

71. As Mathias points out, and as chapter 3 of this book explores, the consistent decline in real interest rates on government bonds through the first six decades of the eighteenth century "evidenced the progressive availability of savings in relation in investment opportunities" (91).

72. Julian Hoppit, "The Use and Abuse of Credit in Eighteenth Century England," in *Business Life and Public Policy: Essays in honour of D. C. Coleman*, ed. Neil McKendrick and R. B. Outhwaite (Cambridge, 1986), 66.

73. Ibid.

74. Ibid., 67.

75. *The Tradesmen Director, or The London and Country Shopkeeper's Useful Companion* (London, 1756), 12–13.

connected markets for goods and credit. The scope and size of these markets expanded across cities and the countryside, and interchange between the mother country and its colonies rose significantly. Caught up in economic transformation, Britons perceived themselves as more and more affected by any circumstances that contaminated or improved the commercial health of the nation. Such perceptions had important political repercussions.

In the midst of increasing commercial integration, urbanization in eighteenth-century Britain grew in rapid and novel ways. During the medieval and early modern periods, the country's urban population had not been particularly large, but this picture began to change significantly in the seventeenth century. Between the last quarter of the seventeenth century and the midpoint of the next, urban dwellers rose from 13.5 percent to 21 percent of the total population. Beyond London the urban population grew even more swiftly, from 4 to 9.5 percent.[76] This urban expansion continued through the entire eighteenth century. The share of towns other than London with more than 5,000 inhabitants climbed substantially, rising from 6 to 17 percent of the national total over the course of the century and by 1800 exceeding London's share.[77] New cities surged ahead. Medieval towns, once regionally or even nationally dominant, fell behind. Wrigley explains:

Several cities which had once figured prominently in the English urban hierarchy, including Norwich, Exeter, and York, grew less quickly than the population overall and ended the century with smaller fractions of the national total than at the beginning. For many centuries such towns had exchanged places in the premier urban league, but the league's membership had not greatly altered. By 1800, however, only Bristol, Newcastle, and Norwich of the old major regional centers remained among the country's largest towns. Manchester, Liverpool, and Birmingham stood second, third, and fourth, after London. They ranged between 70,000 and 90,000 in population, having grown fiftyfold or more since the early sixteenth century.[78]

There were other newly burgeoning towns. Leeds and Sheffield, home to expanding manufacturing enterprises, both saw their populations more than triple in the last five decades of the eighteenth century. The

76. Brewer, *Sinews of Power*, 180.
77. Wrigley, 130.
78. Ibid., 130–31.

port and dockyard centers also expanded significantly. Portsmouth's population trebled between 1750 and 1800; during this same time, the number of Plymouth's inhabitants climbed from 15,000 to 43,000.[79] The pace and magnitude of such urban growth were unprecedented in eighteenth-century Europe.[80]

What was responsible for such swift urbanization? This is a complicated problem, one economic historians have not yet thoroughly unraveled. On the most obvious level, manufacturing growth, transport improvements, and an increase in the relative significance of international trade in the national economy stimulated urban expansion in cities such as Birmingham and Leeds. More efficient transportation and booming international commerce also fueled the growth of various port cities, especially those, like Liverpool and Newcastle, that rode the back of the progressively buoyant Atlantic trade in the eighteenth century.[81]

On a deeper level, historians of the eighteenth-century economy are confronted with a thornier issue: What lay behind the widespread and steady growth that powered all this manufacturing, transport, and overseas interchange? A comprehensive exploration of this problem is beyond the scope of this book,[82] but it is important to observe that on the supply side,[83] much of Britain's eighteenth-century industrial output and thus

79. Ibid., 126.

80. For an analysis of Britain's experience in the context of other European nations, see ibid., 145–65.

81. As Wrigley notes, such reasoning is subject to errors of simplification and oversight, (ibid., 134–35). He concludes, "it remains reasonable to argue, however, that there were important links between some types of urban growth and real income trends in early modern England" (135).

82. Historiographically, the causes of Britain's industrialization and economic growth during the eighteenth century are two of the most important topics in the current research and literature of the industrial revolution. For an overview of recent writings on this topic, see Cannadine; Julian Hoppit, "Counting the Industrial Revolution," *Economic History Review* 43 (1990): 173–93, and idem, "Understanding the Industrial Revolution." More specifically, see Crafts, *British Economic Growth during the Industrial Revolution*; Joel Mokyr, *The Economics of the Industrial Revolution* (London, 1985); G. N. Von Tunzelman, "Technical Progress during the Industrial Revolution," in Floud and McCloskey, 143–63; J. G. Williamson, "Why Was Britain's Economic Growth So Slow during the Industrial Revolution?" *Journal of Economic History* 44 (1984): 687–712; D. N. McCloskey, "The Industrial Revolution: A Survey," in Floud and McCloskey, 103–27; and C. H. Feinstein, "Capital Accumulation in the Industrial Revolution," in Floud and McCloskey, 128–42.

83. Recent research on the causes of British industrialization has focused on the supply side of the economy. That is, economists have (sought and) found the stimuli to secondary and tertiary sector growth as well as the structural transformations inherent in such change in issues of labor supply, capital accumulation, total factor productivity growth, and human ingenuity—all elements in the production of goods and services. Most recently, scholarly attention has focused on the significance of total factor productivity growth—a statistical

urban expansion was predicated on improvements in agricultural efficiency, specifically an increase in output-per-worker ratios. Adam Smith, Arthur Young, and other political economists of the 1760s and 1770s understood this relationship. Smith, for example, articulated the prerequisites for economic success:

A piece of fine cloth, for example, which weighs only eighty pounds, contains in it, the price, not only of eighty pounds weight of wool, but sometimes of several thousand weight of corn, the maintenance of the different working people, and of their immediate employers. The corn, which could with difficulty have been carried abroad in its own shape, is in this manner virtually exported in that of the complete manufacture, and may easily be sent to the remotest corners of the world. In this manner have grown up naturally, and as it were of their own accord, the manufactures of Leeds, Halifax, Sheffield, Birmingham, and Wolverhampton. Such manufactures are the offspring of agriculture.[84]

Smith, like his scholarly counterparts two hundred years later, realized that only if human and material resources were spared from the necessity of supplying an adequate amount of food could a larger and broader scale of industrial manufacturing be attempted.[85] Britain's farming sector during the eighteenth century was clearly capable of releasing resources in significant quantities, and this during a time when population and the need for food were growing quickly.[86]

The relation between improvements in agricultural productivity, industrialization, and urban growth in eighteenth-century Britain is an interesting one. Throughout the period, the average output of individual agricultural workers increased steadily. Because of this, farming could relinquish labor to manufacturing, fueling industrial and urban expansion and the country's rapidly changing occupational structure.

Overseas trade became increasingly important as the century wore on.

residual that measures how much of output expansion we can attribute to elements other than the growth of labor and capital—and issues of labor supply. Epistomologically this represents a significant volte-face from the economic historiography of the 1960s when the demand side of the eighteenth-century economy played a larger role in scholarly reconstructions of productivity growth. What lies behind this significant shift in perspective is an interesting and unexplored question.

84. Smith, 1:43; see also Young, 74–75.

85. Wrigley, 162.

86. Crafts, *British Economic Growth during the Industrial Revolution*, 115–21. For an opposing view, see E. L. Jones, *Agriculture and the Industrial Revolution* (Oxford, 1974), 102.

Between 1700 and 1800, imports into Great Britain expanded by more than 500 percent. Exports grew more than 560 percent and reexports by over 900 percent. The population of Britain increased by just over 250 percent. So foreign trade became progressively more significant per capita.[87] The pace of this expansion in trade, like the growth of national output overall, accelerated over the course of the century. From 1700 to 1740, the rate of growth of the nation's international trade was 0.8 percent annually; during the next four decades it was 1.7 percent; and in the last thirty years of the century it grew at an annual rate of 2.6 percent.

What do these numbers mean for a reconstruction of the perspectives and policies of the first empire? The figures confirm what contemporary political economists and imperial ministers understood about their country's dominion. They knew that Britain's "great machine of trade" was increasingly dependent on foreign consumption of British manufactures and external provision of the raw materials used in manufacturing production and agricultural processing.[88]

As Mildmay, Tucker, and other writers realized in the 1760s, the changing composition of England's growing international trade reinforced the structural transformation already under way in the nation's economy. That is, agriculture's significance as a fraction of exports fell markedly over the century's first fifty years. By 1750 Britain, long a net provider of food to other parts of the world, had become a net importer of grains.[89] In sharp contrast, manufacturing exports grew rapidly—sixfold over the century.[90] British exports had been dominated by trade in woolen cloth for centuries, but this good became a much less significant portion of eighteenth century trade.[91] In place of woolen cloth, the nation's export commerce grew up around metalwares, glass, earthenware, and nonwoolen textiles—linen, fustians, and cotton. The contribution of these rapidly growing manufactured exports to eighteenth-century industrialization is a source of significant controversy among twentieth-century economic historians. Some researchers, such as W. A. Cole, contend that the size, composition, and speed of growth of exports,

87. R.P. Thomas and D. N. McCloskey, "Overseas Trade and Empire, 1700–1860," in Floud and McCloskey, 87.
88. William Mildmay, *The Laws and Policy of England relating to Trade* (London, 1765), 63; Tucker, *Four Tracts*, 199.
89. Cole, 39.
90. Ibid.
91. Ralph Davis, "English Foreign Trade, 1700–1774," *Economic History Review* 15 (1962–63): 286. See also Cole, 39.

coupled with their tendency to outpace domestic consumption, accounted for almost 40 percent of the increase in industrial output over the century.[92] Ralph Davis, R. P. Thomas, Donald McCloskey, and others deny that all this international exchange significantly affected industrial development.[93]

Yet 220 years ago there was much less disagreement about the role of overseas trade in the growth and prosperity of Britain's economy. As the next chapter explores in greater detail, eighteenth-century statesmen and commercial writers conceived of economic expansion as primarily demand driven and export oriented. For these men, Britain's power and plenty increasingly depended on its ability to sell large amounts of manufactures abroad. If past and present economists have not always agreed on the importance of overseas trade in stimulating industrial development, they have generally concurred that the growth in foreign trade induced the economy to become more specialized in manufacturing and reduced its dependence on agriculture.[94]

Where were British exports sent? Like other questions concerning the eighteenth-century economy, the answer to this one depends on the period. In the opening decades of the century, more than 80 percent of England's exports went to Europe. Yet by 1770 Europeans purchased only 30 percent of Britain's exports. In place of Dutch, French, and German consumers, a growing number of American customers—both in the mainland colonies and in the West Indies—bought 44 percent of Britain's exportable goods. India took almost 10 percent and Ireland 5 percent. Although the American markets were not the mother country's only important outlets for its manufactures, they were far and away its most valuable and fastest growing. Over the course of the century, ex-

92. Cole, 41.

93. Ralph Davis, *The Industrial Revolution and British Overseas Trade* (Leicester, 1979), 62–64; Thomas and McCloskey, 100–102. See also Joel Mokyr, "Demand vs. Supply in the Industrial Revolution," in *Economics of the Industrial Revolution*, 100. To a large extent, one's position in this historiographic debate depends on one's stance in a larger, related scholarly controversy over the relative significance of demand and supply forces in England's industrialization. Not surprisingly, those economists who have seen demand as predominant in catalyzing industrialization have been concerned with exports in this regard. Supply siders, who currently represent a large majority of economic historians writing on the eighteenth century, are much less interested in the contribution of international trade. If supply calls forth its own demand, as most cliometricians reason, lower demand for British exports would, ceteris paribus, have been effectively supplanted by higher domestic demand (Thomas and McCloskey, 100).

94. Thomas and McCloskey, 90. On the changing composition of exports and imports, see Crafts, *British Economic Growth during the Industrial Revolution*, 143.

ports to North America and the West Indies climbed 2,300 percent.[95] Political economists and government officials in the 1760s and 1770s were cognizant of this growth and valued these markets accordingly. But members of the wider political nation had other reasons to view these distant outlets as significant. In qualitative terms, Brewer elaborates:

> [The American colonies] received disproportionate emphasis not only because of the swiftness of their expansion, but also because they contributed to some of the most *visible* changes in British economic and social life. The emergence of tobacco, tea and sugar as staples in the domestic economy of all classes; the presence in London of prodigiously wealthy West Indian nabobs whose extravagance made them a byword for tastelessness; the rapid expansion of the cottage industries producing textiles in Yorkshire and metal goods in the West Midlands for transatlantic markets: all were tangible evidence of the colonial contribution to British prosperity.[96]

One commercial writer spoke for many when in 1765 he wrote to Lord Rockingham about the importance of England's geographical offspring across the Atlantic. The American colonies, he said, not only "consume vast quantities of our Manufactures, [produce] . . . many raw materials, but they *are* so situated, their numbers so increased, . . . as to give vast addition to the consequences [commerce and prosperity] of Great Britain."[97] William Shirley, former governor of Massachusetts, calculated in 1755 that the population of North America doubled every twenty years.[98]

Throughout the 1760s, the American colonies represented Britain's most rapidly expanding markets, but imperial experts were by no means ignorant of India's vast economic potential. As the postwar decade wore on and difficulties with North America mounted, the commercial significance of the eastern subcontinent loomed ever larger to Britons. Chapter

---

95. Thomas and McCloskey, 91.

96. Brewer, *Sinews of Power*, 185.

97. Rockingham MSS, Wentworth-Woodhouse Muniments (hereafter WWM), Sheffield City Library, R65–5b.

98. William Shirley to John Robinson, 15 August 1755, State Papers, Colonial America and West Indies, Public Record Office, 82, cited in George Beer, *British Colonial Policy, 1754–1765* (New York, 1907), 142. Social and demographic historians have confirmed Shirley's estimates of population growth: "Between 1700 and 1770, the population of the mainland colonies rose approximately eightfold, from roughly 275,000 to 2,210,000. During the decade of the 1760s, it jumped almost 40 percent"; T. H. Breen, "An Empire of Goods: The Anglicization of Colonial America, 1690–1776," *Journal of British Studies* 25 (1986): 485.

4 of this book examines the interconnections between the empire's eastern and western dominions. Here it is sufficient to note that India's
statistical importance as an outlet for British goods rose throughout the
century: in 1700 India purchased 4 percent of British exports; in 1797
it took more than 12 percent.[99]

Britain's increasingly international economy was vulnerable to disruptions: war, harvest failure, or a domestic or overseas financial crisis could
induce a depression. All three factors buffeted the British economy
between 1763 and 1773.[100] Military conflict, an almost regular occurrence
between 1688 and 1820, usually interrupted the nation's international
trade, pushing import prices up and export prices down. Nominal wages
and prices often rose during wartime as the state issued various debt
instruments—exchequer, navy, and treasury bills—and increased the
effective money supply. But real incomes and thus home demand fell,
and national recessions ensued. For the Wars of Spanish and Austrian
Succession, as well as the American War, these macroeconomic effects
were significant.

The British economic experience during the Seven Years War was
much more ambiguous, however. With its navy usually in command of
the seas, Britain's international trade and manufacturing output continued to expand even during the war. In North America, Prussia, India,
and Ireland, war-induced additions to demand increased England's exports and reexports to these areas by more than 33 percent between the
onset of the fighting and the conclusion of peace.[101] Many imperial experts and observers saw this as an unparalleled achievement by the nation's economy and an important precedent for its future performance.
But this boom did not significantly outlast the war, and shortly after the
signing of the Peace of Paris, Britain suffered a reversal of its usual
postwar fortunes. Instead of an economic recovery accompanying the

99. Thomas and McCloskey, 91.

100. On war and the eighteenth-century economy, see T. S. Ashton, *Economic Fluctuations in England, 1700–1800* (Oxford, 1959); A. H. John, "War and the English Economy, 1700–1763," *Economic History Review* 7 (1955): 329–44; Brewer, *Sinews of Power*, 191–99. On eighteenth-century financial crises, see Julian Hoppit, "Financial Crises in Eighteenth-Century England," *Economic History Review* 39 (1986): 39–58, idem, "Risk and Failure in English Industry" (Ph.D. diss., Cambridge University, 1984), idem, and *Risk and Failure in English Business, 1700–1800* (Cambridge, 1987). On harvest failures, see Ashton, *Economic Fluctuations*.

101. Elizabeth B. Schumpeter, *English Overseas Trade Statistics, 1697–1808* (Oxford, 1960), 15–16.

end of hostilities, the nation endured a postwar recession—a real drop in international commerce from wartime levels. Bankruptcies among City businesses climbed.[102] In 1763 a financial crisis on the Amsterdam stock market spread to London, heightening City worries about the bloated national debt and exacerbating England's recessionary woes.

Macroeconomic conditions did not improve much in the middle 1760s. Relative to their wartime levels, exports to America, Europe, India, and Ireland fell in 1764 and 1765, depressing incomes and domestic demand for manufactured goods. Bad harvests in 1766 and 1767 pushed food prices—on the rise since the late 1740s—up sharply, sparking grain riots throughout the country.[103] In the closing years of the decade, Britain's exports and imports increased, but the nation's real output in 1770 was 2 percent lower than a decade earlier when the exigencies of war had pushed production up.[104] With historical hindsight it seems an almost imperceptible decline—a mere stumble along the British economy's smooth and sure journey toward industrialization.

But for manufacturers, MPs, and other Britons in 1770, the stagnation seemed frightening and unexpected after the boom years of the early 1760s. The nation's victory in the Seven Years War piqued imperial ambitions and anxieties. Shaped in the unique macroeconomic conditions of wartime, commercial expectations were extraordinarily powerful throughout the postwar decade in affecting how British officials viewed and governed the imperial system.

Neither the anticipation nor the fear that eighteenth-century Englishmen manifested toward the new empire was consistently justified by macroeconomic circumstances. As twentieth-century economic historians have confirmed, the nation's continued prosperity after the Seven Years War was contingent on factors beyond the state's control; the fiscal health of the postwar government was sounder than contemporaries understood. Britain's fate was to be less extreme than its citizens prophesied in the 1760s. But economic historians did not make eighteenth-century

102. Hoppit attributes these bankruptcies in 1763 to international stimuli, specifically the collapse of more than twenty major financial houses in Amsterdam ("Financial Crises," 50). Undoubtedly this financial crisis—to apply Hoppit's terminology—was important to contemporary perceptions, but in analyzing the sources of bankruptcies and other business failures, it is essential to be cognizant of other macroeconomic conditions.

103. See Walter J. Shelton, *English Hunger and Industrial Disorders: A Study of Social Conflict during the First Decade of George III's Reign* (Toronto, 1973).

104. This was the only eighteenth-century decline in such ten-year measurements (Cole, 64).

imperial policy; contemporary statesmen did, and they acted on their own contrasting attitudes within a macroeconomic environment that alternately confirmed both the potential and the angst of dominion.

The political role of the eighteenth-century economy extended beyond the shaping and validation of imperial perspectives. Aspects of the transforming economy created new incentives and opportunities for political action by men of movable property. One aspect was the growing significance and integration of credit markets in the national economy. An increasingly interregional structure linked the fortunes of tradesmen in Wakefield and elsewhere with the London money market. The vicissitudes of the capital were now also the opportunities or misfortunes of the wider commercial nation.[105] Provincial businessmen understandably became more concerned with events both in London and abroad, and this concern in turn stimulated their interest in national policymaking.[106]

The growing provincial press fed local appetites for political information. But accurate descriptions of an incompetent government decision or a financial disaster were hardly compensation for many Britons. To those affected by bad policies and vacillations in the credit markets, it seemed that political and economic events often lay beyond their control.[107] Hostility grew toward a political system epitomized by the stockjobber and placeman. As the scope and magnitude of commercial credit and the nation's debt grew, so did the incentives to affect economic policymaking. Throughout the 1760s, more and more men of movable property became concerned with having a greater say in national government.

For the men of commerce, this meant becoming involved in issues of empire. During the postwar decade, financial and other commercial interests from London and provincial cities were heavily involved in the debates surrounding the fate of the East India Company. As the first East India inquiry unfolded in the autumn of 1766, the linkages between the Company's fortunes, the size of the national debt, and the condition of the London stock market came onto the parliamentary stage and into the public eye. To William Beckford and other MPs representing the forces of City radicalism, the Company symbolized the dangers of unsound financial speculation. The trading concern also represented the immense potential of Eastern wealth—prosperity and ostentation being

---

105. Brewer, "Commercialization and Politics," 229.
106. Ibid.
107. Ibid.

enjoyed by the small but conspicuous class of "nabobs" who were thrusting themselves on British society.[108] One contemporary observer commented, "The Interest the Publick hath in the Indian Territories furnishes a strong argument, in favour of a claim on behalf of the Publick to a share of [the] management"[109] of commerce and company financial practices. (The final chapter of this book argues that such sentiments were to acquire much more political momentum by 1772 and the onset of a nationwide credit crisis.)

The new and growing importance of credit was not the only macroeconomic thread tying men of commerce together politically and pulling them toward Westminster and Whitehall. The country's changing occupational structure greatly increased the number of manufacturers and tradesmen, especially after 1750. A shifting output mix, from agriculture to secondary and tertiary sector production, heightened the political significance of the men of movable property in a commercial empire. Versed in the doctrines of political economy, ministers knew that these men and their manufactures mattered to England's power and prosperity. In 1769 Edmund Burke looked back to the economic effects of the Stamp Act:

Our trade felt this to its vitals: and our then ministers were not ashamed to say, that they sympathized with the feelings of our merchants. The universal alarm of the whole trading body of England will never be laughed at by them as an ill-grounded or pretended panick. The universal desire of that body will always have great weight with them in every consideration connected with commerce; neither ought the opinion of that body to be slighted . . . in any consideration whatsoever of revenue.[110]

Burke and other elite politicians had their own reasons for championing the interests of the trading classes—rationales that were rooted in the political configuration of empire. The structural transformations that occurred in the eighteenth-century economy justified and reinforced the political significance of these particular constituencies to ministers and MPs.

108. Lucy S. Sutherland, *The East India Company in Eighteenth-Century Politics* (Westport, Conn., 1979), 147.

109. "Observations on the Heads of a Bill for the Better Regulation of the British Settlements in India," Shelburne Papers, Clements Library, 99/209–11.

110. Edmund Burke, "Observations on a Late State of the Nation" (London, 1769), in *Writings and Speeches of Edmund Burke*, vol 2, *Party, Parliament and the American Crisis, 1766–1774*, ed. Paul Langford (Oxford, 1981), 191.

From the top down and the bottom up, the changing economy altered the balance of political power in England. The growing number of businessmen, producing ever larger quantities of goods and services in the 1760s, became increasingly interested in trying to affect commercial policymaking. For the expanding number of concerns and communities heavily dependent on imperial interchange, this meant coming to the center of dominion—Whitehall and Parliament. And this they did, often acquiring political cohesion and initiating petitions in trade associations. In 1763 merchants and iron manufacturers from London, Birmingham, Wolverhampton, and Walsall joined iron- and steelmakers from Sheffield to successfully lobby the Grenville administration for subsidies on American iron imports.

Three years later, textile and metalware manufacturers from Manchester, Leeds, Bradford, Nottingham, and Leicester testified before Parliament that their trade was being ruined and unemployment was rising in these cities as a result of American boycotts in response to the Stamp Act.[111] During this same year, Samuel Garbett tried to organize a national coalition of manufacturers—a broad-based permanent lobby that would concentrate its efforts on parliamentary factions concerned with promoting industrial interests. He failed in 1766 to achieve this objective, but he succeeded in calling ministerial attention to the industrial wonders of the Midlands. He acted as a kind of one-man chamber of commerce for Birmingham, showing Burke, Grafton, Shelburne, and other statesmen the manufacturing marvels of the region.[112]

This kind of political action was not confined to Yorkshire and the Midlands, but it is not surprising that many manufacturing initiatives in this period originated in the expanding industrial regions. The parliamentary and ministerial debates surrounding imperial governance in the 1760s and 1770s also saw collective inputs from the Bristol Merchant Adventurers, from West Indian traders, from London merchants involved in North American interchange, from Norwich weavers, and from other commercial concerns. Some of these organizations were newly formed; others had existed for decades.

The attempt specific lobbyists and groups made in the postwar decade to secure their own advantage in the policymaking process was not a novel historical occurrence: special interests had been banging on the

111. Langford, *First Rockingham Administration*, 181.

112. J. M. Norris, "Samuel Garbett in the Early Development of Industrial Lobbying in Great Britain," *Economic History Review*, 2d ser., 10 (1957–58): 452. On Shelburne's tour of industrial Birmingham, see Fitzmaurice, 1:274–76.

doors of Parliament since the sixteenth century. But historians have correctly argued that in the twenty years before the American Revolution, more of them were banging louder than in the past.[113] According to Michael Kammen, 1760–1780 constituted an "age of interests,"[114] a period when "the government was susceptible as never before" to influence and pressures from various interest groups.[115] He traces the organizational abilities and ambitions of these groups, so obvious in the imperial debates of the 1760s, to the period two decades earlier. Kammen contends that after 1745 a series of political and economic circumstances greatly amplified the capacities and objectives of interest groups. Macroeconomic growth, Pelham's permissive attitude toward a range of special interests, and the general political instability that followed his death broadened the effectiveness of special interests.[116] Certainly, since the mid-1750s contemporary observers such as Benjamin Franklin and David Hume had been aware of the aggressive emergence of extraparliamentary forces.[117] In the political confusion surrounding the accession of George III in 1760, official concern with interest groups escalated significantly. Kammen is surely right to point to the deterioration of the party system and to general political turbulence in explaining the enlarged importance of extraparliamentary forces in the 1760s and 1770s.

Equally distinctive, if less historically analyzed, is the proliferation of provincial and metropolitan *manufacturing* groups, organized around what were rapidly becoming industrial concerns. As Britain's experience following the Seven Years War demonstrates, this was a decade when some of the fastest growing extraparliamentary concerns were made up of manufacturers. The prominence of manufacturing interests in the policy discussions and decisions of the 1760s owed more to specific macroeconomic transitions than Kammen suggests.[118] Also unique during this

113. Michael Kammen, *Empire and Interest: The American Colonies and the Politics of Mercantilism* (New York, 1970), 95–98; Brewer, *Sinews of Power*, 231–49; Alison Gilbert Olson, *Making the Empire Work: London and American Interest Groups, 1690–1790* (Cambridge, Mass., 1992), 124–25.

114. Kammen, *Empire and Interest*, 95.

115. Michael Kammen, "British and Imperial Interests in the Age of the American Revolution," in *Anglo-American Political Relations, 1675–1775*, ed. Alison Gilbert Olson and Richard Maxwell Brown (New Brunswick, N.J., 1970), 145.

116. Ibid., 143–44.

117. See Benjamin Franklin to Isaac Norris, 19 March 1759, in *The Papers of Benjamin Franklin*, ed. Leonard W. Labaree, 29 vols. to date (New Haven, Conn., 1959–), 8:295–96; Franklin to David Hume, 27 September 1760, ibid., 9:229; Mildmay, 101.

118. Kammen is quick to credit rapid economic growth with political instability, and he rightly contends that such growth in the 1740s contributed to the increased prominence

period was the attention these groups focused on trying to affect *imperial* policymaking in a national forum—on influencing an interconnected and international economy.

For the growing number of Britons who relied on a mostly thriving manufacturing sector, the geopolitical and fiscal circumstances of the Seven Years War changed the rules of the political game. The Peace of Paris enormously expanded the purview and benefits of an "empire of goods,"[119] earning Britain possible dominion over vast new markets and millions of potential customers. For the men of movable property, the incentives to affect government's management of this commercial system had never been higher. As important, many of the leaders of the manufacturing groups recognized how critically the financial foundations of Britain's victory in the Seven Years War had depended on a robust trade in manufactures. Samuel Garbett knew, as did Arthur Young, that customs and excise duties on British manufactures had powered military expenditures and debt service. This recognition—on their part as well as by political elites—provided such men with new confidence and clout in the debates surrounding imperial governance.

This is not to imply that businessmen were not interested in domestic politics during the first empire. Undoubtedly, local and regional issues—where and when to construct a turnpike, what shire lands to enclose, how to regulate prices—occupied much of the time that men like Garbett and Wedgwood chose to devote to collective activity. But as the economy became more nationally and internationally integrated, so too did the political priorities of the organized trading classes. The people who led these groups brought the skills they had acquired in local political struggles to bear on imperial policy debates in Whitehall and Westminster.

One of the most potent weapons these men used was public opinion. On a range of significant issues centering on the imperial system of commerce and inexorably connected to Britain's economic health, provincial and metropolitan lobbyists recognized the political importance of public consensus. Claiming to speak for the commercial health of the country, the various lobbying groups—some permanent, others ad hoc—used this understanding to mobilize and present public opinion on a *national* scale. Thus, during the parliamentary debates concerning the

---

and confidence of a variety of interest groups in the wake of Pelham's death ("British and Imperial Interests," 146). He does not, however, precisely articulate the interconnections between macroeconomic expansion, general political volatility, and the emergence of specific interests.

119. Breen.

repeal of the Stamp Act, manufacturers and merchants testified that the fall-off in their commerce was due to North American boycotts of British goods. They chose to illustrate the deleterious effects of this economic slowdown by documenting how much regional unemployment had resulted. Robert Hamilton, a fustian manufacturer from Manchester, claimed he had laid off 2,400 men, while William Reeve, who led the Bristol merchants, told the Commons that unemployment was high and rising among West Country nailmakers.[120]

Why did the commercial classes play such a prominent role in the imperial debates of the 1760s and early 1770s? Political elites had pragmatic and ideological reasons for soliciting and supporting manufacturing interests. In the struggle for parliamentary supremacy, established politicians used the power of commerce and its social representatives—manufacturers and other tradesmen—to legitimate their positions. Shifts in the eighteenth-century economy buttressed the importance of these new and growing constituencies, as MPs and imperial ministers saw Britain's output and international trade grow at unprecedented rates. They also cannot have been unimpressed by the expansion of Manchester, Leeds, Liverpool, and Birmingham—towns that in their lifetimes had become cities and regional centers built upon manufactured goods. (After his tour of a Birmingham gun-making manufactory, Shelburne marveled, "This trade, great as it is, is not above twenty or twenty-five years' standing.")[121] Small wonder that "the consideration of those great commercial interests,"[122] as Burke dubbed the manufacturers and their issues, had become the overriding frame of reference in which imperial policy was to be debated and evaluated. Less surprising is the role—often carefully orchestrated—that the trading classes were allowed to play in parliamentary rhetoric.

But there is more to explain. Political identities, opportunities, and rhetoric were not imposed solely from above.[123] Particular men, usually in organized coalitions, *chose* to come to Parliament and the ministries to try to influence the politics and policies of the first empire. Mere access to a parliamentary forum does not tell us why men invested their energies

120. Langford, *First Rockingham Administration*, 182. See also Rockingham MSS, WWM, R97, R57.

121. Quoted in Fitzmaurice, 1:278.

122. Edmund Burke, Commons debate, 28 February 1769, in *Sir Henry Cavendish's Debates of the House of Commons during the Thirteenth Parliament of Great Britain*, ed. J. Wright, 2 vols. (London, 1841), 1:266.

123. Linda Colley makes a similar, though broader, point in "Britannia's Children," 22.

this way, how they came to organize themselves, or why they chose to cast their interests in terms of an increasingly commercialized conception of the public interest.

To answer these questions, we need to examine the intersection of politics and economics in the 1760s. Between the fissures of an unstable order, new forces pushed up to the surface of national politics, transforming its patterns and eroding the barriers—structural and ideological—that political leaders had constructed for their own protection.[124] Men of commerce, men of movable property, men dependent on and representative of the country's evolving economy were part of these forces.

By 1760 the overwhelming majority of British citizens did not—could not—live out their lives uncontaminated by trade.[125] Its exuberant growth put Britons from all walks and shires into more frequent contact with each other. Regionalized economies and newly large urban centers spawned trade associations, which became breeding grounds for numerous extraparliamentary organizations. In Bristol and Westminster, cities with eighteenth-century histories of opposition to government, the political soil was already fertile for challenges to oligarchic rule.[126]

Informed by the proliferation of an active provincial press—itself a child of Britain's commercial success—these men tried, with uneven success, to influence the management of the imperial economy. In 1766 manufacturers played a significant role in repealing the Stamp Act. Three years later, they could not convince the same legislature to revoke the tea tax. This was hardly the emergence of full-scale middle-class politics or of nineteenth-century-style liberalism. It was, rather, part of the broader and longer term eighteenth-century challenge to political oligarchy—a challenge whose origins, evolution, and successes grew out of the interconnections between political and economic change. The men of movable property and their attempts to affect the imperial economy were part of this challenge. So too were the politicians in Whitehall and Westminster who responded to commercial interests. In London and beyond, a transforming economy underlay the policies and players of imperial management.

124. Brewer, *Party Ideology*, 267.
125. Colley, "Britannia's Children," 16.
126. Rogers, *Whigs and Cities*, 403–6.

❦ THREE

Managing the "Great Machine of Trade"

MOST HISTORIANS have not lingered over the field of eighteenth-century political economy as it was practiced before 1776. Scholars of economic thought have usually hurried on to the century's main event, Adam Smith's *Wealth of Nations*. This is unfortunate historiographically, because the discipline came of age between 1745 and 1775. Cognizant of the breadth of Britain's macroeconomic transition and the challenges confronting a nation almost habitually at war, a score of informed observers attempted to systematize their theories and observations about the British economy. They also tried to legitimate this sphere of endeavor by establishing the science of commerce. Throughout the middle decades of the century, men like Josiah Tucker and James Steuart strove to educate ministers and other government officials in the emerging field of political economy.

Their efforts affected imperial governance after the Seven Years War. In the particular circumstances that obtained in Britain after 1763, the making of government policy met the study of economy, with important results. As statesmen struggled to manage Britain's newly enlarged empire, commercial observers attempted to describe the functioning of the nation's changing and increasingly international economy. In and outside government, these men confronted a similar dilemma: how to govern the frontiers and finances of a world power.

Within this imperative, policy and political economy fed on each other. Government ministers such as George Grenville and Edmund Burke agreed that Britain's dominions were to be governed as markets for the mother country's manufactures. As important, the colonies and India were to help maintain the fiscal sinews of the nation's military power by providing state revenues. In formulating these objectives and the policies to achieve them, government officials relied heavily on a growing body of economic theory. Political economists, in turn, articulated commercial principles in terms of policymaking as well as the country's transforming economy. They did so within a geopolitical frame of reference. For economic theorists and ministers, one overarching preconception obtained: power equaled wealth. As William Mildmay, author of the *Laws and Policy of England relating to Trade*, explained in 1765,

A *Nation* cannot be safe without *Power*; *Power* cannot be obtained without *Riches*; nor *Riches* without Trade . . . An increase of *National Wealth* may be procured, by enforcing such laws as are most agreeable to the *Maxims* and *Principles* which govern the true interest of *Trade*; such, I mean as can conveniently be put in execution, with regard to the exigencies of our own government; the state of foreign affairs, and the different interests of each independent kingdom.[1]

The equation of power and wealth was not new. Throughout the sixteenth and seventeenth centuries, statesmen and commercial commentators had understood that national prosperity was esential to international ascendancy. What was novel about this connection in the aftermath of the Seven Years War was the specific form it assumed for eighteenth-century British citizens. Elite politicians, economic writers, and others realized that the empire's fate depended on sound fiscal administration and British manufacturing capacity, and this collective understanding informed imperial policymaking.

Was this realization a unique consequence of the war? Several historians, interested in the origins of the American Revolution, have seen the stimuli to colonial policy during the 1760s in a pattern of imperial governance established in the preceding two decades.[2] Jack Greene and

1. William Mildmay, *The Laws and Policy of England relating to Trade* (London, 1765), 3–4.

2. Jack P. Greene, " 'A Posture of Hostility': A Reconsideration of Some Aspects of the Origins of the American Revolution," *Proceedings of the American Antiquarian Society* 87 (1977): 27–68; idem, "The Seven Years War and the American Revolution: The Causal Relationship Reconsidered," *Journal of Imperial and Commonwealth History* 8 (1980): 85–105; idem, "An Uneasy Connection: An Analysis of the Preconditions of the American Revolution," in *Essays on the American Revolution*, ed. Stephen Kurtz and James Huston

P. J. Marshall have each contended that the temporary peace afforded by the Treaty of Aix-la-Chapelle (1748), in conjunction with other factors, gave rise to Board of Trade initiatives in the 1740s and 1750s. These policy proposals were designed to increase metropolitan protection and control of the increasingly valuable American colonies.[3] Most of the attempts at more restrictive imperial administration between 1748 and 1756 were never implemented; those that were rarely achieved their objectives.

Greene attributes this failure to the Board of Trade's inadequate enforcement authority and inattention to colonial issues by British ministers outside the board. American resistance to regulatory initiatives also reduced their effectiveness. Greene views the Seven Years War as a temporary interruption to an ongoing, almost obsessive "metropolitan determination to secure tighter control over the colonies."[4] Imperial policymaking after 1763, he contended, did not represent a radical departure, political or conceptual, from earlier ministerial intentions. With some qualifications Marshall concurs, arguing that most measures put forward by British colonial officials after the Peace of Paris "were neither original nor did they amount to an attempt to create a new relationship between the colonies and the mother country. Increased awareness of the potential value of overseas possessions had merely induced some major politicians to try to remedy defects that had become apparent during the [Seven Years] [W]ar and had indeed been noted for several decades before the war."[5]

The contention that the war did not fundamentally alter colonial administration in the 1760s takes us some way—though not far enough—toward understanding imperial governance. Greene's and Marshall's argument helps explain the spectrum of policy alternatives that confronted British ministers in 1763: why, for example, Grenville chose to levy a stamp tax to raise North American revenues. The Board of Trade had proposed this tax in the 1750s. Analogously, Shelburne's championing of the Proclamation of 1763, which restricted the settlement of recently acquired North American territories, was not completely innovative. In the 1740s, Board of Trade ministers had discussed similar measures for

---

(Chapel Hill, N.C., 1973), 65–80; P. J. Marshall, "The British Empire in the Age of the American Revolution," in *The American Revolution: Changing Perspectives*, ed. William M. Fowler Jr. and Wallace Coyle (Boston, 1979), 193–212.

    3. Greene, " 'Posture of Hostility,' " 33–35; Marshall, 199–202.

    4. Greene, " 'Posture of Hostility,' " 66.

    5. Marshall, 203. See also Richard Koebner, *Empire* (Cambridge, 1961), 125–29.

Canadian government and defense.[6] Throughout the postwar decade, officials relied on policy solutions that were not really new; many proposals enacted between 1763 and 1773 resembled those that had been debated by Board of Trade members and economic observers in the previous twenty years.

Here, however, historiographical detours around the Seven Years War bring us up short. In concentrating on the consistency of policy *solutions* deployed between the 1740s and 1770s, scholars have not fully analyzed the conflict's profound effect on contemporary perceptions of imperial *problems* and *possibilities*. For eighteenth-century Britons, the war fought between 1756 and 1763 greatly increased the geopolitical and commercial stakes of dominion. The problems of colonial control, commerce, and revenue collection had first become obvious to politicians, such as Halifax, in the two decades before the Seven Years War. But these dilemmas had not then attained the urgency, clarity, or public significance necessary to overcome ignorance or opposition from the majority of ministers. Throughout the later 1740s and early 1750s, Newcastle, Pelham—even Pitt—could not be bothered, politically, with stricter imperial management.

But the experience of the Seven Years War radically altered official understanding of the difficulties and possibilities of empire, giving these risks and rewards great exigency in policy debates. Throughout the postwar decade, ministers, commercial writers, manufacturers, and others realized that their country's geopolitical ascendancy and the economic potential of such status would brook no political ignorance. The pressures and incentives of dominion *compelled* widespread attention at all levels of government. After the Peace of Paris, salutary neglect was no longer a metropolitan option.

The war increased the breadth and significance of political debate about the empire. It imbued earlier concerns with the relevance they needed to command widespread attention. The select issues that had interested a half dozen officials during the 1740s had become, through the experience of thoroughgoing international conflict, general political imperatives for the growing number of Britons interested in imperial business. Some of the policies proposed after 1763 had been articulated fifteen years earlier; yet this in no way lessens the uniqueness of the imperial situation after the Seven Years War.

To understand how the issues of empire took on far-reaching urgency

6. Greene, " 'Posture of Hostility,' " 45–46.

and pertinence, we must analyze the dynamic between political economy and policymaking. Commercial writers had long recognized that colonial profit could be converted into British military power. In the seventeenth century, economic commentators had heralded the benefits of a flourishing overseas trade in providing nurseries for seamen. The same writers had also noted that certain territories could serve as strategic outposts. Early eighteenth-century theorists took up similar doctrines, revising them in response to Britain's changing economy and geopolitical stature. During the first half of the century, primarily militaristic conceptions of empire gradually gave way to commercial ones. By the end of the War of Austrian Succession (1739–48), a few political economists and statesmen understood that the connections between British military success and economic success were significant.[7]

What was new about this strategic-commercial equation after the Seven Years War was the proven and interactive strength of the association. British commercial wealth, in forms the government could extract and utilize, had enabled the nation to win a war of unparalleled expense and debt financing.[8] The fruits of that victory were unprecedented: Britain acquired Canada, India, East Florida, the West Indian islands of St. Vincent, Dominica, and Tobago, and Senegal in Africa—lands with enormous economic potential. Commercially, economic theorists and government officials saw the nation's economy grow as domestic and foreign trade rose.[9] The duke of Newcastle, first lord of the treasury, and financiers had negotiated huge loans, sums once deemed fiscally impossible, at relatively stable interest rates.[10] In 1765 the former governor of Massa-

7. Townshend Papers, Clements Library, 8/52/1.

8. During the three previous eighteenth-century conflicts, the government had on average financed 30 percent of wartime costs by borrowing. More than 37 percent of the expenses of the Seven Years War were funded through additions to the debt; see Larry Neal, "Interpreting Power and Profit in Economic History: A Case Study of the Seven Years War," *Journal of Economic History* 37 (1977): 31.

9. In 1750 Britain's national income, in constant prices, was £62.2 million; ten years later it had grown to £73.2 million—a 14 percent increase, the largest ten-year jump in national income thus far in the century. On national income in the eighteenth century, see Peter Mathias, "Taxation and Industrialization in Britain, 1700–1870," in *The Transformation of England: Essays in the Economic and Social History of England in the Eighteenth Century* (New York, 1979), 118.

10. Despite the £60 million the government borrowed on London money markets over the course of the war, market rates of interest did not rise significantly. The return on Bank of England stock hovered between 4 and 5 percent throughout the war. Although the demand for loanable funds increased, the supply grew commensurately. Neal has speculated that this increase in the supply of loanable funds was a result of increased Dutch investment in the British national debt (34). His emphasis on foreign ownership is

chusetts, Thomas Pownall, looked back at Britain's successes. Taking his
cue from contemporary economic theorists, he argued that the forces
of world politics were changing:

In the first uncultur'd ages of Europe, when men sought nothing but to
possess, and to secure possession, the power of the *sword* was the predominant spirit of the world; it was that, which formed the Roman empire;
and it was the same, which, in the declension of that empire, divided
again the nations into the several governments formed upon the ruins of
it.

When men afterward, from leisure, began to exercise the power of
their minds in (what is called) learning; religion, the only learning at that
time, led them to a concern for their spiritual interests, and consequently
led them under their spiritual guides. The power of *religion* would hence
as naturally predominate and rule, and did actually become the ruling
spirit of the policy of Europe . . . (this spirit) formed the ballance of the
power of the whole, and actuated the second grand scene of Europe's
history.

But since the people of Europe have formed their communication with
the commerce of Asia; have been, for some ages past, settling on all sides
of the Atlantic Ocean, and in America, have been possessing every seat
and channel of commerce, and have planted and raised that to an interest
which has taken root;—since they now feel the powers which derive from
this, and are extending it to, and combining it with others; the spirit of
commerce will become that predominant power, which will form the general policy, and rule the powers of Europe: and hence a grand commercial interest, the basis of a great commercial dominion, under the present
scite and circumstances of the world, will be formed and arise.[11]

What constituted the spirit of commerce, and how were statesmen to
manage such power? What did it mean to administer a grand commercial
dominion? In 1763 the answers to these questions were complex and
controversial. But throughout the postwar decade, Britons realized that
the empire they had fought for was primarily a commercial one, whose

---

exaggerated. By 1750 and increasingly as the century wore on, British men (and women)
owned the majority of government stock, suggesting relative slack in the nation's supply
of financial capital. On the issue of debt ownership in the middle decades of the century,
see Alice Carter, *The English Public Debt in the Eighteenth Century* (London, 1968), 3–24. It
is important to note that Newcastle and other fiscal experts were unaware of such slack. They
worried significantly with each new loan offering that there would be too few subscribers.

11. Thomas Pownall, *The Administration of the Colonies* (London, 1766), 3–4.

stature depended on the mother country's ability to exploit a variety of economic transformations. Officials like George Grenville knew that imperial policymaking required a systematic understanding and application of the science of commerce. Statesmen frequently justified their positions toward the empire on explicitly commercial grounds, invoking the doctrines of political economy to rationalize a given decision. The theories of political economists working in the decade before Adam Smith's *Wealth of Nations* pervaded the political debate about imperial governance—a discussion overwhelmingly concerned with the relation between domestic prosperity and international preeminence.

Throughout the later seventeenth century, mercantile writers had been interested in a distinct formulation of the relationship between national wealth and power.[12] Their interest was material and applied: How did Britain's wealth, in the form of colonial territories, a positive balance of trade, and an inflow of gold and silver further the country's international strength? Josiah Child, Thomas Mun, and other seventeenth-century commercial authors wrote extensively on the value of overseas colonies as military strongholds, suppliers of naval stores, outlets for surplus population, and sources of raw materials. According to Child, a positive balance of trade was the "Compass to steer by, in Contemplation and Propagation of Trade for public advantage."[13] An excess of exports over imports was beneficial, wrote Gerard de Malynes as early as 1623, because "if the Native Commodities exported do weigh down and exceed in value the foreign Commodities imported; it is a rule that never fails, that then the Kingdom grows rich, and prospers in estate and stock; because the overplus thereof must needs come in, in treasure."[14] This treasure, the "sinews of war," bought arms, ammunition, and men.[15] The British ships

12. On seventeenth- and early eighteenth-century economic thought, see Joyce Appleby, *Economic Thought and Ideology in Seventeenth Century England* (Princeton, N.J., 1978); A.V. Judges, "The Idea of a Mercantile State," *Transactions of the Royal Historical Society* 21 (1939): 41–70; G. S. L. Tucker, *Progress and Profits in British Economic Thought, 1650–1850* (Cambridge, 1960); Klaus Knorr, *British Colonial Theories, 1570–1850* (Toronto, 1944); Jacob Viner, *Studies in the Theory of International Trade* (London 1937); E. A. Johnson, *Predecessors of Adam Smith* (New York, 1937); Robert Schuyler, *The Fall of the Old Colonial System: A Study in British Free Trade, 1770–1870* (London, 1945).

13. Josiah Child, *A New Discourse of Trade*, 3d ed. (London, 1718), 152.

14. Gerard de Malynes, *Center of the Circle of Commerce* (London, 1623), 117.

15. See Knorr, 16, on the somewhat ambiguous meaning of money and treasure in this literature. Charles Davenant's interpretation of the value of a balance of trade surplus is representative of this ambiguity: see *On the Plantation Trade* (London, 1698; reprinted 1775), 40. Not only does this excess increase the money supply and augment the nation's

that carried this commerce, Child noted, "bring with them a great access of Power (Hands as well as Money); *many ships and Seamen being justly the reputed Strength and Safety of England.*"[16] For men like Charles Davenant and like James Whiston, who wrote *A Discourse on the Decay of Trade* in 1693, specific commercial (and colonial) resources provided—directly or in the form of metals and specie—the instruments of warfare.[17] This was, of course, a relative conception. Britain's resources must be greater than those of other rival states. As specie, ships, or sailors, wealth represented the liquidity needed to acquire a military arsenal. If most seventeenth-century commercial writers valued wealth for the sake of power, as numerous historians of mercantilism have contended, it was in this particular context.[18]

By the midpoint of the eighteenth century, economic thinkers conceived of the connection between prosperity and geopolitical strength in more complex and theoretical terms. The most important political economists were Josiah Tucker, James Steuart, Joseph Massie, Arthur Young, and Malachy Postlethwayt. These men were primarily interested in elucidating what they viewed as the central principles of the evolving science of commerce. Tucker explained this novel perspective:

I hope that these Discourses will throw such new and striking Lights on the Subject of Commerce, as will induce Men of a liberal Education to study it for the future as a *Science* . . . For surely a great part of Mankind have too long submitted to be led blindfold by Writers on Trade, whose private Interest very often clashed with the general Good . . . In short, it is a melancholy Truth, that almost as much implicit Faith and blind Credulity have hitherto prevailed in the Theory of Commerce, as in the darkest Times of Popery, obscured the Principles of Religion.[19]

Writing in 1767, James Steuart was certain he was working in a new field of study. He called it political economy, titling his work *An Inquiry into the Principles of Political Economy, Being an Essay on the Science of Domestic*

shipping and naval capabilities, it is visible "in the improvements of Land, in our magnificent Buildings, in our Quantity of Plate, Jewels, sumptuous apparel and rich Furniture, and in the vast Stores that were lying by us, both of our home Product and foreign Commodities, which were our principal Strength and Support while the War lasted."

16. Child, preface.

17. James Whiston, *A Discourse on the Decay of Trade* (London, 1693).

18. Knorr, 17; E. Heckscher, *Mercantilism*, 2 vols. (London, 1935), 2:31.

19. Josiah Tucker, *Four Tracts Together with Two Sermons on Political and Commercial Subjects* (Gloucester, 1774), xiii.

Policy in Free Nations.[20] Joseph Massie, author of *The Knowledge of Commerce as a National Concern*, saw himself as a kind of educational architect:

For as in founding of Cities, the Streets and Fortifications thereof are first marked out; so in the establishing of Sciences . . . the Divisions and Boundaries of each should be first settled; and the Consequences of not beginning with those fundamental Regulations are much alike in both Cases, for the Error cannot be rectified in either, without pulling down what hath been built, and rebuilding upon a right Plan.[21]

Massie and Steuart saw their efforts as attempts "toward reducing to principles and forming into a regular science, the complicated interests of domestic policy."[22] The maxims these political economists articulated were universal. These theories, one writer commented, were "such as would suit any Kingdom, State or Climate, whatever."[23]

How did commercial writers discern the axioms of political economy, and in what context did they work? Inductive observation of commercial and political activity provided the fuel for their hypotheses. Tucker wrote his first economic tracts while living in Bristol, a city the essayist Daniel Defoe had described in 1753 as "the greatest, the richest and the best Port of Trade in Great Britain, London alone excepted."[24] While composing his *Principles*, Steuart traveled extensively in Antwerp, Rotterdam, and Paris, all major centers of commercial exchange. In *The Elements of Commerce, Politics and Finances* (1772), Thomas Mortimer described the intersection between his experiences, methods, and conclusions:

A *necessity* therefore arises of reducing those arts and sciences . . . to certain concise elementary principles. . .
On this foundation, and animated by this encouragement, (this) Editor . . . ventured to pursue the same plan; and having diligently collated, and

---

20. Steuart was the first to use the term *political economy* in English; it had been coined in French in the middle of the seventeenth century by Antoine de Montchrestien.

21. Joseph Massie, *A Representation concerning the Knowledge of Commerce as a National Concern Pointing out the Proper Means of Promoting Such Knowledge in This Kingdom* (London, 1760), 4.

22. James Steuart, *An Inquiry into the Principles of Political Economy*, 2 vols., ed. Andrew Skinner (Edinburgh, 1966), 1:3. See also Josiah Tucker, *Elements of Commerce and the Theory of Taxes* (privately printed, 1755), frontispiece; Mildmay, 4.

23. Mildmay, 4.

24. Quoted in Robert Schuyler, ed., *Josiah Tucker: A Selection from His Economic and Political Writings* (New York, 1931), 10.

accurately selected, from the best writers of every nation, the fundamental principles of [Commerce, Politics and Finances], he had the honour to attend several of the young nobility and gentry of this kingdom, in the capacity of private tutor; inculcating, in the form of private lectures, a theoretical and practical knowledge of commerce, politics and finances. A few years attention . . . naturally brought with it improvements, drawn from observations on the practicable part of commerce; on the political state of Europe in general; and on the extension of public credit, and of the funded system in England and France during the late war; at the close of which, the Editor being appointed to an honourable station abroad [British vice-consul for the Austrian Netherlands] had a favourable opportunity, in the course of five years residence, to collect and add to his plan, some modern improvements in the commercial and political departments, and also respecting the administration of the public revenues of different states on the continent.[25]

Induction alone was not enough. As Steuart recognized, political economists had to think deductively as well. The Scottish author tried

to collect and arrange some elements relating to the most interesting branches of modern policy, such as *population, agriculture, trade, industry, money, coin, interest, circulation, banks, exchange, public credit, and taxes.* The principles deduced from all these topics, appear tolerably consistent; and the whole is a train of reasoning through which I have adhered to the connection of subjects as faithfully as I could.[26]

The test of economic principles lay in their practical—that is, political—application. As Massie commented, "For all commercial Measures are either good or bad to the Nation which takes them; and since, in most Instances, it is either very plain, or can be demonstrated by a Chain of Reasoning founded on Facts of self-evident Principles, whether a Measure of that Sort is or will be good or bad, commercial Knowledge certainly may be established upon a firm Foundation."[27]

Political economy in the middle of the eighteenth century was an emerging, though still nebulously defined, social science. It was practiced

25. Thomas Mortimer, *The Elements of Commerce, Politics and Finances in Three Treatises on Those Important Subjects* (London, 1772), ii–iii.

26. Steuart, 1:6–7.

27. Massie, 9. See also Malachy Postlethwayt, *Great Britain's True System* (London, 1757), xlviii–xlix.

by men who observed rather than engaged in economic activity. Tucker was a curate by formal training and made his debut as a political pamphleteer in support of the Hanoverian dynasty during the Jacobite Rebellion of 1745.[28] A writer and antiquarian, Joseph Massie owned more than 1,500 economic treatises, extending from 1557 to 1763. He used his collection, together with his own compilation of contemporary trade statistics, to write some fifteen pamphlets on trade and finance. Educated in Edinburgh as a lawyer, Steuart was active in Scottish politics (and supported Prince Charles in the 1745 rebellion) before spending the 1750s traveling in Europe. This experience as well as his friendship with David Hume contributed to his interest in political economy.[29] Mortimer studied modern history and elocution before serving as English vice-consul for the Austrian Netherlands. His series of London lectures on trade in the early 1770s formed the basis of his *Elements of Commerce*.

The political economists studied commercial activity outside university walls. None of them were professionally trained in their field. During the first half of the eighteenth century, British universities and academies did not offer any kind of instruction in economics. This situation began to change in the 1750s. Malachy Postlethwayt explained:

Since I have put my Hand to the Plough upon these Subjects, I have had the Satisfaction to observe not only many more useful Performances published upon this Subject than before, but many beneficial Designs encouraged in the Nation, that have a Tendency to the Promotion of the Trade and Commerce of this Kingdom, and to raise a general Spirit for these Studies. Amongst the rest, there is one in particular which ought to be taken Notice of: I mean That of the Prize Donations bestowed by a most noble and honourable Lord [Charles Townshend] to encourage the Studies of Commerce even at the University of *Cambridge*; and may not this prove the happy Prelude to the Establishment of a *Commercial* and *Mercantile College* at our most learned and illustrious Seminaries?[30]

Broadly defined, commercial policy was the axis around which the field of political economy revolved. The "laboratory" in which the new social scientists gathered the observations they needed was the changing

28. Schuyler, introduction, 9. There is surprisingly little scholarship about this often precocious and articulate vicar turned economist. See George Shelton, *Dean Tucker and Eighteenth Century Economic and Political Thought* (London, 1981).

29. Skinner, introduction to Steuart, 1:xxi–lxxxiv.

30. Postlethwayt, xlix–l.

British economy; their experimental equipment, the existing set of fiscal and regulatory policies pursued by the British state. Economic theories were to be tested by incorporating them into government action. Tucker and other political economists saw themselves as relatively objective educators and advisers to government officials. Eighteenth-century theorists knew that their detachment from specific commercial interests was distinct from earlier mercantile authors and believed it entitled them to more credibility in political debates.

Why did ministers need enlightenment in the aftermath of the Seven Years War? How did the political economists justify establishing their works as indispensable instruments in national policymaking? In 1772 Mortimer explained the newly obvious marriage of politics and economics:

The great increase and extent of the commercial connections of Great Britain, arising from the augmentation of her maritime power, from new territorial acquisitions, and from the flourishing state of her colonies, having totally changed the face of affairs in this kingdom in the course of the present century, and evidently given to the monied interest, great weight and influence in the state; the study of every branch of the public revenues, and of the public funds, which are the grand bulwark of the power and influence of the monied men, becomes a necessary part of education, and should have had its rise with the origin of these funds; but though they have annually increased, with astonishing rapidity, from the [Glorious] Revolution [of 1688] to the present time, yet the generality of those, whose situation in life may afford them reasonable expectations of being chosen directors of those funds, representatives of the people in parliament, or servants of the crown in the revenue department, are often quite uninformed and unskilled in matters of this nature.[31]

Political economists' views mirrored those of government ministers. Narrowly construed, wealth equaled power for Steuart, Massie, war minister William Pitt, and others after 1763, because the British state's fiscal and economic capabilities had enabled the nation to win the recent conflict. Britain owed its new lands and international preeminence to economic sinews of power; it needed statesmen who understood this infra-

31. Mortimer, ix–x. See also Arthur Young, *Political Essays concerning the Present State of the British Empire* (London, 1772), 49; William Dowdeswell to Lord Rockingham, 21 May 1774, Dowdeswell Papers, Clements Library.

structure. The first men to call themselves *political economists* tried to provide such an understanding.

The purview of the discipline extended beyond war and money. Economic observers of the mid-eighteenth century were concerned more generally with articulating theories of commercial growth. Historians of economic thought have overlooked these broader, sophisticated objectives, so quick have scholars been to label all of Adam Smith's predecessors as mercantilists.[32] But it is hard to misinterpret Steuart's intention:

> The principal object of this science is to secure a certain fund of subsistence for all inhabitants, to obviate every circumstance which may render it precarious; to provide every thing necessary for supplying the wants of the society, and to employ the inhabitants (supposing them to be freemen) in such a manner as naturally to create reciprocal relations and dependencies between them, so as to make their several interests lead them to supply one another with their reciprocal wants.[33]

Government played a major role in achieving economic purposes. "It is the business of a statesman," Steuart continued, "to judge of the expediency of different schemes of œconomy, and by degrees to model the minds of his subjects so as to induce them, from the allurement of private interest, to concur in the execution of his plan."[34] Self-interest, according to one theorist, was the "great Mover of created Beings"; it motivated men to aspire to "Wealth, Power, Honour, Pleasure, or Preferment."[35] Government was responsible, noted another political economist, for directing private interests toward the "support and benefit of the whole."[36]

Government regulation of individuals' private pursuits was a mechanis-

---

32. Viner, *Studies in the Theory of International Trade*: Knorr.

33. Steuart, 1:17. See also J. Tucker's introduction to *The Elements of Commerce and Theory of Taxes* (1755), in Schuyler, *Josiah Tucker*, 55–63; Mildmay, 3–12. B. Suviranta, *The Theory of the Balance of Trade in England: A Study in Mercantilism* (Helsinki, 1923), 161, argues mistakenly that the predecessors of Adam Smith were not interested in individual consumption. It is true that they were less concerned with individual consumption than were the classical economists that built on this eighteenth-century scholarship, but it was a more significant objective for these earlier thinkers than most historians of economic thought have acknowledged.

34. Steuart, 1:17.

35. J. Tucker, *Elements of Comerce and Theory of Taxes*, quoted in Schuyler, *Josiah Tucker*, 58.

36. Mildmay, 10. See also Nathaniel Forster, *An Enquiry into the Causes of the Present High Price of Provisions* (London, 1767), 18–19.

tic process. Political economists viewed statesmen as key operators of the "great machine of trade," who managed competing interests, marshaled human and other resources, and oversaw commercial interchange according to the tenets of political economy.[37] In 1757, Tucker elaborated:

The *Circulation* of *Commerce* may be conceived to proceed from the *Impulse* of two distinct Principles of Action in Society, analogous to the *centrifugal* and *centripetal* Powers in the Planetary System . . . universal Commerce, good Government, and true Religion, are nearly, are inseparably connected. For the Directions and Regulations of each of these, are no other, than to make private coincide with public, present with future Happiness. And whoever is conversant with the Affairs of the World, cannot fail to observe, That whenever the Parts of this *extensive System* have been separated by the Arts or Folly of Men, Religion has sunk into Superstition or Enthusiasm, Government has been turned into Tyranny and *Machiavelian* Policy, and Commerce has degenerated into Knavery and Monopoly.[38]

For Tucker, as for other theorists, there was one *political* economy. These writers drew no distinction between public and private sectors. They saw government as a necessary and inherent part of a grand economic system, a system that, like the heavens, was subject to discernible laws. To this extent the political economists inverted the association between wealth and power. Power equaled wealth because a commercially and militarily strong nation enjoyed the stability of government necessary to ensure a successfully functioning economy.

Mortimer devoted the first chapter of his *Elements of Commerce* to tracing the history of commerce in mighty empires. He admired the ancient Egyptians, "a warlike people . . . who extended their commerce . . . by conquests" and "made their passions subservient to their commercial transactions." The Phoenicians understood that "commerce must be supported by maritime power or naval strength." More recently, Amsterdam and London had avoided the licentiousness, "the bane of commerce," that had ruined ancient Rome, Carthage, and Tyre.

A rivalry had grown up between the Dutch and British: "Fired with emulation, all England engaged in the attempt to vie with the neighbouring city of Amsterdam, and to form the basis of a maritime and commercial power that should take in every branch of the commercial art known

37. Mildmay, 11.
38. J. Tucker, *The Element of Commerce and Theory of Taxes*, quoted in Schuyler, *Josiah Tucker*, 60.

or practised throughout the habitable globe." Which country had won the imperial competition? Mortimer was unequivocal:

In process of time this glorious and stupendous plan (for so I may justly term it, considering the small extent of the British Isles, their separation from each other, disunited interests, and various disadvantages) has been accomplished, and so completely accomplished, that we have seen Great Britain, notwithstanding all the opposition of rival commercial powers, who have waged with her the most expensive and bloody wars, in order to impede her progress, rise superior to every obstacle, acquire and maintain the sovereignty of the seas, and distinguish herself as the first maritime and commercial power of Europe. In a word, we see her enjoying at present a manifest superiority in that most profitable branch of ancient commerce, the *East India* trade; and, whether we consider the enlargement of her territories, the strength of her maritime power, the universality of her commerce, the extent of her public credit, the opulence of her chief cities, or the flourishing state of arts and sciences, we may venture to pronounce, that she was at the summit of national glory, and of human grandeur, soon after the conclusion of the late Peace [of Paris].[39]

From across the English Channel, the perspective on British prosperity was similar. Voltaire commented:

Trade, which has made richer the citizens of England, has helped to make them free, and this freedom has, in turn, enlarged trade . . . It is trade which has gradually created the Navy, thanks to which the English are masters of the seas . . . Posterity might be surprised that a small island, which has from her own only some lead, tin, fuller's earth and coarse wool, has become, thanks to its trade, powerful enough to dispatch in 1733 three squadrons . . . to three uttermost ends of the earth.[40]

The Seven Years War made Great Britain a world power, but in the conflict's aftermath, how was it to remain so? What policies should the nation pursue to sustain the economic growth that had made victory possible? There are economic and fiscal answers to these questions, policy suggestions rooted in the prevailing doctrines of political economy. The central objectives of imperial management were increased sales of British manufactures and prudent fiscal administration. These goals found their

39. Mortimer, 16.
40. Voltaire, *Lettres philosophiques* (Paris, 1964), 66.

clearest, most comprehensive articulation in the works of Tucker, Massie, and other contemporary political economists. In the ongoing dialogue between commercial writers and statesmen, the theoretical ambitions of political economy infused the practice of policy. The aims of national strategy frequently clashed: it was not always possible to raise government revenues while simultaneously promoting manufacturing sales. Political configurations, parliamentary and bureaucratic, affected policy choices as well as the spectrum of responses officials pursued. The interaction between policymaking and politics rebounded to political economy, shaping the contours and content of this new social science.

In 1760 other economic thinkers were certain that producing large quantities of affordable manufactured goods was the key to outselling other nations. Massie wrote that "the general Reason why the People of other Nations buy such vast Quantities of our *Woollen Manufactures,* is, their being the best or the cheapest to those Nations."[41] Tucker was more broadly confident in his assessment of Britain's productivity:

Now let anyone cast his Eye over the Bills of Exports from *London, Bristol, Liverpool, Hull, Glasgow,* etc. will soon discover that excepting Gold and Silver Lace, Wines, and Brandies, some sorts of Silks and Linens, and perhaps a little Paper and Gun-powder; I say, excepting these few Articles, *Great Britain* is become a Kind of general Mart for *most other* Commodities: And indeed were it not so, how is it conceivable, that so little a Spot as this Island could have made such a Figure either in Peace or War, as it hath lately done?[42]

Political economists nurtured what today might be called demand-driven conceptions of economic growth. Britain had become a "general Mart" for manufactured goods by selling these items both at home and abroad more cheaply than competing nations. Its trade would continue growing, in absolute terms and relative to other countries', provided the demand for British goods kept rising. Theorists and ministers had watched imperial commerce prosper during the recent conflict. In the context of eighteenth-century warfare, this effect was impressive and surprising.[43] Why shouldn't the situation continue, reasoned Massie and others, assuming domestic and foreign buyers wanted British goods more

41. Massie, 22.
42. J. Tucker, *Four Tracts,* 206–7.
43. Massie, 8; William Knox, *The Present State of the Nation* (London, 1768), 5–6.

than those of other nations?[44] Britain could produce the needed manufactures. Demand, according to economic writers, called forth its own supply, and it was to the demand side of the economy that they turned analytic attention.[45]

How was Britain to keep manufacturing sales high and growing? Political economists and politicians throughout the 1760s and early 1770s grappled with this problem. Two conditions were deemed necessary. First, since "trade will always follow cheapness," according to Tucker, British goods must be less expensive to produce and transport than those of other countries.[46] Second, domestic merchants and manufacturers must have access to expanding, controllable markets. The empire was to be governed toward these ends, the principles of political economy providing the grist for specific policy proposals.[47]

If Britain was to sell large quantities of manufactures at low prices, it needed relatively inexpensive labor and raw materials.[48] Economic writers suggested specific fiscal and regulatory policies designed to keep British labor costs low. One important policy recommendation prohibited

44. I am not suggesting that political economists and government officials were unconcerned with trading rivalry. They worried about increasing European competition in the middle decades of the century, and about the North American colonies' establishing manufacturing capabilities. See Ralph Davis, "The Rise of Protection in England, 1689–1786," *Economic History Review* 19 (1966): 307–17 and idem, "English Foreign Trade, 1700–1774," *Economic History Review* 15 (1962): 285–303; P. J. Cain and A. G. Hopkins, "Gentlemanly Capitalism and British Expansion Overseas: The Old Colonial System, 1688–1850," *Economic History Review* 39 (1986): 501–25, and idem, "The Political Economy of British Expansion Overseas, 1750–1914," *Economic History Review* 33 (1980): 463–92. But imperial experts were primarily anxious about British access to markets rather than their country's capacity to produce large quantities of goods—as many as demanded—efficiently and quickly. Economists and statesmen were not intently concerned with supply-side considerations; they were much more explicitly interested in the consumption end of world markets.

45. Midcentury economic writers did not ignore supply-side considerations. The price and availability of raw materials, transportation, and labor were widely discussed. But this analysis took place within the broader context of market demand for a given manufacture. Low labor, material, and transport costs were desirable to the extent that they allowed British merchants and manufacturers to sell their products more cheaply, thus boosting sales.

46. Josiah Tucker, *The Case of Going to War for the Sake of Procuring, Enlarging or Securing of Trade* (London, 1763), 41.

47. As Edmund Burke remarked in 1769, "[Our] object is wholly new in the world. It is singular: it is grown up to this magnitude and importance within the memory of man; nothing in history is parallel to it. . . . In this new system, a principle of commerce, of artificial commerce, must predominate"; "Observations on a Late State of the Nation," in *Writings and Speeches of Edmund Burke*, vol. 2, *Party, Parliament and the American Crisis, 1766–1774*, ed. Paul Langford (Oxford, 1981), 194.

48. See Young, 205.

excise taxes on necessities. Taxes on essentials, the political economists argued, would raise wages because laborers, living at the margin of subsistence, could not afford such impositions.[49] Since "people without property, who work for their daily bread," Postlethwayt explained, " . . . live but from hand to mouth, whatever is laid on them they must, therefore, shift off or they cannot subsist."[50] According to Postlethwayt's reasoning, employers bore the ultimate burden of levies on necessities, in the form of higher wages. Increased labor costs damaged Britain's relative trading position by raising the price of its manufactured goods. During the 1760s these objections to taxes on essentials proved economically and politically potent.[51]

Government officials such as Newcastle and Grenville took up the argument against taxes on necessities from political economy. Despite the omnipresent revenue needs of the British state in the postwar decade, each administration consistently refused to countenance domestic levies on essentials. Thomas Whately, one of Grenville's subministers in the Treasury, explained the government's refusal in 1763 to continue wartime increases in beer and malt taxes:

And the demands of the War still crowding on, recourse had at last been had to those Supplies which an universal Home-consumption could raise: The common Beverage of the people was chosen, and the Duties were laid on Malt, on Beer, and on Cyder. These pressed immediately on the middling and lower Ranks, on Husbandmen and Manufacturers, who were not indifferent to many of the other duties; the Wages of Labour were raised; the value of foreign Commodities and even of our native pro-

49. See especially Jacob Vanderlint, *Money Answers All Things* (London, 1734); Matthew Decker, *Serious Considerations on the Several High Duties Which the Nation in General Labours Under* (London, 1744); Francis Fauquier, *An Essay on Ways and Means for Raising Money for the Support of the Present War without Increasing the Public Debts* (London, 1756); Forster.

50. Malachy Postlethwayt, *Universal Dictionary of Trade and Commerce*, 2 vols. (London, 1755), 2:3.

51. As William Kennedy notes, commercial arguments against taxes on necessities had first been raised in 1732 during the parliamentary debate over a proposed salt tax. Kennedy convincingly demonstrates that these arguments remained powerful through much of the later eighteenth century, while noting the various challenges to them. Although Steuart and Adam Smith admitted that, empirically, wages did not seem to rise with the imposition of taxes on necessaries, both men opposed such taxes on the grounds that these levies indirectly boosted wage payments. Crudely put, Smith argued that since labor supply depends (through marriage and infant mortality rates) on real wages, a tax that lowers the real wage (by increasing the cost of necessities) will ultimately decrease the labor supply and thus increase real wages. William Kennedy, *English Taxation, 1640–1799* (London, 1964), 113–20.

duce was enhanced; and these are circumstances always prejudicial, frequently dangerous, and sometimes fatal to Trade and Manufactures. Was this a time to impose a new tax which must have been heavy to have been effectual; and which, so far as our Commercial Interests might have been affected by it, would not in the end have been a benefit, though it should be a present Relief to Public Credit?[52]

Revenue needs boxed the Grenville ministry (1763–65) into a fiscal corner. Facing a Parliament completely hostile to increased land levies, the prime minister and his cabinet could not impose direct taxes. A direct levy was scorned politically because it involved, in Adam Smith's words, "inquisition into every man's private circumstances, and an inquisition which . . . would be a source of such continual and endless vexation as no people could support."[53] A tax on profit or income was bad economic policy. As Steuart explained, merchants "ought not to be subjected to any tax upon their industry. They ought to be allowed to accumulate riches as fast as they can: because they employ them for the advancement of industry; and every deduction from their profits is a diminution upon so this useful a fund."[54] Higher customs duties were not viable because they angered the merchant classes and restricted trade. In the interests of Britain's competitiveness, Grenville was unwilling to propose a domestic excise on essentials. His ministry was forced to look to North America for government funds. The ministers who followed George Grenville, such as Chatham and North, faced analogous difficulties. Caught between the Scylla and Charybdis of prevailing economic theories and political priorities, officials found their policy options circumscribed.[55]

Economic theory imposed other implicit constraints on imperial management. If taxes on essentials forced wages up, as most commercial writers contended, a rise in food prices would have the same effect. Using arguments similar to those leveled against taxes on necessities,

52. Thomas Whately, *Considerations on the Trade and Finances of This Kingdom and on the Measures of Administration with respect to These Great National Objects Since the Conclusion of the Peace* (London, 1769), 6. See also Kennedy, 114; Sir John Barnard's speech in Parliament in 1737, quoted in *Parliamentary History of England from the Earliest Period to the Year 1803*, ed. William Cobbett, 36 vols. (London, 1806–20), 10:155; Forster.

53. Adam Smith, *An Inquiry into the Nature and Causes of the Wealth of Nations*, ed. Edwin Cannan, 2 vols. (Chicago, 1976), 2:375.

54. Steuart, 2:688.

55. Patrick O'Brien, approaching this issue from a different perspective, reaches similar conclusions. See "The Political Economy of British Taxation," *Economic History Review*, 2d ser., 41 (1988): 18.

writers such as Nathaniel Forster, author of *An Enquiry into the Causes of the Present High Price of Provisions* (1767), asserted that labor costs depended on workers' cost of living:

There is, no doubt, a certain point in which these three interests (farmer, manufacturer, labourer) coincide; a certain situation of things, more favourable to them all than any other situation; namely when the farmer and manufacturer has such demand, the one for his produce, the other for his goods, as will fairly enable them to find full employment for the working hands, and to give them wages answerable to the prices of the several necessaries of life which they sell to them. Every deviation from this situation of things, though it be perhaps at first favourable to one set of men, will be immediately detrimental to the rest, and in the end even to that one. The guardians of the state will therefore keep a watchful eye upon every such deviation and endeavour to stop the progress of it as soon as it in any degree makes itself felt.[56]

How could the government keep food prices and thus wages down? The state should endeavor to secure "plenty of provisions," according to one political economist. This theorist advocated government encouragement of husbandry and state intervention to ensure the free circulation of all agricultural goods.[57] In addition, foreign trade in foods must be strictly regulated. Britain should import grain and other commodities in bad harvest years and sell its produce abroad in more bountiful times.[58] The author of *Propositions for Improving the Manufactures, Agriculture and Commerce of Great Britain* (1763) recommended increasing the quantity of Irish cattle and provisions imported into England. At the same time, this writer added, Ireland's exports to destinations other than England and the West Indies should be prohibited. By augmenting supplies at home, this proposal would lower food prices and keep domestic wages low. As important, a prohibition on Irish exports of livestock and produce would prevent Holland and France from enjoying the competitive advan-

---

56. Forster, 21–22; see also Mildmay, 13–20, and *Propositions for Improving the Manufactures, Agriculture, and Commerce of Great Britain* (London, 1763), 63–65.

57. Mildmay, 13–20.

58. Mildmay, 18–19. Forster also called for government regulation of agricultural production to ensure adequate supplies. Specifically, he advised encouraging the export of grain so as to guarantee farmers a "full vent for their produce" (72).

tages of cheaper food, forcing up labor costs and goods prices in these countries.[59]

Government ministers realized the importance of keeping Britain supplied with cheap food, and they looked to Ireland for livestock, dairy products, and other foods. Britain's experience over the Seven Years War underscored the political economists' interest in Irish food supplies. The rise in wartime demand for British food exports from India, North America, and Prussia had been satisfied largely by increasing imports of Irish grain, tallow, and dairy products and then reexporting these goods. In 1758, amid considerable argument, the Board of Trade had raised the quota on Irish agricultural goods allowed into the mother country.[60] When peace came five years later, imperial ministers decided to maintain Irish trade at these higher levels.

Longer-term macroeconomic conditions also helped shape official priorities after the war. During the 1740s and 1750s, food prices rose as Britain's long-standing position as a net exporter of grain gave way to an increasing dependence on agricultural imports. From 1763 to 1774, the nation's imports from Ireland climbed to an average of over £1.1 million per year. This represents almost a 100 percent increase over Irish imports in the early 1750s.[61] Undoubtedly accelerated population growth, burgeoning urbanization, and improved transport contributed to the about-face England experienced in its agricultural trade.[62] As these factors intensified and the nation's reliance on outside food sources grew during the 1760s, keeping the mother country supplied with inexpensive provisions became a more important concern of imperial policymaking.

The interest in ensuring cheap food supplies was most clearly manifest in the disastrous harvest years of 1765 and 1766. Confronted with significant grain shortages in various parts of the country and popular riots in provincial cities, Lord Rockingham's administration (1765–66) debated its policy options. Charles Townshend, the future chancellor of the Exchequer, considered several possibilities: a prohibition on wheat

59. *Propositions for Improving the Manufactures*, 63–69.

60. *Scots Magazine* (1758), 121. Historian A. H. John has described the controversy surrounding the higher quota as foreshadowing "that over the Corn Laws a century later. . . . [A]s the *Scots Magazine* observed [at the time], 'It was a dispute between the trading interest and the present landed interest of the kingdom" ("The Course of Agricultural Change, 1660–1760," in *Studies in the Industrial Revolution*, ed. L. S. Pressnell (London, 1960), 155.

61. John, 155.

62. Ibid., 152.

exports once its price had risen above five shillings a bushel, the construction of public granaries in all cities to stockpile grain, and the imposition of government price controls.[63] Townshend received numerous petitions from provincial merchants and manufacturers calling for government relief from the social and economic consequences of widespread crop failures. Businessmen in Norwich asked for a stop to all grain exports, writing, "If it should continue your petitioners humbly apprehend it will not only render the condition of the Labouring poor here truly deplorable, but will produce very pernicious consequences to the Woollen trade of this city."[64] The Committee of London Merchants Trading to North America offered an alternative proposal: "Effectual relief may be obtained by a speedy importation of wheat and flour from the Continent of America, where the Crops this year have been remarkably plentiful and the grain particularly good in quality." In advocating increased American imports, the merchants denied self-interested motives. "All the grain shall be sold for the benefits of the Manufacturers, Mecanics and Labourious Poor, without any profit to the subscribers whatsoever."[65]

The merchants' advice proved prophetic. Although Parliament granted ministers the authority to suspend all grain shipments out of Britain if necessary, most of the nation's food needs in the mid-1760s were not met by forgone exports. Imports from Ireland and North America made up the lion's share of the shortfall.[66] The value of England's annual imports of grain rose more than tenfold over the middle years of the 1760s, from £85,000 in 1764 to £987,000 in 1767.[67] Issues of social order were undoubtedly very important in determining the government's response to these food shortages.[68] But just as certainly,

63. Shelburne to Charles Townshend, "Hints for Preventing the Scarcity of Corn" (1766), Townshend Papers, Clements Library, 8/14/12.

64. Townshend Papers, Clements Library, 8/14/25.

65. Ibid., 8/14/6.

66. During the summer of 1765, Parliament authorized duty-free grain imports.

67. Elizabeth Boody Schumpeter, *English Overseas Trade Statistics, 1697–1808* (Oxford, 1960), 51. It is useful to note that although eighteenth-century trade statistics were recorded as values rather than quantities, such entries were valued at fixed prices selected at the beginning of the century. These statistics thus provide an approximate quantity index of the physical volume of foreign trade. See R. P. Thomas and D. N. McCloskey, "Overseas Trade and Empire, 1700–1860," in *The Economic History of Britain since 1700*, vol. 1, ed. R. Floud and D. McCloskey (Cambridge, 1981), 88. See also R. Davis, *The Industrial Revolution and British Overseas Trade* (Leicester, 1979).

68. On issues of social order and the government response to the hunger riots of 1765 and 1766, see Walter J. Shelton, *English Hunger and Industrial Disorders: A Study of Social Conflict during the First Decade of George III's Reign* (Toronto, 1973), and John Stevenson, *Popular Disturbances in England, 1700–1870* (London, 1979).

ministers such as Townshend and Shelburne never lost sight of the perceived commercial repercussions of high domestic food prices. Whately explained what this meant for imperial management:

For tho' the Inhabitants of these Kingdoms and of America are equally Subjects of *Great Britain,* yet they serve the State in different Capacities; and if to make unwarrantable Distinctions between them would be Oppression; on the other hand to preserve the Distinctions which the Difference of their Situation has made, is true policy, which has the general Good for its Object: Extent of Country, Fertility of Soil, Cheapness of Land, Variety of Climate and scarcity of Inhabitants, naturally lead the *Americans* to Cultivation . . . the [North American] Continent alone can produce Provisions for Subsistence, Commodities for Commerce, and the raw Materials for Manufacturers to work with, in much greater Variety, in Quantities immeasurably larger, and on Terms by far more easy than they could be raised in *Great Britain.*[69]

Even before the dearth years of 1765 and 1766, British officials had been concerned with colonial agriculture. In 1763 Shelburne and other Board of Trade officials hoped that the North American and West Indian colonies would continue to supply the mother country with grain, rice, fish, sugar, and rum. Perhaps, Shelburne reasoned, more exotic commodities, such as pepper and safflower, could be cultivated in the empire's new lands.[70] John Ellis, a colonial agent for Florida, wanted to grow tea and rhubarb in Britain's semitropical territory. "The encouraging [of] our Colonies in North America and the West Indies to raise those commodities, which we take from Foreigners, would be a means to extend and promote the exportation of our own Manufactures, and to lessen the Balance of Trade against us in our commerce with other Nations."[71]

To ministers and economic writers, it seemed a simple but important formula. With adequate supplies of American and Irish grain, British food prices would remain relatively low. If the laboring poor also faced low taxes, domestic wages as a function of subsistence costs would stay down too. Lower labor costs meant cheaper prices for British manufactures and thus more sales.

69. Thomas Whately, *The Regulations Lately Made concerning the Colonies and the Taxes Imposed upon Them Considered* (London, 1765), 63–64.

70. Shelburne Papers, Clements Library, vol. 48.

71. Ibid., 48/52, "Catalogue of Such Useful Foreign Plants as Will Thrive in the Different Climates of Our American Dominions," 1767.

With few exceptions, imperial experts took little notice of the income effects of low wages.[72] While most politicians and economic theorists advocated measures to keep wages down, they were unconcerned with how such efforts would affect *domestic* sales of manufactures. Ceteris paribus, a Norwich weaver earning two shillings, sixpence a day could buy more nails and cutlery than the same man making two shillings daily. Why didn't government officials and political economists pay more attention to the income side of the economy? Theorists understood the circular nature of commercial interchange, at least in rudimentary form. Perhaps these men mistakenly envisioned a distinction between most laborers and the preponderance of men and women who purchased British manufactures. If suppliers of manufacturing labor were not necessarily consumers of such goods, then it made commercial sense to focus on the importance of low wages for the former group.[73]

Manufacturing success depended not only on low-priced labor, but on inexpensive raw materials as well. Eighteenth-century political economists consistently called for government involvement in the markets for manufacturing inputs. Specifically, commercial writers advocated bounties on rough and intermediate goods imported from North America, Ireland, and India. Mortimer explained:

It is the interest, and we know it is the inclination of our most gracious sovereign, to prevent [the North American colonies from forsaking] . . . their true interest, which is the clearing and cultivating the vast quantities of land lying waste in their different soils and climates so, as to make them produce every rough material for our manufactures, every naval store, and . . . every other commodity we find ourselves necessitated to purchase on exorbitant terms from foreign countries. If all or most of these can be produced in our own settlements and paid for with our manufactures, it must surely be the heighth of folly, or of blind prejudice and

72. Josiah Tucker is a precocious exception. See *Elements of Commerce and Theory of Taxes,* quoted in Schuyler, *Josiah Tucker,* 125–29; and *Instructions for Travellers* (London, 1758), 241–42, 246.

73. See Neil McKendrick, "Commercialization and the Economy," in *Birth of a Consumer Society: The Commercialization of Eighteenth Century England,* ed. Neil McKendrick, John Brewer, and J. H. Plumb (Bloomington, Ind., 1982), 9–33. McKendrick points out that economic commentators like Forster were aware that the propensity to consume in British society transcended class lines. But eighteenth-century economic writers also contended—fallaciously, to judge from economic research on the nineteenth century—that the upper and middling classes bought far more manufactures than the lower ranks.

partiality, not to give the colonists all possible encouragement to convert their uncultivated lands to mines of commercial treasure.[74]

India was also to be encouraged to supply raw silk, sugar, and other commodities to be used in manufacturing.[75] In addition to bounties on colonial production of raw materials, Tucker wanted the Board of Trade to pay a "personal premium to such Merchants as shall import the most of these Commodities, and the best in their Kind." He saw another advantage in this proposition: "How gladly would our Colonies *embrace* such Proposals, and *quit* the Pursuit of the Manufactures they are now engaged in? It is certain, these Manufactures, tho' highly detrimental to us, are not *so* advantageous to them as the Raising [of Commodities]."[76]

The interest in Britain's dominions as suppliers of raw materials was not created in the wake of the Seven Years War. Since the midpoint of the seventeenth century, commercial writers had been concerned with colonial production of commodities and naval stores. Josiah Child had realized that British territories represented more reliable sources of raw materials than imports from rival nations; he and other contemporaries had understood as well that replacing foreign with colonial supplies diminished the dreaded outflow of bullion and improved the balance of trade.[77] What was new about this discussion in the 1750s and 1760s was the emphasis on encouraging colonial provision of raw materials in order to secure them *at lowest cost.*

But eighteenth-century political economists did not completely abandon earlier theories. The author of *Elements of Commerce* (1772) continued to worry about the precariousness of foreign supplies of raw materials. But even this seventeenth-century concern was now expressed in terms of Britain's interest in making cheap manufactures: "For supposing your government to be at war with the country from whence you draw the first materials for your manufacture . . . the manufacture, in these cases will either so enhance in price, from scarcity, that it will neither sell at home, nor at foreign markets; or it will be totally demolished."[78] Mildmay

74. Mortimer, 156; see also J. Tucker, *Instructions*, 252; Patrick Lindsay, *The Interest of Scotland Considered* (London, 1733), 135; Mildmay, 33.

75. M. Postlethwayt, *Britain's Commercial Interest Explained and Improved* (London, 1757) 2, 238; Commons debate, 27 February 1769, Cavendish Diary, Egerton MSS. 218, fols. 153–54.

76. J. Tucker, *A Brief Essay on the Advantages and Disadvantages Which Respectively Attend France and Great Britain with regard to Trade* (London, 1767), 103.

77. Knorr, 85, 50–56, 81–95.

78. Mortimer, 66.

recommended that Britain purchase raw materials from the cheapest supplier, whether colony or competing nation.[79] He and Tucker favored removing customs duties from imports of manufacturing inputs. Mildmay justified this suggestion on the grounds that "every tax thus laid upon any *material* or *ingredient* necessary toward the composition of a MANUFACTURE is a tax on the manufacture itself which must enhance the price, and obstruct the sale in every foreign market."[80]

Government ministers realized the importance of abundant, inexpensive inputs. They had long encouraged colonial production of naval stores and had offered bounties on importation of hemp, flax, pitch, tar, and rosin since the reign of Queen Anne (1702–14).[81] In 1715 a Board of Trade memorandum had explained that the rationale behind such subsidies was primarily strategic: to employ New Englanders in furnishing goods for the mother country, "lest they should hereafter be obliged to depend on the pleasure of the Danes, Swedes and Russians for leave to set a fleet to sea."[82] Fifty years later, officials such as Grenville, Rockingham, and North continued to subsidize colonial production of hemp, flax, and indigo. But these statesmen justified the expense of these bounties during a decade of fiscal stringency on a *commercial* rather than a *military* basis. As Whately explained the Grenville ministry's subsidies in 1765:

A Bounty upon *American* Flax, imported into *Great Britain*, will give the *British* Manufacturer a still further Advantage over the *Americans* and enable him even to purchase his Materials cheaper . . . The same Observations apply to the prohibited *East India* Goods, the wrought Silks and the printed Callicoes, they are prohibited [from import into England] in order to oblige the [East India] Company to import the Silk raw, and the Callicoes white for our Manufactures.[83]

There were other advantages to encouraging colonial cultivation and production of manufacturing inputs, as the governor of Quebec recognized after Britain's accession of Canada. A bounty on hemp and flax

79. Mildmay, 64, 35, 52–53.

80. Ibid., 65.

81. G. L. Beer, *The Commercial Policy of England toward the American Colonies: Studies in History, Economics and Public Laws* (New York, 1893), 91–106.

82. Letter to the Board of Trade (1715), cited in Beer, 92.

83. Whately, *Regulations*, 69–70; see also "Hints respecting the Settlement of Our American Provinces," 24 February 1763, Jenkinson Papers, Add. MSS 38,335, fols. 15–17.

imports, he wrote to imperial officials in Whitehall, "will be one means of Employing [Canadian] Women and Children during the long Winters, in breaking and preparing the Flax and Hemp for Exportation, [and] will divert them from Manufacturing Coarse things for their own use, as it will enable them to purchase those of a better sort Manufactured [in] and Imported from Great Britain."[84] As president of the Board of Trade in 1763, Shelburne was anxious about this particular consequence. He wanted the colonies to produce raw materials for Britain's expanding manufacturing sector, but he worried that such production might lead to more advanced forms of manufacturing and thus breed competition for the mother country's goods.

American manufacturing potential had interested specific British officials in the 1740s and 1750s. But the issue had not galvanized general recognition, much less political action. After the Seven Years War, the possibility of colonial manufacturing became a much greater concern to British ministers and political observers. Many officials and political economists in the 1760s envisioned a regulatory balancing act with regard to raw material production in the periphery. The government should encourage the colonies to supply certain inputs without promoting their conversion into rival manufactures. While he headed the Board of Trade (1763), Shelburne formulated several schemes for checking North American manufacturing attempts, and he monitored all such efforts assiduously.[85]

The Grenville administration's policies, as the following chapter of this book argues, formed the legislative backdrop against which the postwar debate about imperial governance played itself out. Virtually the only one of Grenville's regulatory measures that remained immune to controversy during these years was the promotion of raw material production in the periphery. North America and, to a lesser extent, India and Ireland were to supply Britain with manufacturing inputs. During parliamentary discussions over repeal of Grenville's Stamp Act in 1766, one MP criticized the former prime minister's attempts at raising a colonial revenue, saying that stamp levies had turned North American eyes away from their real concerns in husbandry and toward manufacturing.[86]

Regulating colonial production of raw materials had additional advan-

84. Report of the Governor of Quebec and Its Dependencies (June, 1762), Shelburne Papers, Clements Library, 64/78.

85. See Shelburne Papers, Clements Library, vol. 48.

86. House of Commons, 12 February 1766, in *The Parliamentary Diaries of Nathaniel Ryder, 1764–1767*, ed. P. D. G. Thomas, vol. 23 (London, 1969), 297.

tages, as ministers and MPs were quick to note. North American flax cultivation and Indian production of raw silk provided these dominions with the means to purchase British goods. The larger objectives of this system of commercial interchange seemed clear to Mildmay:

Whatever our soil and climate may be incapable of producing, let us take from our *own colonies*: for whilst they can supply us with the *products* we want, and they can raise, and we in return send them such *manufactures* as they want, and we can make, we shall mutually assist each other; and the encrease of their employment abroad will increase our employments at home; new Materials will introduce new Manufactures; new Manufactures will introduce new Trades; and new Trades will introduce new Wealth and Power to the Kingdom in general.[87]

The first condition of promoting British manufacturing—sell the goods as cheaply as possible—fed the second condition—keep open British access to controllable, growing markets. Throughout the 1760s and early 1770s government officials, economic theorists, and the political populace regarded British dominions as the mother country's most important outlets. Several scholars have recently depreciated the contribution of colonial consumption to British economic growth.[88] But revisionist arguments do not diminish the strength of eighteenth-century assessments of imperial markets. As Pownall explained in 1766:

The view of trade, in general, as well as of manufactures in particular, terminates in securing an extensive and permanent vent; or to speak more precisely (in the same manner as shop-keeping does) in having many and good customers: the wisdom therefore, of a trading nation, is to gain and to create as many [markets] as possible. Those whom we gain in foreign trade, we possess under restrictions and difficulties, and may lose in the rivalship of commerce: those that a trading nation can create within itself, it deals with under its own regulations, and makes its own, and cannot lose. In the establishing [of] colonies, a nation creates people whose labour, being applied to new objects of produce and manufacture, opens new channels of commerce, by which they not only live in ease and affluence within themselves, but, while they are labouring under and for the

---

87. Mildmay, 35; see also Lindsay, 137.

88. See especially Patrick O'Brien, "European Economic Development: The Contribution of the Periphery," *Economic History Review* 35 (1982): 1–18; Thomas and McCloskey, 87–102.

mother country (for there all their external profits center) become an increasing nation, of appropriated and good customers to the mother country.[89]

Political economy at midcentury was Janus-faced. In many respects theorists looked back to commercial ideas of the 1680s and 1690s. But writers like Tucker and Young also anticipated the late eighteenth and early nineteenth-century genesis of classical economic theory, articulating doctrines that Smith and Ricardo would take up. Older commercial conceptions took on new form and importance in a period of macroeconomic and geopolitical transition and commingled with new and at times precocious theories.

Interest in colonial markets was no exception. Mercantile writers had been concerned with securing controlled trade since 1624. In that year the author of the *Plaine Path-Way to Plantations* called for trade "between one and the same people, though distant in Region, yet united in Religion, in Nation, in Language and Dominion."[90] The author of *Reasons for Raising a Fund for the Support of a Colony at Virginia* (1607) had deemed Britain's territories more reliable markets for the mother country's products than Spanish, French, or other foreign outlets. "It is publicly known," the writer had contended; "that traffic with our neighbor Countries begin[s] to be of small request, the game seldom answering the merchants adventure, and foreign states either are already or at this present are preparing to enrich themselves with wool or cloth of their own which heretofore they borrowed from us."[91]

Political economists working in the mid-eighteenth century recognized similar advantages in maintaining prosperous colonies.[92] As Young commented in 1772, "It may be observed that our colonies are of infinite consequence to this nation; for the wealth resulting from the exportation

89. Pownall, 25–26.

90. *Plaine Path-Way to Plantations* (London, 1624), 11.

91. *Reasons for Raising a Fund for the Support of a Colony at Virginia* (1607).

92. "The History of Europe," *Annual Register* 9 (1766): 35. Josiah Tucker's work again stands as a precocious exception. For although his early tracts (*Essay on Trade*) evince concern with the benefits of colonial markets, his later writings (*Four Tracts, The Case of Going to War, Four Letters*) show skepticism about the value of such possessions. Indeed, in words that anticipate Ricardo, Tucker contended that it was unnecessary for Britain to control markets, since price and supply rather than regulatory purview govern the flow of goods across national borders. To the extent that Britain could continue to produce as many manufactures as demanded at the lowest relative prices, it would continue to enjoy economic prosperity in international markets without legislative control.

of £3,571,365 in British commodities, the largest part of which are our own manufactures, is of the most truly valuable kind, and will be found hereafter to bear a prodigious proportion to what we gain by all other branches of our commerce."[93] The author of *The Importance of the British Dominions in India . . . Compared with That in America* looked eastward:

With regard to commerce, if we are to consider it on that general footing, of an intercourse commenced, by the free and unconstrained choice of two countries, upon the motive of mutual necessity and utility, which is the source of all commerce, and without which it cannot subsist; we must perceive, that the commerce of India will ever continue to be highly advantageous to Britain . . . For the natural necessity and utility of commerce, arises from the difference of production in the two trading countries. And from this cause, the productions of India whether of nature or art being altogether different from those of Britain, it proceeds that the articles which India receives at present from Britain can never cease to be necessary to India.[94]

This writer estimated that Britain's trade surplus with India in 1770 was £300,000.[95]

Concern with imperial markets in the 1760s and 1770s was distinct from seventeenth-century interest in two respects. First, eighteenth-century writers were less concerned with dominion as a motivating force than were their mercantile predecessors. Trade between countries was governed as much by reciprocal needs and utility as by national loyalty, according to writers like Tucker. Global interchange, one economist observed, "takes its rise from numbers of people employed in cultivating and improving the first productions of nature, for common use and conveniency; from whence all nations, according to their skill and industry . . . endeavour to support their own interest, by mutually supplying each other with what the one wants, and the other has in too great abundance."[96] Within this context, America and to a lesser extent India were important as large, growing markets comprising consumers who would purchase British goods because they were cheaper and more useful than other nations' products. In 1774 Tucker was sufficiently

93. Young, 339.
94. *The Importance of the British Dominions in India Stated, and Compared with That in America* (London, 1770), 10–11.
95. Ibid., 20.
96. Mildmay, 3.

confident of British manufacturing capabilities to offer an interesting conjecture:

Granting, therefore, that *North America* was to become independent of us, and we of them, the Question now before us will turn on this single Point,—Can the Colonists, in a general Way, trade with any other *European* State to greater Advantage than they can with *Great Britain*? If they can, they certainly will; but if they cannot, we shall still retain their Custom, notwithstanding we have parted with every Claim of Authority and Jurisdiction over them . . . Let us now consider their *Imports.* And here one Thing is very clear and certain, That whatever Goods, Merchandize, or Manufactures, the Merchants of *Great Britain* can sell to the rest of *Europe*, they might sell the same to the Colonies, if wanted: Because it is evident, that the Colonies could not purchase such Goods at a cheaper Rate at any other *European* Market.[97]

The economic thinkers of the 1760s and 1770s did not deny the benefits of reliability and security in colonial markets. Judicious regulation of Britain's dominions would augment manufacturing sales. But the ability to satisfy colonists' appetite for inexpensive, reputable goods was equally important. "Yet we are to consider not only what we can most advantageously supply," Mildmay wrote, "but what it is others chiefly want; and accordingly imitate the Dutch."[98] As Postlethwayt explained, "It is the Fruit of the Efforts of Industry to suit the Taste of the Consumer, and even to anticipate and spirit up that Taste."[99] It was clear to political economists and politicians, in the wake of the Seven Years War, that Britain could produce the wares its colonies and other countries wanted.

A second distinctive facet of concern with imperial markets involved domestic labor. Seventeenth-century commercial writers had not been overtly interested in connections between imperial commerce and the number of British wage earners.[100] By contrast, political economists in

97. J. Tucker, *Four Tracts*, 204, 206. See also Burke, "Observations on a Late State of the Nation," in *Writings and Speeches*, ed. Langford, 2:192–96. It is interesting to note that Smith echoed these confident predictions in *Wealth of Nations*, 2:103–30.

98. Mildmay, 52–53.

99. Postlethwayt, *Great Britain's True System*, 234.

100. See Knorr, 95–105. A few seventeenth-century writers, such as Josiah Child, had worried about Britain's balance of employment relative to that of its trading rivals. These concerns had centered on maintaining domestic population; see Josiah Child, *A Discourse about Trade* (London, 1690), 165. Seventeenth-century interest in imperial markets as props

the 1760s were vitally concerned with American and East Indian consumption as a means of augmenting Britain's employment.[101] "Numbers of people being the Strength of a nation," wrote one theorist in 1765, "and their skill and industry the foundation of its riches; to promote their *Encrease*, and procure means for their *Employment*, must be the chief maxim of every government."[102] Economic writers viewed domestic employment as a way to increase national population. "There is not a demonstration in Euclid clearer than [this]:" Young wrote; "increase employment and you will increase the people."[103] Toward this end, he continued, manufactures, especially those produced as exports, were significant because these industries employed people who "would either starve or remain a dead weight upon the public."[104]

Why couldn't low-skilled laborers find work in agriculture? With reference to sectoral change, Young addressed this question: "Agriculture being at a stand, or improving but slowly, a vast number of the lower people do not find employment in it."[105] He estimated that the woolen industry alone provided work for 1.5 million Britons; the metal trades employed some 900,000; and cotton and silk manufacturing supplied a livelihood for almost 500,000 British men and women.[106] Through the 1750s and early 1760s, Young, Tucker, and others watched British exports of manufactures to imperial markets rise significantly. The author of an *Essay on the Trade of the Northern Colonies* (1764) estimated that in 1748 the North American colonists bought £830,000 of British exports. Ten years later they purchased more than £1.8 million, an increase of more than 100 percent.[107] The importance of expanding exports to British employment was not lost on that keen observer of imperial affairs, Ben Franklin:

---

to British population was a less significant concern than other considerations. Strategic issues, including balance of trade problems, specie shortages, and provision of raw materials dominated earlier commercial debates about empire.

101. Viner, *Studies in the Theory of International Trade*, 51, contends the balance of employment argument dates back as far as 1538 and "persists without break throughout the literature of the 17th and 18th centuries." He denies, incorrectly I believe, that this doctrine was more important in the eighteenth-century debate on political economy than a century earlier.

102. Mildmay, 5; see also Steuart, chap. 30.

103. Young, 195.

104. Ibid., 193.

105. Ibid., 194.

106. Ibid., 197.

107. *Essay on the Trade of the Northern Colonies* (London, 1764), 36–37.

But sure experience in those parts of the island teaches us, that people increase and multiply in proportion as the means and facility of gaining a livelihood increase; and that this island [Britain], if they could be employed, is capable of supporting ten times its present number of people. In proportion therefore, as the demand increases for the manufactures of *Britain*, by the increase of people in her colonies, the numbers of her people at home will increase, and with them the strength as well as the wealth of the nation.[108]

Macroeconomic transformation stimulated political economists' interest in the relation between domestic employment and the imperial economy. As Britain's manufacturing sector grew, it became increasingly apparent to economic observers that agriculture, husbandry as well as farming, could no longer employ the majority of domestic laborers. Young explained: "The immense importance of manufacturing all the product at home, appears in the clearest light . . . for it is a melancholy instance to see such numbers of unemployed poor, and feel so heavily the weight of employing them, and at the same time suffer a raw commodity to be carried out of the country, which would give industry and maintenance to such numbers of people."[109]

The changing patterns of eighteenth-century trade focused attention on Britain's imperial markets. Throughout the middle decades of the century, political economists and government ministers watched European markets for British manufactures, especially woolen cloth, shrink as France, Spain, Portugal, Germany, and other nations began to produce competing goods in large quantities.[110] At the same time as older markets

108. Benjamin Franklin, *The Interest of Great Britain Considered with regard to Her Colonies* (London, 1760), 25.

109. Young, 181.

110. *Proposals for Carrying on the War with Vigour, Raising the Supplies Wtihin the Year, and Forming a National Militia* (London, 1757), 54. With attention to the woolen market, historian Ralph Davis has summarized eighteenth-century shifts in trading patterns: "Meanwhile continental development towards self-sufficiency nibbled . . . at the market abroad for English woollens. France, of course, had built up her woollen industry and closed her gates to imports in the seventeenth century, and was becoming a serious competitor in south European markets. The growth of the German industry threatened many of the oldest English markets in central Europe, and it began to receive some measure of protection from the Imperial government. . . . Even Spain and Portugal, which against the general European trend, took increasing quantities of English woollens throughout the first half of the century, began to foster their own industries in the fifties and sixties, and their demand for English manufactures at last slackened and fell away" ("English Foreign Trade," 288).

contracted, exports to the mother country's dominions—India and especially the American colonies—rose substantially.[111] Political economists
realized that the country could no longer rely on European outlets for
its manufactures. To maintain employment and prosperity, Britain
would have to sell its goods in America and India. Young summarized
this perspective:

If this nation preserves her colonies securely to herself, and prevents
their interfering with the manufactures and products of their mother-
country; and a political attention be given to other trades . . . any one
may venture to assert, that it is impossible the trade of Britain should decline; on the contrary, it must regularly increase with the increase of the
colonies. And this branch of our commerce is, and must be, (under these
circumstances) so very considerable, that, added to our coasting trade and
fisheries, it will occasion such a circulation of industry, such large stocks
in merchant hands, and such an extensive navigation, that a nation possessing so much must possess more; a share of other trades must be enjoyed by it in spite of all rivalry. Here then are the great means of preserving, and even increasing the commerce of Great Britain: the
particular methods of managing this business ha[s] been treated already
in another place. Let her manage her colonies in a political manner.[112]

Seven years of war underscored the importance of colonial outlets.
During the conflict British manufactures—metalwares, textiles, glass,
and more—poured overseas to North American colonies and Bengal,
where thousands of troops demanded food, clothing, and equipment.
It was the most rapid growth in exports to America that Britons had
witnessed thus far.[113] To the extent that British taxpayers funded war
expenditures, wartime additions to American *and* East Indian demand
for British manufactures represented a replacement of home demand
by colonial consumption. But this was not apparent to most economic
observers.[114] From the perspective of political economists, statesmen, and

111. Economic historians have corroborated the growth in Britain's imperial trade across
the eighteenth century. See Thomas and McCloskey.

112. Young, 550. For contemporary perceptions of India's role on the imperial economy,
see Mortimer, 131.

113. Davis, "English Foreign Trade"; Schumpeter, 17.

114. William Knox, a meticulous (and zealous) observer of the imperial economy, was
cognizant of the extraordinary nature of colonial demand for British exports during the
war (8). Other imperial experts, in and outside government, looked less carefully at this
phenomenon, inferring (mistakenly) that British exports to America and India would
continue to grow from their wartime levels.

manufacturers, the war was a harbinger of Britain's commercial future. Pownall's confidence was hardly unique:

The great question at this crisis is, and the great struggle will be, which of the states of Europe shall be in those circumstances, and will have the vigour and wisdom so to profit of those circumstances, as to take this interest under its dominion and to unite it to its government. This lead seemed at the beginning of the late war to oscillate between the English and French, and it was in this war that the dominion also hath been disputed. The lead is now in our hands, we have such connection in its influence, that, whenever it becomes the foundation of a dominion, that dominion must be ours.[115]

The Seven Years War set new standards for British imperial trade; it also illuminated the fragility of this intercourse. Although the Navigation Acts prohibited American customers from purchasing specific goods from any nation except Britain, French and Spanish trade with the colonies had expanded during the war. By shipping goods through the neutral Dutch Caribbean islands of Curaçao and St. Eustatius and later through Spanish Santo Domingo, American colonists carried on significant wartime commerce with Britain's enemies.[116] This illegal interchange during the conflict did not trouble imperial experts unduly. When Massachusetts Bay merchants sold lumber to Martinique traders, declared the author of *Thoughts on Trade in General* (1763), the North Americans "drain[ed] off some of the riches of the French West Indies."[117] Colonists then used this specie to buy British manufactures.

When the war ended, political economists worried that contraband trade would continue and escalate. Political dominion and national fealty were not sufficient incentives to keep the colonists loyal customers. As one naval official, charged with controlling this illegal trade during the Seven Years War, commented, "Here it is an Island Interest, There it is the Interest of the Colonies; What opposes this Interest is, of all other Things the most obnoxious to them, For the Public or National Interest is out of the Question with both."[118] How was Britain to ensure colonial consumption? Tucker asked:

115. Pownall, 9.
116. George Louis Beer, *British Colonial Policy, 1754–1762* (New York, 1907), 72–113.
117. *Thoughts on Trade in General* (London, 1763), 37.
118. Charles Holmes to William Pitt, 4 January 1761, Colonial Correspondence, Jamaica 2, PRO. See also Josiah Tucker, *The True Interest of Great Britain Set Forth in Regard to the Colonies* (Philadelphia, 1776).

What then shall we say in Regard to such Colonies as are the Offspring of a free Constitution? And after what Manner, or according to what Rule, are our own in particular to be governed, without using any Force or Compulsion, or pursuing any Measure repugnant to their own Ideas of civil and religious Liberty? In short, and to sum up all, in one Word, How shall we be able to render these Colonies more subservient to this Island, and more obedient to the Laws and Government of the Mother Country, than they *voluntarily choose to be?*[119]

If Britain was to keep the lion's share of the growing American markets in the postwar world, it would have to supply the goods colonists wanted at the lowest possible prices.

The importance of colonial self-interest extended beyond the problem of illegal trade. It became, as chapters 4 and 5 of this book explain, an agitating force in imperial policymaking, spilling over to affect Britain's relationship with its colonies. As the postwar decade wore on and difficulties in Boston and Bengal multiplied, government ministers found the strength of legal sanction wanting. Without the cohesive power of a shared imperial identity, laws made in Whitehall and applied to the periphery held scant authority. As many economists before Smith realized, unless New York merchants believed they would benefit more from obeying the Sugar Act than from violating it, colonists were unlikely to comply. The task, therefore, as Burke understood, was to devise policies in the shared interests of Great Britain and the colonies. But as British ministers discovered in the postwar decade, the commercial priorities of the mother country, America, and India did not always coincide. Within the constraints of parliamentary, ministerial, and popular politics, metropolitan statesmen struggled to use legal precedent, economic interest, and constitutional sanction as tools in imperial governance. The strategic decisions of empire—whether to tax the North American colonists, how to manage the East India Company revenues and commerce—were also shaped by the evolving boundaries of political economy.

In Whitehall, government officials shared economic theorists' interest in imperial markets. Long regarded as advantageous, after the Seven Years War colonial outlets became a central focus of policymaking. Statesmen like Grenville and Rockingham saw other benefits in Britain's accessions. These lands could serve as strategic strongholds and suppliers of raw materials. But politicians viewed these advantages as subordinate.

119. J. Tucker, *True Interest of Great Britain*, 164.

In late 1762, speaking in support of the preliminary articles of peace, Shelburne explained the novelty of ministerial priorities:

Heretofore, the Extension of Limits was the Single Point aimed at. But now the Possession of Territory is but a secondary Point, and is considered as more or less valuable as It is subservient to the Interest of Commerce, which is now the great object of ambition . . . It is apparent that the Value of our Exports to North America as far as they consist of our Manufactures which are the greater part, is a clear profit to the Nation, and in its present State may be fairly said to Yield full half the Natural Balance Great Britain gave by Trade, the annual profits of which are thought not to exceed two Million.[120]

Officials knew, as did political economists, that foreign markets had become increasingly precarious. In 1765 the former colonial officer Thomas Pownall compared European and colonial outlets: "Those whom we gain in foreign trade, we possess under restrictions and difficulties, and may lose in the rivalship of commerce." By contrast, Britain's colonies, "labouring under and for the mother country (for there all their external profits center) become an increasing nation, of appropriated and good customers to the mother country."[121]

Demographic considerations underscored ministerial interest in colonial markets. In 1755 William Shirley, governor of Massachusetts, estimated that the population of North America doubled every twenty years, contending that Britain's export growth correlated with this population increase. The conquest of Canada, he predicted, would further expand burgeoning North American markets. Canada's "extensive Trade with the Indians, the increase of the Fishery, the Rich vacant Country for new Settlements, and the quick Growth of their Estates would make the Inhabitants increase if not in a Duplicate proportion to what they have hitherto done, yet in a much greater degree."[122] The population and commercial potential of India did not escape British attention. With the war's end, most of the continent's trade was controlled by the East India

120. Shelburne Papers, Clements Library, vol. 165. See also Whately, *Regulations*, 6; "Observations relating to North America," Shelburne Papers, Clements Library, vol. 48.
121. Pownall, 23.
122. William Shirley to Thomas Robinson, 15 August 1755, State Papers, Colonial, America and West Indies, PRO. See also "Hints respecting the Settlement of Our American Provinces," Liverpool Papers, Add. MSS 38,335, fol. 14.

Company. Robert Clive, a company official and MP, explained what this eastern monopoly meant for the British economy:

Whoever reads the accounts of India, will find that the British Nation there [has] been attended with a series of successes almost unparalleled in any age . . . The East India Company are at this time Sovereigns, of a rich, populous, fruitful Country, in extent beyond France and Spain united; they are in possession of the Labour, industry and manufactures of 20 million of Subjects; they are in the actual receipt of between five and six millions a year. They have an army of 50,000 men.[123]

India's role as a market for domestic manufactures grew slowly but steadily in British perceptions over the 1760s. In the conflict's immediate aftermath, statesmen viewed the expanded eastern territories as lands with enormous fiscal and commercial potential. Commenting in 1762 on the wartime increase in British exports to India, John Pownall, secretary of the Board of Trade, said: "This remarkable Change in the Circumstances of this [commerce] is occasioned partly by the Great Acquisitions of Territorial Property which at the same time that it produces a large Revenue to the [East India] Company does also open a vent for the greater Quantity of our Manufactures."[124]

During the mid-1760s, government officials were uncertain how to exploit Indian markets. As North American difficulties mounted—both in collecting taxes and in securing British access to markets there—India's financial significance in the empire became more prominent. In 1766 the Chatham administration considered regulating the East India Company and launched a parliamentary inquiry into its finances and operations. A year later the British state began collecting £400,000 annually from Company revenues.[125] Prime Minister North was certain by 1769 that the East India Company's interest in revenue collection was restricting sales of British goods:

Before the Company acquired these revenues, it was their interest to export manufactures . . . In that case, they made a profit from Exports as

123. Commons debate, 27 February 1769, Cavendish Diary, Egerton MSS 218, fols. 149–50.

124. John Pownall to East India Company directors, 23 December 1762, Shelburne Papers, Clements Library, 90/413.

125. In 1765, acting on behalf of the East India Company, Clive had secured the *diwani* of Bengal and several other Indian regions. The *diwani* was the right to collect and administer these regions' territorial revenues. Clive estimated the Company's net gain from

well as Imports. There was no doubt upon that case that they would export as much as the Indian markets would want. But from the time they came possessed of the revenues in India, it ceased to be the interest of the Company to export the manufactures of Great Britain, that stood in the way of so much revenue they should have brought home. That being the case, that being so material a consideration with regard to all our trade, with regard to all our manufactures, industry and internal Wealth, it called upon the Treasury to be careful as far as they could, to secure to the Publick the continuation of those advantages, which our manufacturers and industry drew from the East India Company in its foreign dominions.[126]

North's concern about the Company's export trade was not unique. Ministers and MPs worried that the Company's new reliance on territorial revenues would adversely affect the volume and value of its exports to India. Declining exports could significantly damage the health of British industry.[127]

How could the mother country keep imperial markets open to British manufactures? Throughout the 1760s, officials ironed out older and more novel policy responses to this problem. Grenville tried to regulate American consumption of British goods by tighter, more comprehensive enforcement of the Navigation Acts. The Rockingham ministry reduced the force of the preceding administration's policies and lowered colonial tax burdens in an effort to secure commercial loyalty. Chatham favored state intervention in East India Company operations. North gave the trading company permission to export tea duty free to the American colonies. His administration also sought guarantees from the trading concern that it would export a fixed amount of manufactures to India each year.

Scholars have not always seen imperial policies as the effective and distinctive solutions that eighteenth-century politicians declared them to be before contemporary parliaments. Interested in the origins of the American Revolution, historian John Shy has argued that British states-

---

such collections at over £1.6 million a year. Robert Clive to the [East India Company] Court of Directors, 30 September 1765, *Fort William–India House Correspondence*, vol. 4, *1764–1766*, ed. C. C. Srinivasachari (Delhi, 1962), 337.

126. Commons debate, 27 February 1769, Cavendish Diary, Egerton MSS 218, fol. 106. See also Egerton MSS 218, fol. 108.

127. H. V. Bowen, *Revenue and Reform: The Indian Problem in British Politics, 1757–1773* (Cambridge, 1991), 111.

men confronted a relatively limited spectrum of policy alternatives in the 1760s.[128] This was also true for metropolitan action toward India.

Why were the possibilities of imperial governance limited? The answer lies in the interrelation between the changing British economy, contemporary economic theory, and the alignments and perceptions of elite politicians. Throughout the decade before the Boston Tea Party (1773) and the East India Company Regulating Act (1773), ministers and MPs attempted to manage the power of commerce toward geopolitical ends. To do this, they relied heavily on the theories of Young, Postlethwayt, and others. Certainly scholars like Shy, Greene, and Marshall are correct to point out that Halifax had acted similarly as president of the Board of Trade in the early 1750s. He and a few other British officials had been concerned with pursuing commercial objectives by rational, enlightened means.[129]

The Seven Years War accelerated the diffusion, urgency, and relevance of economic priorities, linking these aims inextricably to issues of international ascendancy. In the aftermath of the conflict three dozen officials, several hundred MPs, and countless other Britons devoted enormous amounts of time and attention to managing the great machine of imperial trade. Such management was one of the most consistently important issues confronting Britons in the 1760s.

Married, albeit tempestuously, to commercial aspirations were significant fiscal concerns. Economic writers and statesmen recognized that to sustain its global preeminence, Britain would have to remain more solvent than its rivals. The nation needed money to wage war, to man and defend its empire, and to service the fiscal engine of eighteenth-century warfare, the national debt. Like so many issues of political economy in the 1760s, these were not born anew in the economic fallout of the Seven Years War. But questions of state finance took on a novel urgency and importance after the Peace of Paris.

Foremost among fiscal worries in 1763 was the issue of debt service. The war had been financed principally by borrowed money, and the nation's funded liability had grown almost £60 million over the course of the conflict, fueling a national debt that in 1764 had climbed to an unprecedented £141 million. Stretching out for decades, annual interest costs were over £5 million, a sum that represented approximately half

128. John Shy, "Thomas Pownall, Henry Ellis, and the Spectrum of Possibilities, 1763–1775," in *Anglo-American Political Relations, 1675–1775*, ed. Alison Gilbert Olson and Richard Maxwell Brown (New Brunswick, N.J., 1970), 155–86.

129. Ibid., 183.

of the government's yearly expenditures in peacetime.[130] In addition to service charges, ministers faced the problem of financing an army— some 10,000 men strong—now stationed on the western borders of the much enlarged North American territories. The estimated annual cost of this force was £360,000.[131]

The problem of paying debt service and imperial costs was intertwined with commercial considerations. William Knox, undersecretary of state to the (American) colonies in the early 1770s, explained these:

Such part of this heavy burden as falls upon our artificers and mariners, superadded to all former impositions must either sink them to poverty, and thence force them into foreign service, or oblige them to demand an increase of wages, which must advance the price of our freights; and in either case, our carrying trade cannot be recovered . . . Effects equally ruinous must be produced by the increase of taxes upon our manufactures; heavy taxes and low wages must force the manufacturer to seek a cheaper country, and with him departs the manufacture: increasing his wages must raise the price of the manufacture, and diminish its consumption at home, and lessen the demand for it from abroad. In either case, the nation loses its trade, and with that its people, and the public revenue moulders away of course.[132]

For Knox, other statesmen, and economic theorists, a rough tradeoff obtained between raising revenue and promoting British commerce.[133] Throughout the postwar period, the state needed revenue. But raising funds at home or in the periphery compromised Britain's interest in selling as many manufactures as possible. According to the doctrines of political economy, domestic taxes on necessary goods raised domestic wages and thus the price of Britain's finished goods, making them less attractive relative to those of other countries. Significant levies on colonial consumers reduced their purchasing power. As the duke of Grafton said during the parliamentary debates over repeal of the Stamp Act, "It is said America is not taxed. I answer they pay Taxes in taking your

130. B. R. Mitchell and Phyllis Deane, *Abstract of British Historical Statistics* (Cambridge, 1962), 390.

131. Committee of Ways and Means, 9 March 1764, estimate quoted in *Ryder Diaries*, 235.

132. Knox, 29. See also Postlethwayt, *Great Britain's True System*, letters 1 and 2.

133. See Samuel Garbett, "Thoughts on the Colonies," Shelburne Papers, Clements Library, 49/21; see also Shelburne Papers, 90/243, and Burke, "Observations," in *Writings and Speeches of Edmund Burke*, ed. Langford, 2:191.

manufactures."[134] In 1763 the author of *Propositions for Improving the Manufactures* argued that commercial prosperity and public solvency were incompatible as policy ends:

This island seems to be arrived at a crisis which must either turn to our future glory, or our destruction; and this peace will either introduce a general decay in our trade and commerce, in consequence of those of our neighbours being revived, and of the additional taxes which our heavy debts must keep on our industry; or otherwise, if, by care and economy, we are eased at home, we shall see every individual exerting himself in all parts of his majesty's dominions, and not only many new manufactures established, but every useful plan carried into execution which may tend to promote our foreign trade in all parts of the world.[135]

How should the state balance its revenue needs with national commercial priorities? Officials confronted this challenge throughout the postwar decade. Grenville tried unsuccessfully to pursue both objectives simultaneously. Through a combination of regulatory and fiscal measures, he attempted to finance imperial costs by taxing North America while securing markets there for British goods. In the wake of colonial riots and trade boycotts, staged to protest Grenville's stamp tax, it seemed clear to Rockingham and his subministers that the mother country could have outlets for its goods or else state revenue, but not both. As the Birmingham industrialist Samuel Garbett commented:

The *greatest* Commercial object to this Nation is to obtain a *Medium* to enable the Americans to purchase the Manufactures of Britain—and such of our Manufactures which employ the most Labourers, and consequently pay their proportion of all our Taxes; and judicious methods should be devised *to restrain such commodities* going there, as neither *employ* our people, nor pay our *great Taxes*.
Every means of taxing America is playing with Edge-tools, and however easy the Americans may appear, or really be, under any mode of taxation the above mentioned *Capital and Primary Object* will not be accommodated thereby, and though it may artfully, it will injudiciously increase the Revenue, for every Shilling obtained to the Revenue will, as Trade is now circumstanced with America, stop the circulation of many Shillings in Our

134. Lords Debate, 11 March 1766, Add. MSS 35,972, fols. 82–87.
135. *Propositions for Improving the Manufactures*, 10.

Manufactures, and thereby prevent an annual Clear Gain to Our Country.[136]

Markets were what mattered to the Rockingham government and its constituencies. But the need for state revenues did not die with the revocation of the Stamp Act in 1766. North America, it seemed, could not be viably taxed without risking its markets. Fiscal exigency motivated the Chatham administration's effort to tax India. But here too the perceived tradeoff between raising revenues and selling large quantities of manufactures intervened. As the author of "Thoughts on the Present State of the East India Company" noted,

There is a motive, even stronger than that of Compensation, why an Incentive to increase their Trade ought to be left, which is that as the principal Advantage accruing to the State (let the Amount of the revenues be what it will) arises from the Duties paid in England, and the Balance of Foreign Trade, everything which contributes to increase the Trade augments the Duties and turns the Balance more in our favour. The Commerce of the Indies secured to Great Britain is the first Object of the State; the Revenues are only a secondary consideration.[137]

Although ministers wanted both imperial markets and revenues, they believed they must choose between the objectives. The relative weight each administration assigned the two priorities depended on political considerations, official perceptions, and the particular macroeconomic context in which specific decisions were made. That such a tradeoff—explicitly acknowledged or implicitly present—pervaded legislative debates concerning imperial governance was a result of the dynamic between policymaking and the doctrines of political economy. In articulating commercial theories, Tucker, Steuart, and others were responding to the macroeconomic transformations occurring around them.

Geopolitical power and domestic prosperity, including employment, were functions of the "general perfection" of British manufactures. The growth of national manufacturing capabilities was demand driven and depended on the country's ability to produce inexpensive buckets, fustians, and tools in large quantities. Statesman could not tax domestic essentials because the political economists contended that this raised

136. Garbett.
137. "Thoughts on the Present State of the East India Company," Shelburne Papers, Clements Library, 90/243.

British wages. Raw materials must be imported duty free or the price of final goods would climb. If, after the repeal of the stamp levy, North American colonists could not be taxed without ruining British commerce, the profitability of the East India Company could perhaps be tapped to meet the state's revenue needs. The maxims of political economy mattered to imperial officials in the postwar decade. So too did the macroeconomic transitions that men like Tucker and Steuart sought to articulate and systematize to Britain's geopolitical and commercial advantage.

But the vectors of historical reconstruction point two ways. The decisions ministers made, the policies they enacted, and the results of their actions reverberated back to the field of political economy, subtly shaping the observations, methods, and conclusions of its practitioners. It is surely more than coincidental that Tucker and others became increasingly concerned with freer trade in the early 1770s, when the North American colonies grew more rebellious and the loss of these markets seemed progressively more likely. Symbiotically, political economists and government officials struggled to promote the power of commerce, the lifeblood of the first British empire in the years after its inception.

❧❧❧ FOUR

The Political Configurations of Dominion

IN 1769, looking outward from Westminster, Edmund Burke summarized the challenges of imperial governance:

We have a great empire to rule, composed of a vast mass of heterogeneous governments, all more or less free and popular in their forms, all to be kept in peace, and kept out of conspiracy, with one another, all to be held in subordination to this country; while the spirit of an extensive and intricate trading interest pervades the whole, always qualifying, and often controlling, every general idea of constitution and government. It is a great and difficult object; and I wish we may possess wisdom and temper enough to manage it as we ought. Its importance is infinite.[1]

What did it mean to rule a dominion pervaded by an "intricate trading interest"? To what ends was Britain's commercial empire to be governed? Versed in the doctrines of political economy, a small group of men—in and outside government—developed generally shared visions of empire. These men harbored imperial ambitions that were a hybrid of older colonial theories and emerging, often surprisingly modern notions of international authority. They envisaged an imperium founded on the

---

1. Edmund Burke, "Observations on a Late State of the Nation" (London, 1769), in *Writings and Speeches of Edmund Burke*, vol. 2, *Party, Parliament and the American Crisis, 1766–1774*, ed. Paul Langford (Oxford, 1981), 194.

demonstrated power of commerce—on Britain's ability to sell increasing quantities of manufactures as well as to raise the money and men necessary to maintain its preeminence. In this system the mother country's children were considered primarily as reliable markets and potential revenue sources, "calculated," as Shelburne's aide Maurice Morgann wrote in 1765, "to increase the Growth and Opulence of Great Britain."[2]

Most MPs and much of the political nation agreed. But *how* was Britain to accomplish this? How, within the exigencies of elite politics, were officials to manage the empire in order to sustain the country's international preeminence while simultaneously promoting economic growth at home? As the 1760s wore on and imperial turmoil mounted, statesmen and pamphleteers debated this question. By 1774 even Burke was stumped:

No topic has been more familiar to us and to the peace and prosperity of this whole empire. For nine long years, session after session, we have lashed round and round this miserable circle of occasional arguments and temporary expedients. I am sure our heads must turn, and our stomachs nauseate with them. We have had them in every shape; we have looked at them in every point of view. Invention is exhausted; reason is fatigued; experience has given judgement; but obstinacy is not yet conquered.[3]

Given the rough consensus about imperial objectives, why were the politics of dominion so fractious? Why did metropolitan statesmen find it so difficult to rule the empire toward geopolitical ends—ends on which most Britons agreed?

This chapter explores how, within a changing domestic political order, the demands of international ascendancy and their perceived relation to British economic growth conditioned specific imperial decisions. Such choices were not the result of ministerial incompetence or confused ambition, as some scholars have alleged.[4] The Seven Years War had

2. Maurice Morgann, "On the Right and Expediency of Taxing America" (1765), Shelburne Papers, Clements Library, 85/71.

3. Burke, "Speech on American Taxation," 19 April 1774, in *Writings and Speeches,* ed. Langford, 2:409.

4. Robert W. Tucker and David C. Hendrickson, *The Fall of the First British Empire: Origins of the War for American Independence* (Baltimore, 1982), 4, 390–93; Richard Koebner, *Empire* (Cambridge, 1961), 117–18; Michael Kammen, *Empire and Interest: The American Colonies and the Politics of Mercantilism* (New York, 1970), 93–94; Michael G. Kammen, *A Rope of Sand: The Colonial Agents, British Politics, and the American Revolution* (Ithaca, New York, 1968), 92, 104, 314; Bernhard Knollenberg, *Origin of the American Revolution, 1759–1766* (New York, 1960), 13–31; Lawrence H. Gipson, *The British Empire before the American*

elucidated the importance of Britain's economic strength to its global position, increased the stakes of dominion, and compelled widespread official attention to the problem of imperial governance. With newfound clarity and urgency, well-informed statesmen understood the objectives of empire.

Throughout the postwar decade, working within the constraints imposed by the demands of elite politics as well as collective attitudes toward empire, government officials tried to promote the nation's manufacturing growth and harness colonial revenues. The results of these efforts—imperial policy outcomes—were thus a product of the interaction between economic and political influences. It is this relationship that accounts for the complex, seemingly chaotic nature of policymaking in the decade after the Seven Years War.

Elite factions used their positions on specific imperial issues as political weapons. In an order characterized by ideological realignment and parliamentary instability,[5] ministers and MPs tried to clarify and strengthen their positions. One of the issues around which various factions attempted to do so was how Britain was to rule its empire. Imperial governance—the means for achieving the ends of empire—thus became a touchstone for political identity.

The debates about imperial governance unfolded mostly within a commercial frame of reference. In Westminster as well as at Leeds and Liverpool, the political nation argued over how to rule Britain's dependencies. Would a duty on glass imported into North America affect sales of other manufactures there? How important was the American trade to the city of Bristol? Was the East India Company more valuable to the imperial economy in a financial or a trading capacity? The central issues of empire were conceptualized, evaluated, and addressed in terms of their commercial contribution to economic prosperity.[6] Burke and other

---

Revolution, 15 vols. (New York, 1936–70), 11:70–82. Koebner contends that after the Seven Years War British conceptions of empire were incoherent and disorganized. As such, they "could have no part in determining the course of events" (118). As I argued in the preceding chapter and as John Shy has pointed out ("Thomas Pownall, Henry Ellis, and the Spectrum of Possibilities, 1763–1775," in *Anglo-American Political Relations, 1675–1775*, ed. Alison Gilbert Olson and Richard Maxwell Brown [New Brunswick, N.J., 1970], 37), the evidence does not support Koebner's argument. Indeed, a careful analysis of contemporary sources, including those cited by Koebner, suggests the systematic and consensual nature of imperial conceptions.

5. John Brewer, *Party Ideology and Popular Politics at the Accession of George III* (Cambridge, 1976), 8–9.

6. Contemporary French commentators thought Britain was obsessed with commerce. A prominent physiocrat, François Quesnay, had scant regard for a country like Britain,

politicians understood that the newly expanded dominion was to be governed to promote domestic manufacturing, trading, and financial capabilities. The nation's commercial interests were critical not only to economic well-being at home, but also to Britain's international authority. Statesmen knew that victory in the Seven Years War owed much to the nation's manufacturing and trading potential. Customs and excise taxes on manufactures had fueled debt service and military outlays, two elements critical to England's triumph. As Rockingham commented, "Commerce is the basis on which the Power of this country has been raised, and on which it must ever stand."[7]

In the wake of the war, representatives of Britain's commercial interests exercised newfound influence on elite politicians. This influence was partly attributable, as historian Michael Kammen has noted, to transformations rooted in the 1750s. Economic expansion, general political instability, and the growing organizational abilities of various interest groups extended their potential influence.[8]

But there is more to understand. The British government's susceptibility to commercial interests in the 1760s was also a product of geopolitical and macroeconomic transition. Throughout the middle of the eighteenth century, manufacturing activity and international trade, especially with Britain's colonies, increased significantly. The men of movable property—who produced and traded ever larger quantities of goods—became progressively more concerned to try to affect imperial management. Britain's victory greatly heightened this concern. By earning the nation potential dominion over vast new markets and millions of customers, the Peace of Paris raised the stakes of empire. For British merchants

---

"where the interests of the soil and of the state are subordinated to the interests of the merchants; where commerce in agricultural products, the ownership of the land, and the state itself are regarded merely as accessories of the metropolis, and the metropolis as composed of merchants." "Dialogues sur le commerce," in *Physiocratie, ou Constitution naturelle du gouvernement le plus avantageux au genre humain,* ed. Pierre Samuel Dupont de Nemours (Paris, 1768), 283. A dominating commercial spirit, the marquis de Mirabeau said, had "deceived" the British nation and prevented its citizens and statesmen from embracing other values. Marquis de Mirabeau, *Théorie de l'impot* (1761), 241, quoted in Frances Acomb, *Anglophobia in France, 1763–1789: An Essay in the History of Constitutionalism and Nationalism* (Durham, N.C., 1950), 50. According to French observers, Britain's obsession with commerce shaped imperial governance. England was portrayed as the modern Carthage, "unjust, proud and grasping" (Acomb, 9).

7. Rockingham to the merchants of Leeds (ca. 1766), Rockingham MSS, Wentworth-Woodhouse Muniments (hereafter WWM), Sheffield City Library, R59/6.

8. Michael Kammen, "British and Imperial Interests in the Age of the American Revolution," in Olson and Brown, 143–44. See also Kammen, *Rope of Sand*, 99–107.

and manufacturers, the incentives to try to influence its governance were very strong.

Government officials could not afford to ignore the commercial lobbyists who came to Whitehall and Parliament. Men like the Birmingham industrialist Samuel Garbett often served as important sources of information about the empire—its trade, inhabitants, and general health. Metropolitan officials needed this information to formulate specific policies for a far-flung dominion. As significantly, the men of movable property represented new, potentially important constituencies for elite politicians. Concerned to legitimate and increase their parliamentary authority during a decade of political confusion, elites looked to the trading classes. From the perspective of statesmen like Grenville and Burke, commercial interests were increasingly important in the domestic and imperial economy. They had proved crucial in winning the recent war, and at times their objectives appeared significant to national prosperity. For the Rockinghams and other elite factions, championing the priorities of manufacturing and mercantile lobbyists was another tool, possibly an important one, in the struggle for parliamentary power.

On the "tessellated pavement" of politics[9] that emerged after George III's accession and the Seven Years War, Grenville promised to find external funds to pay the costs of empire. His administration initiated a combination of regulatory and fiscal measures in North America, culminating in 1765 in the passage of the Stamp Act. A year later, responding to colonial and metropolitan discontent with these policies, Rockingham and his supporters repealed the stamp tax and dismantled the force of the Navigation Acts. Not long after, the earl of Chatham denied the constitutional propriety of the stamp levy while simultaneously upholding the British state's claim to East India Company revenues. Professing in 1770 to be "a friend to trade, a friend to America,"[10] Lord North advocated retaining the tea tax but revoking the other Townshend duties. Again, claiming to act in the commercial interests of the empire, in 1773 North and his subministers prepared to assume significant state responsibility for the governance of India.

Yet beneath the political disagreements of the 1760s, an underlying consensus was developing about the fundamental source of imperial authority. By 1773 most metropolitan officials believed that Parliament—not the monarch, executive departments, or colonial governors—had

9. Edmund Burke, quoted in Brewer, 44.
10. Commons debate, 5 March 1770, Cavendish Diary, Egerton MSS 221, fol. 22.

The Great Financier, or British Œconomy for the Years 1763, 1764, 1765. British Museum Catalogue 4128 (1765). Printed shortly after George Grenville proposed the stamp tax, this cartoon depicts the fiscal and commercial dilemmas confronting Britain after the war. Grenville tries to balance a national debt of £140 million with savings, but the former far outweighs the candle ends that Grenville's servant, "Economy," adds to the savings scale. William Pitt, complete with gouty shoes and crutch, stands on the other side of Grenville, gestures toward Britain's recent military conquests, and contends that "conquests will ballance it." Behind Pitt an American colonist, burdened by taxes imposed by the mother country and dogged by British stamp tax collectors, argues that imperial commerce will outweigh the debt. Accompanying verse suggests the political tradeoffs British ministers confronted between raising revenues and obtaining markets for domestic manufactures: "For Conquests, or Commerce [Grenville] cares not a Straw / Nor if French, Dutch or Spaniards in Trade give us Law; / Œconomy only shall cure every Evil, / Pitt, Merchants and Soldiers may go to the Devil."

the sovereign right to regulate the Indian and North American economies. This parliamentary superintendence, Britons understood, was to
be directed toward promoting their country's economic and geopolitical
stature.

In 1763 government officials could not see ex ante that various policies
enacted to exploit the power of commerce would meet with significant
resistance at home and in the periphery. When discontent with specific
policies appeared to threaten the commercial health of the empire, as
in 1766 and 1773, statesmen revised earlier policy decisions, consistently
struggling to sustain Britain's international stature. In doing so, ministers
bumped up against a general imperative of political theory, one with
enormous practical consequences. As Burke said, how was the British
polity to reconcile "the strong presiding power, that is so useful towards
the conservation of a vast, disconnected, infinitely diversified empire
with that liberty and safety of the provinces which they must enjoy?"[11]

Over the postwar decade, British officials confronted this question
in both explicit and implicit forms. Despite what numerous ministers
regarded as responsive governance on the part of the mother country
toward its dominions, the challenges to imperial management mounted.
By 1774 these challenges, according to Burke, "ha[d] shaken the solid
structure of this Empire to its deepest foundations."[12] On the surface
and below, the configurations of politics in the 1760s anticipated the
trauma and success of the future empire.

How then is Britain's political landscape to be apprehended? Since the
1720s the nation had known single-party government, dominated by
Whig rule and characterized by significant political stability. Although
this stability deteriorated in the mid-1750s, the wartime coalition headed
by William Pitt and the duke of Newcastle garnered support from a
spectrum of interests. Ministerial unity, so essential to the successful

11. Edmund Burke, "Letter to John Farr and John Harris, Esqrs. (Sheriffs of the City
of Bristol) on the Affairs of America," in *Edmund Burke: Selected Works*, ed. W. J. Bate,
(New York, 1960), 212. On the development of political theory in the context of imperial
politics, see Paul Langford's incisive analysis, "Old Whigs, Old Tories, and the American
Revolution," *Journal of Imperial and Commonwealth History* 8 (1980): 106–30. On the constitutional debates surrounding the governance of the North American colonies, see Jack P.
Greene's cogent study, *Peripheries and Center: Constitutional Development in the Extended Politics
of the British Empire and the United States, 1607–1788* (Athens, Ga., 1986).

12. Edmund Burke, "Speech on American Taxation," in *Writings and Speeches of Edmund
Burke*, ed. Langford, 2:411.

conduct of the Seven Years War,[13] concealed deeper divisions in the political order. One of these divisions concerned the changing structure of politics under the new king. Unlike the first two Georges, both of whom distrusted Tories and served as willing, important actors in the Whig oligarchy, George III hated organized political parties. He also harbored an intense personal resentment toward the leaders of the dominant political group, the Old Corps of Whigs.[14]

At his accession in 1760, the monarch set out to forge a new alliance that he hoped would put an end "to those unhappy distinctions of party called Whigs and Torys,"[15] and constrain Whig control of Parliament and patronage. The king invited Tories and independents into government. He immediately appointed a political outsider, the earl of Bute, to an influential cabinet position. When Bute, the monarch's former tutor and the Favorite, took up the seals as first lord in late 1761, he sought a speedy end to the Seven Years War and with it, the Newcastle government.[16]

The close of the war thus signaled the end of the Old Corps of Whigs. Practically, the conclusion of peace destroyed the raison d'être of the Newcastle government. Ideologically, Bute's controversial peace settlement exposed the numerous divisions in the Old Corps and shattered what had long been an uneasy alliance of political groups. But worse was yet to come for many members of the coalition. In late 1762 and early 1763 the Old Corps was dispatched in the "Massacre of the Pelhamite Innocents," a sweeping dismissal of Newcastle's supporters from office that completed the process by which a new configuration of politics had emerged.[17] The once stable Whig oligarchy had given way to a patchwork

13. On the fiscal, strategic, and political management of the war, see Richard Middleton, *The Bells of Victory: The Pitt-Newcastle Ministry and the Conduct of the Seven Years War* (Cambridge, 1985).

14. Brewer, 10.

15. Memorandum (n.d.), Royal Archives of Windsor, RA 15672, printed in Herbert Butterfield, *George III, Lord North and the People, 1779–80* (London, 1949), 3.

16. The connection between Bute's conciliatory posture on what kind of peace Britain should make and his interest in breaking the Old Corps's dominion is relatively unexplored by scholars of eighteenth-century politics. See D. A. Winstanley, *Personal and Party Government: A Chapter in the Reign of George III, 1760–1766* (Cambridge, 1910), 29, on the Favorite's interest in a swift peace. Winstanley contends that Bute's stance on the peace terms was conditioned by his desire to be rid of Pitt. This argument does not explain Bute's willingness in mid-1762—some ten months after the Great Commoner's resignation—to support peace on virtually any terms. As the following chapter demonstrates, the Favorite's position on the peace treaty and the reaction this position provoked, in and outside the government, were representative of broader, more ambivalent attitudes to empire.

17. Brewer, 44.

of factions over which no group held consistent sway. In the space of a few years the accession of George III, the conclusion of the Seven Years War, and the exacerbation of older party tensions had transformed Britain's fairly peaceful political landscape into a mosaic of factions.

In the confusion, elite politicians scrambled to define their ideological and partisan positions.[18] They did so with reference to familiar divisions. Those now outside government, such as Newcastle, Rockingham, and Pitt, termed themselves Whigs and thus true "friends to the Revolution System of Government."[19] Ousted Whigs labeled George III, Bute, and the administration's followers slaves to the "Doctrines of Toryism"[20] for their purportedly dangerous dedication to the concept of personal royal government.

What did it mean to be "friends to the Revolution," and who was to lead the factionalized Whig party? In the struggle for parliamentary predominance, the issues of empire became important litmus tests by which the Rockinghams, Grenvillites, and others could define and project their own political identities. They did this using both political theory and specific policy decisions. At the theoretical level, questions concerning the British legislature's authority to tax America and to regulate East India Company practices were debated within an ideological framework constructed to curb the influence of the monarchy and preserve Parliament's supremacy. On a more pragmatic plane, elite factions argued extensively over how Britain should harness the power of commerce. Were outlets for British goods more important than taxes raised in the periphery? Was it possible to secure simultaneously both colonial markets and revenues? Throughout the 1760s, spokesmen from various groups, including the Crown, tried to use such issues to legitimate their positions.

The growth of out-of-doors political activity in the 1760s presented elites with an additional source of instability. For decades the potential influence of extraparliamentary politics had been intermittently obvious to ministers and MPs.[21] But it had generally proved very difficult for

18. Brewer, 39–54; Langford, "Old Whigs, Old Tories."

19. Manchester to unknown, 9 January 1776, Henry E. Huntington Library, HM22513, quoted in Langford, "Old Whigs, Old Tories," 107.

20. *Observations on Public Liberty* (London, 1769), 15.

21. On the significance of popular politics before 1760, see Linda Colley, "Eighteenth-Century Radicalism before Wilkes," *Transactions of the Royal Historical Society*, 5th ser., 31 (1981): 1–19; idem, *In Defiance of Oligarchy: The Tory Party, 1714–1760* (Cambridge, 1982), 146–74; Nicholas Rogers, *Whigs and Cities: Popular Politics in the Age of Walpole and Pitt* (Oxford, 1989); idem, "Aristocratic Clientage, Trade and Independency: Popular Politics in Pre-radical Westminster," *Past and Present* 61 (1973): 70–106; idem, "Popular Protest

those excluded from the political process to affect national issues directly.[22] After 1760 and a realignment in the elite order, however, popular interventions registered greater impact on Westminster politics. The burgeoning press provided extraparliamentary interests with an important public forum. Britain's evolving economy increased the focus and the number of people concerned to affect national politics. A particular set of issues—Wilkes, parliamentary reform, and the empire—helped once amorphous extraparliamentary groups define their priorities and strategies.[23] Armed with specific objectives, focused on frequently urgent issues, and fueled by growing participation, special interests tried to expand their influence on elite decision making. The men of movable property, heavily involved in the imperial economy, constituted an important subset of these special interests.

Within a chaotic political environment, a small, fairly constant group formulated imperial policies. These ministers and subministers, such as Grenville, William Dowdeswell, and John Pownall, were well informed about imperial issues. Most had served at one time or other as Treasury or Board of Trade officials. They had access to a wide variety of information about the political arithmetic, the commerce, and the health of the empire.[24] The letter books of customs commissioners, Navy Board minutes and accounts, the boxes of Treasury memoranda, and the Board of Trade colonial reports testify to the cumulative industry of clerical staffs in an age without typewriters and copying machines.[25]

In addition to official information, there were other sources of knowl-

in Early Hanoverian London," *Past and Present* 79 (1978): 70–100; George Rudé, *Hanoverian London, 1714–1808* (London, 1971); idem, *The Crowd in History: A Study in Popular Disturbances in France and England, 1730–1848* (London, 1964); idem, *Ideology and Popular Protest* (New York, 1980); and Kathleen Wilson, "Empire, Trade and Popular Politics in Mid-Hanoverian Britain: The Case of Admiral Vernon," *Past and Present* 121 (1988): 74–109.

22. Brewer, 8–9.

23. Ibid., 15. A detailed analysis of how the indigenous and heterogeneous political culture that had existed for decades in Britain acquired focus and viability during this time is beyond the scope of this book. On such issues, see Brewer, *Party Ideology and Popular Politics*; idem, "English Radicalism in the Age of George III," in *Three British Revolutions*, ed. J. G. A. Pocock (Princeton, N.J., 1980), 322–67; Linda Colley, "Britannia's Children: Images and Identities" (unpublished paper, Davis Center Colloquium, Princeton University, October 1989); Kathleen Wilson, "Imperial Culture, Imperialist Ideologies: Empire and the British Political Nation, 1720–1785" (unpublished paper, Davis Center Colloquium, Princeton University, October 1989).

24. On the relation between the emergence of the modern fiscal-military state and the proliferation of public information, see John Brewer, *The Sinews of Power: War, Money and the English State, 1688–1788* (New York, 1989), 221–49.

25. Ibid., 221.

edge. Shelburne, briefly president of the Board of Trade in 1763 and secretary of state for the southern department in 1766, corresponded with North American colonial agents and entrepreneurs as well as with East India Company directors.[26] His communications spanned a spectrum of subjects and included plans for developing iron and pearl ash production in Canada, settlement proposals for Ohio, histories of the Indian subcontinent, and state revenue calculations. Grenville, Burke, North, Townshend, and Dowdeswell all gathered and synthesized enormous amounts of qualitative and numerical information.[27] They used their knowledge widely, becoming, as the decade wore on, de facto experts on governance in both North America and India.

They shared their expertise, frequently writing and talking to each other about specific issues, especially those concerning the state's commercial and fiscal role in imperial governance. Despite significant contention in 1766 between the Rockingham Whigs and the members of the Chatham ministry, Dowdeswell and Townshend kept in regular contact about financial issues.[28] Although Thomas Whately, Grenville's secretary to the Treasury, collected information about the religious practices of Illinois Indians as well as trade statistics on interchange between Bristol and Boston, he was more concerned with the latter. But Whately and other officials were by no means ignorant of cultural and social matters in the periphery.[29] Ministers used their extensive knowledge to devise a variety of proposals, ranging from plans to curb rum consumption in North America[30] to schemes for transferring authority in Bengal from East India Company servants to state officials.[31]

Throughout the 1760s, the men at high levels of government were served by a score of informed subministers. Relatively isolated from the vagaries of elite politics, these civil servants acquired significant expertise

26. Shelburne Papers, Clements Library.

27. For Grenville's public account of information collection surrounding the proposed stamp tax, see Commons debate, 5 March 1770, Cavendish Diary, Egerton MSS 221, fol. 33.

28. Dowdeswell Papers, Clements Library; Townshend Papers, Clements Library, box 296.

29. Officials compiled memoranda on the subjects, settlements, resources, religions, and histories of Britain's dominions. See Grenville MSS, Add. MSS 57,834, fol. 114; Shelburne Papers, Clements Library, 99(1)/107–20; Townshend Papers, Clements Library, 8/3/26, 8/34/55.

30. Colonial Office Papers, PRO, CO5/216, fol. 33.

31. Memorandum from Nathaniel Smith to Shelburne (undated), "Observations on the Heads of a Bill for the Better Regulation of the British Settlement in India, Shelburne Papers, Clements Library, 99/209–10.

and consequent power on colonial affairs.[32] The career of John Robinson, secretary to the Treasury under North, was representative. Active in East Indian issues throughout the 1760s, he did much of the groundwork on the Regulating Act of 1773 and was recognized as an official expert on the subcontinent and its governance.[33] During the 1770s he and Charles Jenkinson, a Treasury subminister for the Grenville, Chatham, Grafton, and North ministries, bore significant responsibility for political management at India House. Seven years after the Regulating Act's passage, Burke acknowledged Jenkinson's experience: "I know you to be remarkably conversant in India affairs and that you had taken a leading part in the Act for altering the constitution of the [East India] Company and establishing the Interference of the King's Government in their Affairs, by enacting, that the most capital part of their affairs should be regularly laid before the Ministers."[34]

In an analogous career path, John Pownall, a junior minister at the Board of Trade between 1741 and 1769 and an undersecretary of state for America in the 1770s, acquired considerable knowledge about North America and the West Indies. After the Peace of Paris, he had primary responsibility for organizing the mass of data, projections, and recommendations that Shelburne had collected and for preparing a formal report on American policy for the Lords of Trade.[35] He and his fellow undersecretary of state William Knox regularly exchanged letters with colonial agents and governors. These communications were very important in keeping ministers informed about American events.[36]

The government's need to know often extended beyond the purview of those in Whitehall. Throughout the postwar decade, officials were forced to seek facts, numbers, and counsel from outside parties. These consultants fell generally into two categories. The first group comprised the political economists, who considered themselves disinterested observers of international commerce. These were men such as Josiah Tucker, who knew Shelburne well and spoke often with him during the 1760s about the empire. Both Adam Smith and David Hume talked regularly with James Oswald, a Trade and Treasury board member; in 1766 Smith

32. On professional administrators in the eighteenth-century state, see Brewer, *Sinews of Power*, 79–87.

33. Lucy S. Sutherland, *The East India Company in Eighteenth Century Politics* (Westport, Conn., 1979), 252, 267–68.

34. Edmund Burke to Charles Jenkinson, 2 October 1780, Add. MSS 38,404, fol. 202.

35. Leland J. Bellot, *William Knox: The Life and Thought of an Eighteenth Century Imperialist* (Austin, Tex., 1977), 51.

36. Ibid., 119.

also advised Townshend on specific revenue matters.[37] Malachy Postle-thwayt sent his *Universal Dictionary of Trade and Commerce* to numerous well-placed imperial officials.[38]

The second group of outside advisers were less objective. Often organized into specific coalitions with individual political agendas, the men in this category were generally merchants, manufacturers, and financiers. By virtue of their business, they had amassed information about certain colonies. Barlow Trecothick, for example, was chairman of the Committee of London Merchants Trading to North America, a prosperous transatlantic trader, and a large landowner in the West Indies. In November 1765 he wrote to Rockingham seeking repeal of the Stamp Act, grounding his case on domestic economic considerations.[39] His knowledge of American commerce helped make him an important participant in the Rockingham Whigs' efforts to reform imperial policy. So too did Trecothick's connections with numerous merchants, manufacturers, and city officials in London and the provinces.[40]

Joseph Salvador was another influential lobbyist. A Dutch-born financier who became a director of the East India Company, he had negotiated large loans for Newcastle's wartime government. In the ten years following the peace, Salvador served every administration as an informal liaison between the Company and government officials, especially Grenville and Jenkinson.[41]

Another consultant, John Bindley, was a distiller by trade. Although he served as a subminister in the Excise Commission for the Bute and Grenville ministries, he completed most of his work on various revenue schemes in the later 1760s and early 1770s, after he had left public service to become a wine seller. He was friendly with Townshend, Jenkinson, and North, who granted him a pension for his fiscal contributions. When Bindley died in 1786, the *Gentleman's Magazine* described him as a man

37. See W. R. Scott, "Adam Smith at Downing Street, 1766–1767," *Economic History Review* 6 (1935–36): 79–89. See also Edmund Burke to Adam Smith, 1 May 1775, on the effect of patent legislation on British manufactures, in *The Correspondence of Adam Smith*, ed. Ernest Campbell Mossner and Ian Simpson Ross (Oxford, 1977), 180–81.

38. On the significance of information gathering for the eighteenth-century state, see Brewer, *Sinews of Power*, 221–49.

39. Trecothick to Lord Rockingham, 7 November 1765, Rockingham MSS, WWM, R43a.

40. Paul Langford, *The First Rockingham Administration, 1765–1766* (Oxford, 1973), 119–24.

41. See especially Salvador's correspondence with Jenkinson in *The Jenkinson Papers, 1760–1766*, ed. Ninetta S. Jucker (London, 1949), and in the Liverpool MSS, Add. MSS 38,197–38,469.

"to whose abilities the revenue of this country is considerably indebted as well for its augmentation as [for] improvement in several capital branches."[42]

Many of the outside consultants, of course, had material interests to promote. For example, Rose Fuller was a Sussex landowner and ironmaster with large holdings in Jamaica, who wanted specific legislation to promote West Indian trade. With Trecothick, he advised the Rockingham government on American policy. Several East India Company officials, such as Henry Vansittart and Harry Verelst, consulted with state servants about regulating the concern's enterprises on the eastern subcontinent.

Why did ministers trying to manage a vast commercial empire listen to lobbyists? Government officials understood that special interest groups were useful because they were frequently better informed about distant territories and imperial commerce.[43] Manufacturers and merchants often heard international news before government officials did. For this reason Dowdeswell, chancellor of the Exchequer for the first Rockingham administration, and other ministers encouraged lobbyists to come forth with information about the facts and finances of empire.[44] As head of the Board of Trade in 1763, Shelburne collected information on Jamaica from the Committee of London Merchants Trading to America.[45] A year later, London merchants involved in North American interchange advised him on the use of paper currency in the colonies;[46] and in the later 1760s an East India Company commander informed Shelburne about British settlement on the subcontinent.[47]

In inviting lobbyists to provide information, public servants knew they were allowing pressure groups an opportunity to shape policymaking.[48]

42. *Gentleman's Magazine* 56 (1786): 183.

43. Brewer, *Sinews of Power*, 232. On the politics of information and lobbyists' interaction with the state, see 231–49; John M. Norris, "Samuel Garbett and the Early Development of Industrial Lobbying in Great Britain," *Economic History Review*, 2d ser., 10 (1958): 450–60; Alison G. Olson, "The Board of Trade and London-American Interest Groups in the Eighteenth Century," *Journal of Imperial and Commonwealth History* 7 (1980): 33–50; John Styles, "An Eighteenth Century Landed Ruling Class? Interest Groups, Lobbying and Parliament in Eighteenth Century England" (unpublished paper, 1987).

44. Rockingham MSS, WWM, R1/599, R35.

45. Shelburne Papers, Clements Library, vol. 62.

46. Ibid., 48/57.

47. Ibid., 99/209.

48. This is not to say that imperial governance was a crudely functionalist endeavor, with lobbying groups dispensing information in exchange for sympathetic policies. As

But there was more to this than a simple exchange of information for influence. In the turmoil of the 1760s, organized interest groups offered other attractions to elites. For politicians seeking parliamentary authority, such coalitions represented new, potentially significant constituencies. For example, Rockingham and his followers regarded the London Merchants Trading to North America, a group that also included provincial traders and manufacturers, as an important subset of the British citizenry.[49] "It is with no small Satisfaction," Rockingham wrote to Bristol merchants in 1766 after the repeal of the Stamp Act, "that I can look back at the Measures of the last Session of Parl[iamen]t, because I think at no Time the Commercial Interest of this Country was more the Object of Government."[50] Analogously in 1767, Chatham recognized the support he would command among a variety of City trading interests by challenging the East India Company's right to its territorial revenues.[51]

The emphasis ministers and MPs placed on appealing to the commercial classes, particularly those concerned with imperial trade and manufacturing, was relatively new. It cannot be attributed to Whig tradition or to the political connections of former leaders. During his wartime administration, Newcastle's commercial contacts had been principally financial. Almost monthly throughout the conflict, the Treasury minister had dined with Bank of England officials, Change Alley brokers, and other men who made the availability of credit their business. These men

---

Brewer has noted in analyzing the evolution of the eighteenth-century British state, lobbyists' influence varied considerably across coalitions, issues, and time (*Sinews of Power*, 246–48). Yet at no time in the ten years following the birth of the first British empire did pressure groups control its governance. In 1766, during the repeal of the stamp tax and the enactment of the Free Ports Act, special interests enjoyed their biggest policymaking role of the decade. But even at this time government officials were actively involved at each stage of the process, from the earliest discussions of repeal until the final parliamentary vote on West Indian free ports.

49. Burke, "Short Account of a Late Administration" (London, 1766), in *Writings and Speeches of Edmund Burke*, ed. Langford, 2:54–57; George Savile to Lord Rockingham, 1 November 1765, Rockingham MSS, WWM, R1/519; Lucy Sutherland, "Edmund Burke and the First Rockingham Ministry," *English Historical Review* 47 (1932): 46–72; D. H. Watson, "Barlow Trecothick and Other Associates of Lord Rockingham during the Stamp Act Crisis, 1765–66" (M.A. thesis, Sheffield University, 1958), 50; Langford, *First Rockingham Administration*, 109–14.

50. Rockingham MSS, WWM, R1/670.

51. Lucy Sutherland, "Lord Shelburne and East India Company Politics, 1766–9," *English Historical Review* 49 (1934): 450–86, and idem, "Edmund Burke and the First Rockingham Ministry"; H. V. Bowen, "British Politics and the East India Company, 1766–1773" (Ph.D. diss., University of Wales, 1986), 276–79.

had long represented desirable, at times essential, constituencies for any governing coalition. During the postwar decade, statesmen continued to regard financial interests as important props to political legitimacy.[52]

But alongside elite support for such traditional groups appeared a new, general, and publicly proclaimed concern with representing trading and domestic manufacturing interests.[53] In the imperial policy debates of the 1760s, politicians from diverse factions championed and courted these commercial groups, consistently equating their well-being with the economic health of the empire.[54] Perhaps Burke, writing in 1766, gave clearest expression to this new political aim:

[The Rockingham] Administration was the first which proposed, and encouraged public Meetings, and free Consultations of Merchants from all Parts of the Kingdom; by which Means the truest Lights have been received; great Benefits have been already derived to Manufacture and Commerce; and the most extensive Prospects are open'd for further Improvement . . .

52. Kammen, "British and Imperial Interests in the Age of the American Revolution," 145.

53. In the speech from the throne in 1766, George III did not hesitate to court commercial interests. He praised Parliament for "extending and promoting the trade and manufactures of Great Britain, and for settling the mutual intercourse of my kingdom and plantations, in such a manner as to provide for the improvement of the colonies on a plan of due subordination to the commercial interests of the mother country." *Parliamentary History of England from the Earliest Period to the Year 1803*, 36 vols., ed. William Cobbett (London, 1806–20), 16:234.

54. Elite concern with representing British commercial interests coincided with the declining influence of American lobbyists in London. In *Making the Empire Work: London and American Interest Groups, 1690–1790* (Cambridge, Mass., 1992), Alison Gilbert Olson contends that ministerial turnover, bureaucratic transition, parliamentary inflexibility, and new lobbying methods underlay the deteriorating influence of colonial interests between 1755 and 1775 (134–48). Kammen points to the changing roles of colonial agents, the isolation of North America's London interests from their traditional British counterparts, and the strategic disadvantages faced by American lobbyists ("British and Imperial Interests in the Age of the American Revolution," 148–51). Also important in explaining the dwindling power of colonial groups to affect metropolitan policy was the increased number, organization, focus, and political commitment of *British* commercial interests. Not only did domestic manufacturing and trading groups represent new, potentially important constituencies to elites in Whitehall and Westminster, but most of these interests professed to represent Britain's economic health. Although American lobbyists—most consistently Franklin—claimed to speak on behalf of imperial prosperity, in the eyes of British officials the events of the postwar decade undermined the legitimacy of such avowals. In the wake of the colonial boycotts staged to protest the Stamp Act and the Townshend duties, many MPs found it difficult to consider colonial and British merchants "Links of the Chain that binds both countries together" (Committee of Merchants of Philadelphia to the Committee of Merchants of London, 25 November 1769, *London Chronicle* [3 March 1770]).

[T]hat Administration provided for the Liberty and Commerce of their Country, as the true Basis of its Power, they consulted its Interests, they asserted its Honour Abroad, with Temper and with Firmness.[55]

The Rockinghams were not the only party to claim the commercial classes and their concerns as paramount. Grenville and his supporters consistently asserted that their positions represented the "Real and Substantial" priorities of government, which "are the Commercial Interests of Great Britain."[56] During the debates on the Stamp Act's repeal, Shelburne conceded that Parliament had the right to tax America, but he grounded the execution of this right on commercial criteria.[57] When in 1770 Parliament discussed revoking the Townshend duties, North noted the importance of merchant opinion to his stance. It was a view based on commercial, rather than explicitly financial, considerations:

When we look over the duties, we shall find that some of them are really such duties founded on such anti-commercial principles, that every Member of Parliament will be of the same opinion this year he was the last, as to wish they never had passed, and be desirous of taking the first opportunity of removing those parts, which according to the general rules of com-

55. Burke, "Short Account," in *Writings and Speeches of Edmund Burke*, ed. Langford, 2:55–56. In "Thoughts on the Cause of the Present Discontents" (1770), Burke contends that public officials need prior experience with the landed or commercial interest in order to have "*connexion with the interest of the people*" (reprinted in *Writings and Speeches of Edmund Burke*, ed. Langford, 2:280). In 1774 Burke was more explicit: Commerce "has ever been a very particular and a very favorite object of my study, in its principles, and its details . . . This I know, that I have ever had my house open, and my poor services ready, for traders and manufacturers of every denomination." See "Speech at His Arrival at Bristol," in *The Works of the Right Honorable Edmund Burke*, 12 vols. (Boston, 1865–1871), 2:87; See also Dowdeswell Papers, Clements Library.

56. Thomas Whately, *The Regulations Lately Made concerning the Colonies and the Taxes Imposed upon Them, Considered* (London, 1765), 3–4. In 1764 Grenville said he "would lose all he has in the world rather than suffer diminution of the honour of the King his master, or of the commerce of the kingdom." *The Grenville Papers: Being the Correspondence of Richard Grenville, Earl Temple, and the Right Honourable George Grenville, Their Friends and Contemporaries*, ed. W. J. Smith, 4 vols. (London, 1852–53), 2:516. See also *A Reply to a Letter Addressed to the Right Honourable George Grenville* (London, 1763), 7; Grenville's letter to the duke of Bedford, 19 May 1763, in *The Correspondence of John, Fourth Duke of Bedford*, ed. John Russell, 3 vols. (London, 1846), 3:230.

57. Shelburne to the earl of Chatham, 21 December 1765, in *The Correspondence of William Pitt, Earl of Chatham*, ed. William Stanhope Taylor and John Henry Pringle, 4 vols. (London, 1838–40), 2:355. See also "Observations relating to North America" and "Observations on British Policy towards America," Shelburne Papers, Clements Library, 48/17/197, 85/81.

merce strike everybody as injurious to trade. I mean those duties which bear upon the manufactures of this country.[58]

In the decade after the Seven Years War, what was novel about elite politicians' attitudes toward commercial opinion? Certainly the government's awareness of such views was not new. Since the Excise Crisis, popular politics had included sporadic input from the mercantile community outside the London financial sector.[59] Throughout the 1740s and 1750s, ministers and legislators had been cognizant of commercial objectives in the context of opposition ideology and organization. But before 1763 only Pitt had considered actively wooing commercial representatives while in power. When in 1757 he courted London merchants as needed allies, he did so without publicly favoring their concerns, certainly without reference to the national significance of these aims.

The nation's experience in the Seven Years War greatly expanded the geopolitical significance of British commercial interests. At the war's end, statesmen realized with new clarity that Britain's global ascendancy depended heavily on its capacity to sell increasing quantities of manufactures and raise needed revenues. The war had demonstrated how closely these capabilities were related and how important trade and taxes had proved to England's victory. As William Knox wrote to Shelburne in 1763, "It is, certainly, to Commerce that Great Britain owes every Advantage she at present possesses. Commerce has meliorated the Constitution, promoted Population and introduced every kind of Wealth. It has availed itself of Accidents and Mistakes, seemingly the most untoward, and converted them to the most important uses."[60]

When the Great War for Empire ended, officials understood that colonial trade would have to be managed to maximize the return from Britain's victory. As Knox continued, the "Colonies are to be regarded in no other Light, but as subservient to the Commerce of their Mother Country."[61] Specifically, wrote one of the Rockinghams, "The intent and

58. Commons debate, 5 March 1770, Cavendish Diary, Egerton MSS 221, fol. 11. During the same parliamentary debate, North outlined his criteria for assessing revenue proposals: "We therefore must consider this Act of Parliament as I hope we shall consider all Taxes with regard to America, upon a ground properly British, properly commercial" (fol. 18).

59. Rogers, "Aristocratic Clientage"; Wilson, "Empire, Trade and Popular Politics"; and idem, "Imperial Culture, Imperialist Ideologies."

60. William Knox, Memorandum to the earl of Shelburne, 1763, Shelburne Papers, Clements Library, 85/26. In 1766 the duke of Newcastle commented to the archbishop of Canterbury that "the trade of this nation is the sole support of it" (2 February 1766, Add. MSS 32,973, fols. 342–44).

61. Knox, 85/29.

use of colonizing to a commercial nation is generally admitted to consist in securing and augmenting a vent for [the mother country's] trade and manufactures . . . and by adding to the number of subjects abroad, to provide a beneficial employ for those who remain at home from whence Power and Wealth will ensue."[62] Imperial trade was, as Burke noted, "a new world of commerce in a manner created."[63] This "new world of commerce" required extensive government superintendence. After the Seven Years War, metropolitan officials tried to manage the imperial economy to maintain Britain's preeminence.

The conflict and the geopolitical ambitions it bred had important political consequences. For practical and conceptual reasons, the men of movable property exerted newfound influence on British officials in the postwar period. The financial and managerial exigencies caused by the sudden accession of so much land increased the government's informational needs, forcing statesmen to rely on merchants and manufacturers for facts about the empire. As important, the proven association between imperial trade and global authority afforded commercial spokesmen and issues new importance in Parliament and Whitehall. The unprecedented cost of the conflict, the inability of the land tax to support such a burden, and the growing contribution of excise and customs levies to government revenues further legitimated mercantile and manufacturing priorities in the eyes of elites. As Thomas Whately wrote in 1769,

That the Wealth and Power of Great Britain depends upon its Trade, is a Proposition, which it would be equally absurd in these times to dispute or to prove: . . . but on the other hand, the Abilities of this Country were stretched to their utmost extent, and beyond their natural Tone: Trade must suffer in proportion; . . . by the Number and the Weight of the new Taxes, . . . These [duties on soap, paper, licenses, calicoes, plate, beer, cider, malt] pressed immediately on the middling and lower Ranks, on Husbandmen and Manufacturers . . . Was this a time [at the war's end] to impose a new tax which must have been heavy to have been effectual; and which so far as our commercial Interests might have been affected by it, would not in the end have been a benefit, though it should be a present Relief to public Credit?[64]

62. Rockingham MSS, WWM, R65/26.

63. Burke, "Observations," in *Writings and Speeches of Edmund Burke*, ed. Langford, 2:195.

64. Thomas Whately, *Considerations on the Trade and Finances of This Kingdom and on the Measures of Administration with respect to These Great National Objects since the Conclusion of the Peace* (London, 1769), 3–5.

Throughout the 1760s the connection between commercial priorities and imperial well-being increased the significance to elites of manufacturing and merchant constituencies.[65] This association, together with the state's information needs and realignments in the elite order, provided commercial interests greater potential influence than in earlier decades.

This is not to say that the large financial and trading institutions were in any sense eclipsed in their connections to state departments. Ministers, especially those in the Treasury, continued to deal regularly with directors of the Bank and the East India Company in order to manage the government debt and its connections with the London stock market. But beginning in the mid-1760s groups of manufacturers, often under the umbrella of a larger mercantile organization, came regularly to Whitehall and Westminster. By 1773 these men had become consultants on the issues of empire; they were altogether desirable new constituencies for elite politicians.

At times commercial representatives brought manufacturing and mercantile concerns directly to bear on parliamentary debate. As Burke, North, Garbett, and others recognized, the organized men of movable property and their priorities had the potential to affect legislative decisions. By aligning commercial interests with broader issues of imperial prosperity and security, these new constituencies achieved intermittent success in altering policy outcomes. Their influence was not consistent. In 1766 commercial representatives played an important part in convincing ministers and MPs to repeal the Stamp Act. Three years later many of the same lobbyists failed to persuade Parliament to revoke the tea tax. But during the postwar decade, the men of commerce, along with their concerns, became a political force that parliamentary elites acknowledged, frequently chose to use for their own purposes, and occasionally answered.

With input from manufacturing and mercantile representatives, gov-

---

65. As Burke said before the electors of Bristol in 1774: "When I first devoted myself to the public service, I considered how I should render myself fit for it; and this I did by endeavoring to discover what it was that gave this country the rank it holds in the world. I found that our prosperity and dignity arose principally from two sources: our Constitution and commerce ... The other source of our power is commerce, of which you [Bristol residents] are so large a part, and which cannot exist, no more than your liberty, without a connection with many virtues. It has ever been a very particular and a very favorite object of my study, in its principles and details. I think many are acquainted with the truth of what I say. This I know,—that I have ever had my house open, and my poor services ready, for traders and manufacturers of every denomination" ("Speech at His Arrival at Bristol," in *Works of the Right Honorable Edmund Burke*, 2:87).

ernment officials formulated imperial policies toward two often conflicting commercial objectives. The proposals that came before Parliament
attempted to keep colonial markets open to the mother country's goods
or to raise additional revenues in Britain's dominions. The importance
government officials (and the larger political nation) attached to these
priorities was a legacy of Britain's victory in the Seven Years War, a
victory that had come at enormous cost. Not surprisingly, the aims of
postwar imperial management reflected the ambivalent experience of
military triumph. Seeing how statesmen and others chose between two
imperatives they often believed to be in conflict takes us some way toward
understanding the seemingly confused politics of dominion.

As head of the government in 1763 and 1764, George Grenville wanted
both colonial markets and enhanced public revenues. Speaking before
the Commons in early 1764, he was explicit about his administrative
intentions toward the empire:

The House comes to the resolution to raise the revenue in America for
defending itself. We have expended much in America. Let us now avail
ourselves of the fruits of that expense. The great object [is] to reconcile
the regulation of commerce with an increase of revenue. With this view,
[it is] particularly desirable to prevent [the] intercourse of America with
foreign nations. And yet many colonies have such a trade. Such a trade
has been opened by three or four colonies with France to the amount of
£4[00,000] or 500,000 a year. Great attention [must be] given to prevent
this practice by giving directions to the commissioners [of customs] to prevent smuggling. This has been attended with success, the proportion [of
colonial exchange] from England has increased. But this is not enough;
you must collect the revenue from the plantations.[66]

Toward such ends, Grenville and his subministers undertook an extensive reform of the Navigation Acts and revenue collection in North
America. Although the prime minister knew there would be some resistance to the policies, he was certain that colonists would comply.[67] There
was little doubt among metropolitan officials that North Americans could
afford additional taxes without undue hardship. Grenville, Shelburne,

66. Commons debate, 9 March 1764, in *Parliamentary Diaries of Nathaniel Ryder, 1764–
7*, ed. P. D. G. Thomas (London, 1969), 234.
67. Edward Hughes, "English Stamp Duties, 1664–1764," *English Historical Review* 56
(1941): 259–64.

and other statesmen saw strong evidence of colonial prosperity: North American demand for British goods had doubled over the 1750s; the thirteen colonies had discharged their war debts swiftly; the North American colonies' clandestine trade with Europe—estimated in 1763 at £500,000 annually—continued to grow.[68]

In championing their proposals before Parliament, the Grenvillites were interested in raising colonial consumption of domestic manufactures as well as ameliorating the state's fiscal problems. As Whately said of the government's initiatives, "In the Colonies, they are a political Regulation, and enforce the Observance of these wise Laws to which the great increase of our Trade and naval Power are principally owing."[69] The major components of the ministry's program were the Sugar Act and the Stamp Act. The Sugar Act, which passed easily through both houses of Parliament in 1764, was designed to improve the enforcement of colonial trade regulation and increase American revenue collection on foreign goods, such as molasses and sugar, imported into the colonies.[70] The Stamp Act, which levied duties on colonial documents ranging from newspapers to land grants to ships' clearance papers, was intended to produce considerable revenues while asserting Britain's right to tax America.[71] Levies ranged from £10 on licenses for attorneys to the four-

68. See William Knox, *The Present State of the Nation: Particularly with respect to Its Trade, Finance etc. Addressed to the King and Both Houses of Parliament* (London, 1768), 35; Josiah Tucker, *A Letter from a Merchant in London to His Nephew in North America relative to the Present Posture of Affairs in the Colonies* (London, 1766), 27; Shelburne's speech on the preliminaries of peace, December 1762, Shelburne Papers, Clements Library, vol. 165; 11 March 1766, *Lords Journals*, 31:302, 303–5, quoted in *Proceedings and Debates of the British Parliaments respecting North America, 1754–1783*, ed. R. C. Simmons and P. D. G. Thomas, 3 vols. (Millwood, N.Y., 1982–83), 2:332. Even if the stamp levies yielded more than £60,000 annually—and many officials estimated revenues of £100,000—the per capita incidence of the tax did not appear excessive. Recently economic historians have argued that per capita tax burdens in eighteenth-century Britain were ten times higher than those in the North American colonies; see L. Davis and R. Huttenback, "The Cost of Empire," in *Explorations in the New Economic History: Essays in Honor of Douglas C. North*, ed. Roger Ransom, Richard Sutch, and Gary Walton (New York, 1982), 48–50.

69. Whately, *Regulations*, 87.

70. On the Sugar Act's background and passage, see P. D. G. Thomas, *British Politics and the Stamp Act Crisis: The First Phase of the American Revolution, 1763–1767* (Oxford, 1975), 44–50, 55–61; John L. Bullion, *A Great and Necessary Measure: George Grenville and the Genesis of the Stamp Act, 1763–65* (Columbia, Mo., 1982), 78–98.

71. Although the initial rationale behind the duties was largely fiscal, by late 1764, according to Thomas, the Grenville ministry was concerned about colonial protests against the proposed taxes. For administration members, passing the Stamp Act became a means of asserting Britain's right to tax its colonies. Despite riots and other expressions of American defiance, Grenville and his subministers believed colonists would accept the measure once it was sanctioned by Parliament. In early 1765 colonists had not disputed Parliament's

penny duty on ships' bills of lading. The vast majority of levies were designed to be one shilling or less.[72] Most Treasury officials estimated the stamp tax would produce annual revenues of £100,000, which would be used to help defray the £360,000 required yearly to support some ten thousand British troops stationed in America.[73]

Legislators strongly supported the stamp tax on its first reading.[74] William Meredith of Liverpool objected to the levy on the grounds that it would hinder North American consumption of British goods,[75] but most legislators, including Rockingham's supporters and those of the duke of Bedford, disputed neither the commercial propriety nor the constitutional right of taxing America. Townshend spoke for many: "Will these Americans, children planted by our care, nourished up by our indulgence until they are grown to a degree of strength and opulence, and protected by our arms, will they grudge to contribute their mite to relieve us from the heavy weight of that burden which we lie under?"[76]

As several scholars have demonstrated, the broad outlines of Grenville's policies were not new.[77] The Navigation Acts had first been applied to America in 1651. A century later in the 1750s, Board of Trade members had discussed colonial defense and the possibility of a stamp tax.[78]

---

right to tax them (Thomas, *British Politics and the Stamp Act Crisis*, 85–88). Britons themselves were subject to stamp taxes. Some of the costs of empire would have to be borne by Britain's dominions. Ministers and commercial writers believed the British economy alone could not support the price of remaining a world power (see, for example, Knox, *Present State of the Nation*, 60; Whately, *Regulations*, 56–58).

72. Thomas, *Stamp Act Crisis*, 84.

73. Committee of Ways and Means, 9 March 1764, in *Ryder Diaries*, 235.

74. Commons debate, 6 February 1765, in *Parliamentary Diary of James Harris*, quoted in Simmons and Thomas, 2:15.

75. Ibid., 2:13. The objections raised against the Sugar Act were also voiced in terms of Britain's manufacturing interests. One MP, John Huske, defended the mainland colonies' trade with foreign islands because such interchange afforded the colonists the specie they needed to purchase British goods: "The more North America gets, the more it will be able to remit to us for manufactures" (Commons debate, 9 March 1765, in *Ryder Diaries*, 238).

76. Commons debate, 6 February 1765, J. Ingersoll to T. Fitch, in *Fitch Papers: Correspondence and Documents during Thomas Fitch's Governorship of the Colony of Connecticut, 1754–1766*, vol. 2, Collections of the Connecticut Historical Society 18 (1920): 317–26.

77. Jack P. Greene, " 'A Posture of Hostility': A Reconsideration of Some Aspects of the Origins of the American Revolution," *Proceedings of the American Antiquarian Society* 87 (1977): 27–68; P. J. Marshall, "The British Empire in the Age of the American Revolution," in *The American Revolution: Changing Perspectives*, ed. William M. Fowler Jr. and Wallace Coyle (Boston, 1979), 193–212; Tucker and Hendrickson, 106–27.

78. Add. MSS 11,514, fols. 93–94; Add. MSS 32,874, fol. 310; Add. MSS 32,996, fol. 265. See also Hughes.

Grenville and his subministers believed the measures they proposed were consistent with past regulation. Yet in fact, with Parliament's sanction, the government had embarked on nothing less than a reformation of imperial governance in North America.

In the aftermath of the Seven Years War, as the first lord of the Treasury understood, the problems and potential of a vast commercial empire had become much greater and more urgent. In 1765, however, he did not yet recognize that existing policy solutions would ultimately prove inadequate in dealing with such issues. What was clear—the reason the first lord *reorganized* colonial administration and Parliament approved the comprehensive plan—was that the stakes of dominion were now too high for metropolitan inaction. Whately described the government's motivations:

the [Commercial] Principles are great, the Policy is right, upon which this conduct is founded: The prevalence of these Principles at present is the il-lustrious Characteristic of the Times: No period of our History can within the same compass boast of so many Measures, with regard to the Colo-nies, founded upon Knowledge, formed with Judgement, and executed with Vigour, as have distinguished the beginning of his Majesty's Reign. The glorious Peace that ushered it in so auspiciously to his People, is a heap of Concessions forced from our Enemies, in favor of the British Plantations. The Tranquility it Procured us has been employed in improv-ing the Advantage both of our new and our former Possessions: In the protection of which great Work, the true Principles of Commerce have been attended to with so much discernment and care; the Interests of the Mother Country and those of the colonies have been blended with so much skill; and their Union has been strengthened by so many Bonds of Connection, Obligation and Advantage.[79]

A year later, in 1766, ministers, MPs and others were less certain that the circumstances of Britain's victory were legitimate bases for more stringent imperial governance. After consulting with merchants and manufacturers involved in transatlantic trade, officials in the Rocking-ham government considered revoking the Stamp Act. Supporters of repeal justified their position on commercial grounds. They argued that North American reaction to the stamp tax, in the form of colonial boycotts of British manufactures, was seriously damaging Atlantic trade and thus

79. Whately, *Regulations*, 43.

affecting the nation's social and economic stability. According to Rocking-ham administration accounts, British exports to America had fallen by 15 percent, from £2.1 million in 1764 to £1.8 million in 1765.[80] Imperial commerce as well as British prosperity and power now appeared to be more precarious. A kind of collective angst seeped into the arena of public debate about the empire, coloring perspectives and policy discussions. In early 1766 one group of traders wrote to Rockingham,

This Commerce [with North America], so beneficial to the State and so necessary for the support of Multitudes, now lies under such difficulties and discouragements that nothing less than its utter Ruin is apprehended without the immediate interposition of Parliament . . .

[Y]our Petitioners apprehend the passing the said Bill [for repeal] into a Law would be the most probable means to preserve them and their Fam-ilys from Ruin, to prevent a Multitude of Manufacturers from becoming a Burden to the Community or from their seeking their bread in other Countries, to the irretrievable loss of this Kingdom.[81]

Lobbyists and administration officials successfully used similar argu-ments in Parliament. In early March the Commons voted 250 to 122 to repeal the legislation they had so recently approved.[82] It is important to note the political implications of the government's new position. In sponsoring repeal of the Stamp Act, the Rockinghams were developing an ideological (and rhetorical) niche for their party. As Burke explained in February 1766, before a noisy House, "We granted revenue upon commerce and did not grub up commerce in order to plant revenue in the room of it . . . [S]ome say commerce ought to be neglected till dignity is established. It is wrong, because our dignity is derived from our com-merce . . . [W]e have had experiments enough."[83]

Burke went on to say, "It is by the providence of God that we have escaped out of our own hand, not the shuttlecock of faction."[84] He could appreciate the significance of a compelling justification of faction—a rationalization of the Rockingham party that was rooted in the defense

80. WWM, R61/9.

81. January 1766, "Petition of the Merchants of London Trading to North America," Rockingham MSS, WWM, R57.

82. The last chapter of the book analyzes the debate over the stamp tax in some detail.

83. Commons debate, 21 February 1766, in *Ryder Diaries*, 307.

84. Ibid.

of Britain's commerce, specifically in promoting manufacturing sales.[85] He used the group's position on imperial issues to legitimate its claim to political authority.[86] As chief spokesmen for Rockingham's supporters, Dowdeswell and Burke understood that Britain's international stature depended on both the imperial economy *and* the national legislature's authority to manage this commercial exchange. For if Parliament did not control the power of commerce, either by promoting domestic manufacturing or by regulating state finances, then Britain's capacity to wage war and exploit its geopolitical position lay beyond the purview of the elected assembly. Such implications were unacceptable to all the major political factions, including the Rockingham Whigs.

In this sense the repeal of the stamp tax, coupled with the Declaratory Act, which asserted the British legislature's broad authority over the American colonies,[87] was representative of the party's position on imperial issues: Parliament retained the right to tax the outlying territories of the empire, but the exercise of such power should be contingent upon ad hoc considerations of commercial strength. The Rockinghams did not support colonial levies that inhibited British manufacturing sales and trade.

The Rockingham Whigs and Grenvillites were not the only elites to comprehend the political significance of imperial issues. Since 1759, the annus mirabilis of Britain's war effort, William Pitt had recognized the patriotic importance of military success and its relation to domestic economic activity. As the nation's victories in North America, the Caribbean, India, and Europe had increased, so too had British exports, climbing 15 percent in one year to an unprecedented total of £10 million in 1759.[88] Not surprisingly, commercial opinion had strongly supported Pitt's prosecution of the war, and that year had seen the Great Commoner's popularity and political power at their peak.[89]

85. On the Rockingham Whigs' defense of party distinctions and its importance to political argument, see Brewer, *Party Ideology*, 13–15.

86. This is not to say that the Rockingham Whigs consistently supported colonial interests. Paul Langford has demonstrated convincingly that the party's stance on North America was more ambiguous and authoritarian than Whig historians have alleged ("Old Whigs, Old Tories").

87. The resolution stated that "the Parliament of Great Britain had, hath, and of right ought to have full power and authority to make laws and statutes of sufficient force and validity to bind the colonies and people of America in all cases whatsoever" (Add. MSS 32,973, fols. 246–47).

88. B. R. Mitchell and Phyllis Deane, *Abstract of British Historical Statistics* (Cambridge, 1962), 280.

89. Marie Peters, *Pitt and Popularity: The Patriot Minister and London Opinion during the Seven Years War* (Oxford, 1980), 149–51. See also "A Character of Mr. Pitt," WWM, R93/ 8.

After George III's accession in 1760 and his own resignation from office in 1761, Pitt never regained the parliamentary and general influence he had once commanded. But in the political confusion of the postwar decade, his followers in the House as well as his support out of doors ensured the former minister a viable role in public debates.[90] Although he did not consistently choose to play such a part,[91] the Great Commoner tried to use several imperial issues to reinforce his political authority. On the controversies concerning North America in 1766, he steered clear of both the Grenvillites and Rockinghams. The former were determined to enforce Parliament's right to tax the colonies, at least rhetorically; the latter, while never denying the constitutional propriety of raising colonial revenues, expressed significant reluctance to see the supremacy of Parliament asserted in this way. Both factions justified their positions on commercial rationale, claiming to speak for British manufacturers and merchants.

So too did Pitt, but he staked out a different viewpoint. The former minister condemned direct or internal taxes on the colonies as unconstitutional, although he affirmed Parliament's power to impose external levies such as customs duties.[92] Speaking in January 1766 before a crowded House, he underscored the economic importance of American trade and its relation to imperial governance:

There is a plain distinction between taxes levied for the purposes of raising a revenue, and duties imposed for the regulation of trade, for the accommodation of the subject; although, in the consequences, some revenue might incidentally arise from the latter . . .

[T]he profits to *Great Britain* from the trade of the colonies, through all its branches, is two millions a year. This is the fund that carried you triumphantly through the last war. The estates that were rented at two thousand pounds a year, threescore years ago, are at three thousand pounds at present. Those estates sold then from fifteen to eighteen years purchase; the same may now be sold for thirty. You owe this to *America*

90. See, for example, Rockingham's letter to George III, 15 January 1766, in *Memoirs of the Marquis of Rockingham and His Contemporaries*, ed. George Thomas, 2 vols. (London, 1852), 1:270, and H. Walpole, *Memoirs of the Reign of George III*, 4 vols. (London, 1894), 2:185.

91. Peters, 262–64; Brewer, *Party Ideology*, 12–13, 107–10.

92. See Ian Christie's convincing analysis of Pitt's position, "William Pitt and American Taxation, 1766: A Problem of Parliamentary Reporting," *Studies in Burke and His Time* 17 (1976): 167–79. See also Commons debate, 21 February 1766, in *Ryder Diaries*, 309; William Rouet to William Mure, 22 February 1766, in *Selections from the Family Papers Preserved at Caldwell*, 3 vols. (Glasgow, 1854), vol. 2, pt. 2, 60–61.

[North America and the West Indies]. This is the price that America pays you for her protection. And shall a miserable financier come with a boast, that he can fetch a pepper-corn into the Exchequer, to the loss of millions to the nation! I dare not say, how much higher these profits may be augmented. Omitting the immense increase of people, by natural population, in the northern colonies, and the migration from every part of *Europe*, I am convinced the whole commercial system of *America* may be altered to advantage. You have prohibited, when you ought to have encouraged; and you have encouraged when you ought to have prohibited.[93]

It is not clear why Pitt championed the distinction between internal and external taxation. Ian Christie has speculated that he may have been influenced by his longtime ally Beckford, who in 1765 had pointed out that "the North Americans do not think an internal and external duty the same."[94] Various colonial resolutions against the Stamp Act differentiated between this tax and port duties.[95] Perhaps Pitt believed he could relieve the Americans' unease without relinquishing too much parliamentary power.[96] Certainly he was "playing the great game for office and power," as Christie puts it.[97] Pitt sought a position that would discredit the current and preceding administrations while appeasing George III and MPs worried about Britain's economic condition.

The problem of raising colonial revenues and its relation to parliamentary sovereignty persisted after the repeal of the Stamp Act. In the autumn of 1766 Pitt, now the head of government and the first earl of Chatham, considered further regulation for the East India Company, the chartered trading concern that monopolized goods and specie exchange between Britain and India. The Company's Indian position had altered dramatically since the Seven Years War. Beginning in 1757, a series of successful military campaigns under the direction of Robert Clive had earned the trading corporation enormous territory as well the de facto political and economic responsibility for governing the newly acquired lands.[98]

---

93. Commons debate, 14 January 1766, in John Almon, *The Debates and Proceedings of the British House of Commons, from 1743 to 1774*, 11 vols. (London, 1766–75), 7:61–77.

94. Christie, 175; Commons debate, 6 February 1765, in *Ryder Diaries*, 256–57.

95. Christie, 175–76.

96. Ibid., 176.

97. Ibid., 179.

98. For a concise explanation of the Company's activity in India during and after the Seven Years War, see H. V. Bowen, *Revenue and Reform: The Indian Problem in British Politics, 1757–1773* (Cambridge, 1991), 5–15 and P. J. Marshall, *Bengal, the British Bridgehead: Eastern India, 1740–1828* (Cambridge, 1987), 70–92.

During and after the war, Company servants had become embroiled in regional power struggles, successfully overthrowing specific local rulers to replace them with dependent viceroys.[99] By 1765 the Company governed, in historian H. V. Bowen's words, as the "undisputed masters of Bengal."[100] That same year, acting on behalf of the Company, Clive had secured from the Mughal emperor the *diwani*, the right to collect territorial and customs revenues in the regions of Bengal, Bihar, and Orissa. Clive estimated the Company's gain from such collections, after expenses and tribute, at over £1.6 million per annum.[101] Many British observers expected that the *diwani*, together with the Company's territorial sovereignty in India, would prove very profitable to the trading concern.[102]

Clive had seriously overestimated the value of the *diwani*, but this error was not apparent in mid-1766, when news of the financial spoils reached London. Most believed that the Company's assumption of the right to territorial and customs revenues meant an immediate, dramatic increase in the Company's wealth. Speculation in East India stock soared as financiers at home and abroad hurried to claim a piece of the action.[103] Politicians, commercial writers, and pamphleteers debated the Company's role in the imperial economy and argued over whether Indian territorial revenues were a national rather than a private asset.

In this environment, government officials discussed parliamentary intervention in Company affairs. They did so with a view to securing a new source of state revenues. If the costs of empire could not be collected in America then perhaps, reasoned Chatham, Charles Townshend, and

99. Bowen, *Revenue and Reform,* 5–6. On British expansion in India, see Marshall, *Bengal, the British Bridgehead,* 70–92.

100. Bowen, *Revenue and Reform,* 5. India's political situation in the aftermath of the war is summarized in *Fort William–India House Correspondence,* vol. 4, *1764–1766,* ed. C. S. Srinivasachari (Delhi, 1962), xvii–xxxvi.

101. Robert Clive to the Court of Directors, 30 September 1765, *Fort William–India House Correspondence,* 337.

102. The financial spoils of Clive's Indian victories included £1 million for the East India Company, £500,000 for the European inhabitants of Calcutta, £50,000 each for members of the Company's governing council in India, and nearly £250,000 for Clive himself, plus the *jagir,* the assignment to him of quit rents from lands south of Calcutta. The *jagir* was estimated at between £27,000 and £30,000 a year. Stanley Ayling, *Edmund Burke: His Life and Opinions* (London, 1988), 66; *Fort William–India House Correspondence,* xxvii.

103. Between April 1766, when news of the *diwani* reached London, and September, East India stock prices rose over 17 percent. On the repercussions of this speculative boom, see Sutherland, *East India Company,* 141, and idem, "Lord Shelburne and East India Company Politics."

Modello for "Robert Clive and Mir Jaffir after the Battle of Plassey," Francis Hayman (c. 1760). National Portrait Gallery. This painting was completed (along with "The Triumph of Britannia") as part of a four-canvas commission depicting Britain's victories during the Seven Years War. One of the first British artists to exploit Indian scenes and subjects, Hayman here portrayed Robert Clive, victor of Plassey, receiving homage from Mir Jaf[fir], the future Nawab of Bengal. In representing this event, Hayman abandoned the classical conventions of mid eighteenth-century history painting in favor of a vernacular rendition in which modern costume and period details predominate. Unlike "The Triumph of Britannia," which celebrates the country's naval prowess, "Clive" focuses on the theme of imperial mercy in the flush of conquest. As the author of the 1762 guidebook to Hayman's paintings wrote: "The subject of this picture is of the most interesting nature to every Briton, who regards the honour and prosperity of his country. For the better understanding it, it is necessary to observe that General Clive, after gaining the Battle of Plassey in the East Indies, which restored the English interests that had been ruined in those parts of the world, found himself under a necessity of deposing the reigning Nabob; for that purpose sent from the field of battle for Meer Jaffer, a principal General under the Subah or Nabob, and an enemy to the French. Meer Jaffer, when sent for, seeing the General surrounded by his victorious troops, approaches him with every symptom of doubt and diffidence in his countenance. The General is represented in the attitude of Friendship, by extending his hands to receive him. . . . [Mir Jaffer's] dejection seems to be faintly alleviated by the general's manner of receiving him. The extension of his arms, and the inclination of his body, is most movingly expressive of doubt, submission, and resignation."

George III, the solution lay to the east. Obtaining Company revenues, according to the king, was "the only safe method of extracting this Country out of its lamentable situation owing to the load of Debt it labours under."[104] It was an ambitious but as yet indeterminate plan. The wealth of India, Chatham confidently asserted, "would be the redemption of the nation."[105]

Some were more conservative in assessing the benefits of taxing the chartered company. But many in and outside Westminster agreed that in addition to the fiscal rationale, there were political reasons for parliamentary involvement in Company business. A public inquiry, the first since the late seventeenth century, allowed the government to exploit the distrust many MPs harbored toward the Company and its servants.[106] These legislators viewed the trading concern's gains as a monopoly's ill-gotten spoils, reaped at the expense of violations in India and destructive stock speculation at home. Beckford voiced such sentiments before the Commons when he took the opportunity

to abuse the Company as an unconstitutional monopoly, and [to contend] that their conduct merited the inquiry of parliament; that they had a revenue of two millions in India, acquired God knows how, by unjust wars with natives. That their servants come home with immense fortunes obtained by rapine and oppression, yet the Proprietors received no increase of dividend: that it was necessary to know how these revenues were consumed and whence these oppressions so loudly talked of.[107]

The financier Thomas Walpole spoke for many when he told the prime minister that the state might have to intervene in "that which is too unwieldy for a subordinate body of merchants."[108]

Numerous MPs, particularly the country gentlemen, also resented the position (and ostentation) of retired Company servants, whose recent commercial wealth secured them social place. Without birth and breed-

104. The King to the duke of Grafton, 9 December 1766, *The Correspondence of King George III*, ed. J. Fortescue 6 vols. (London, 1927–28), 1:424.

105. *Autobiography and Political Correspondence of Augustus Henry, Third Duke of Grafton*, ed. Sir William Anson (London, 1896), 110.

106. Philip Lawson, "Parliament and the First East India Inquiry, 1767," *Parliamentary History* 1 (1982): 101.

107. L. Scrafton to Robert Clive, 12 April 1766, Powis MSS, quoted in Sutherland, *East India Company*, 148.

108. Thomas Walpole to the earl of Chatham, 9 September 1766, in *Chatham Correspondence*, 3:62.

ing, many of the nabobs were able to purchase landed estates and, as Robert Clive did, command parliamentary patronage.[109] To those antagonized by the nabobs' new status, a parliamentary inquiry offered the possibility of reducing their influence and the certainty of venting collective frustration.

The two main groups of parliamentary opposition under Rockingham and Grenville objected to taxing the Company. Members of both factions based their arguments on an appeal to property rights, maintaining that the ministry's proposal to collect revenues from the trading concern constituted an invasion of the Company's charter.[110] "The violation of property was sounded high," wrote Walpole, describing the opposition parties' strategy.[111] Never one to ignore the larger political possibilities of a given issue, Burke grounded his defense of property in commercial considerations. Meddling in the East India Company's affairs would

make a most important Revolution indeed in the whole Policy of this Country with regard to its Laws its Commerce and its Credit. [If Parliament regulates Company practices] you [Parliament] are going to restrict by a positive arbitrary Regulation the enjoyment of the profits which should be made in Commerce. I suppose there is nothing like this to be found in the Code of Laws in any Civilised Country upon Earth—you are going to cancel the great line which distinguishes free Government. I always took it to be an invariable rule and what distinguished Law and Freedom from Violence and Slavery is, that the property vested in the Subject by a known Law—and forfeited by no delinquency defined by a known [power] could be taken away from him by [no] power or authority whatsoever.[112]

In the larger context of eighteenth-century politics, such affirmation of "the sacredness of charters, property, and public credit" was a reliable tack that attracted the crucial support of independent legislators.[113]

109. Lawson, 101. The career of Francis Sykes was not atypical. In 1769 Sykes returned home from military service with the Company. He used a small fraction of the fortune he had acquired in India to build a huge Georgian mansion, complete with Ionic columns, picture gallery, and grand saloon, in Basildon Park, Berkshire. In 1771 Sykes became an MP from Dorset and was nick-named "Squire Matoot" after the *matoot*, the supposedly extortionate tax by which he gained his Indian wealth. James Holzman, *The Nabobs in England: Study of the Returned Anglo-Indian, 1760–1785* (New York, 1926), 72, 164.

110. Walpole, 2:277; Lawson, 102.

111. Walpole, 2:280.

112. Burke, "Speech on the East India Dividend Bill," 26 May 1767, in *The Writings and Speeches of Edmund Burke*, ed. Langford, 2:65.

113. Walpole, 2:289. Lawson, 102; Colley, *In Defiance of Oligarchy*, 149, 158–59.

Also important in appealing to independent MPs was the charge, leveled by both the Grenvillites and Rockinghams, that closer financial
ties between the state and the Company promoted political corruption.
Opposition spokesmen argued that allowing additional government
involvement in Company affairs provided ministers as well as the king
with access to vast patronage and commercial control. With reference
to Revolution principles, Grenville observed that "if these territories were
adjudged not to belong to the Company they would immediately of
course vest in the Crown, and took notice of the danger of trusting such
an immense revenue a year to an election in the hands of the Crown
who, however he might be disposed to give them to the public, might
have a Minister wicked and base enough to advise him to keep the whole
or part of them."[114]

These comments by Grenville and Burke were directed primarily at
two groups in the House: the country gentlemen, including those with
commercial interests, and the men of movable property.[115] A year earlier,
both these groups had been convinced of the economic necessity of
repealing the Stamp Act. At that time a majority of MPs had been per-
suaded that the power of commerce was best promoted by *not* exercising
the legislature's authority. A year later, before the same assembly, the
Grenvillites and the Rockinghams attempted to stake out an ideologically
viable opposition to state intervention in the East India Company and
the territories it controlled.

But in 1767 such arguments could not override legislators' interest in
securing an external source of state revenues to pay the continuing costs
of empire. Annual interest charges of £4.6 million on the national debt
consumed almost half of government income.[116] Military expenditures
alone in India and North America totaled more than £1.3 million in
1767.[117] For commercial, distributive, and political reasons, many MPs,
including most independent legislators, believed Britain had reached the
limits of its revenue-raising capacities.[118]

114. Commons debate, 14 April 1767, in *Ryder Diaries*, 339. On the ideological significance of "revolution principles" in the context of partisan politics, see Brewer, *Party Ideology*,
52–53.

115. On the commercial connections and priorities of MPs, see Lewis Namier and John
Brooke, *The House of Commons, 1754–1790*, 3 vols. (London, 1964), 1:104–9, 131–38, and
Dora Mae Clark, *British Opinion and the American Revolution* (New Haven, Conn., 1930),
220–22.

116. Mitchell and Deane, 388, 390.

117. *Ryder Diaries*, 235; Bowen, *Revenue and Reform*, 12.

118. Clark, 123–28. On 27 February 1767 the Chatham government experienced a
minor tax revolt in Parliament—an eighteenth-century version of Proposition 13. When
the chancellor of the Exchequer, Charles Townshend, moved for the customary land tax

After six months of parliamentary debate and negotiation with Company officials, the government pushed a compromise bill through the Commons.[119] In its final form, the act required the Company to pay the state £400,000 per annum for two years—a sum that equaled approximately 4 percent of annual government revenue at the time.[120] But the act also confirmed the trading concern's right to Indian territories. Accompanying legislation limited Company dividends to 10 percent. The result of the Chatham ministry's search for revenues, this legislation introduced ministers and MPs to the financial, political, and managerial challenges of Indian governance and established a precedent for future state relations with the Company.[121]

Already divided by the East India Company inquiry, the political landscape in mid-1767 was further complicated by Charles Townshend's plans for North American revenue. His proposal called for a series of import duties on glass, paper, lead, and tea shipped to America. The proposed tax on tea had originated during recent government negotiations with the East India Company. In an effort to assist the Company in expanding its tea sales, the state's agreement with the trading concern had included important concessions on the 25 percent duty it paid on tea exported to America and Ireland. To help make up the ensuing revenue loss and to reestablish the practice of colonial taxation, Townshend suggested an American import duty on tea.[122] He projected that the colonial tea tax would raise £20,000 annually, with the remaining duties on glass, lead, and paper yielding an additional £20,000.[123] He intended to use the revenue to help defray the cost of civil government and the administration of justice in the colonies, "making a more certain and adequate provision for the charge of the administration of justice and the support of civil government" in America.[124]

---

levy of four shillings in the pound, an opposition movement for three shillings, led by Dowdeswell, swept the House 206 to 188. It was a smashing victory for the opposition, and it cost the government £500,000 in forgone revenue.

119. Sutherland, *East India Company*, 138–76, and Lawson analyze in detail the ministerial debate surrounding state intervention.

120. Mitchell and Deane, 388.

121. Lawson, 111.

122. On the negotiations between the Chatham administration and the East India Company surrounding drawbacks on imported tea, see P. D. G. Thomas, *The Townshend Duties Crisis: The Second Phase of the American Revolution, 1767–1773* (Oxford, 1987), 19–30.

123. Ibid., 30; J. W. Barnwell, ed., "Correspondence of Charles Garth," *South Carolina Historical and Genealogical Magazine* 29 (1928–29): 295.

124. *Journals of the House of Commons*, 31 (1767): 329. As Peter Thomas has noted, Townshend's objectives were primarily political, not financial. The minister sought to

Grenville objected to the proposed taxes as trifling because they raised so little revenue, and Burke attacked the levies with commercial arguments similar to those the Rockinghams had used against the Stamp Act.[125] But most MPs accepted the new duties without protest. Why did legislators vote for new colonial taxes less than a year after repealing the stamp tax? Why did they support a revenue scheme that very quickly proved so destructive to imperial relations? For most statesmen, as Peter Thomas has noted, there seemed precious little political or constitutional ground on which to oppose the Townshend duties.[126] In the words of Thomas Townshend, a member of the Treasury Board and a cousin of the chancellor, "It was not the humour of the time to oppose them."[127] The Declaratory Act had clarified Parliament's right to tax its colonies, and in 1767 a majority of MPs strongly favored assertion of that right in the form of colonial revenue measures.Geopolitical exigencies underscored the importance of affirming Parliament's authority. The national debt was enormous; the costs of empire in the west were high, and Americans had indicated a willingness to pay external taxes or port duties of the type Townshend proposed. Most statesmen believed that the long-term sustainability of Britain's international stature depended on the legislature's power to regulate imperial trade and revenues. In 1769 Thomas Townshend described the climate in which his cousin's revenue-raising measures were approved:

It was not the opinion of one man, but of numbers. It had pervaded the nation that it was absolutely necessary to do something. It was the opinion of that gentleman [Charles Townshend]. He exerted all that ability which made him the delight of this House and all who knew him. He desired taxes agreeable to the Americans themselves. He flattered himself too far. In those hopes he was misled by the Americans themselves, who told him, take the tax, let it but bear the appearance of port duties, it will not be ob-

---

reestablish the practice of colonial taxation and "the making of Parliamentary provision for the costs of civil government and the administration of justice in the colonies" (*Townshend Duties*, 30).

125. Edmund Burke, "Speech on the Townshend Duties," 15 May 1767, quoted in *Writings and Speeches of Edmund Burke*, ed. Langford, 2:61–64. Langford notes that Burke may or may not have delivered this speech. "It is reasonable to suppose that he made his prepared observations on American policy generally, but no report records sufficient of his speech to make certainty possible. The point is particularly important since in 1768 Burke was to insist that he had opposed Townshend's duties from the beginning, a claim which gains credence from this draft" (61).

126. Thomas, *Townshend Duties*, 32.

127. Commons debate, 5 March 1770, Cavendish Diary, Egerton MSS 221, fol. 49.

jected to. A Chancellor of the Exchequer at that time who had not attempted something of the kind would have been looked upon as blameable.[128]

Two years after Parliament approved the Townshend duties, political priorities shifted again. Colonists had strongly protested the Townshend Revenue Acts and had organized resistance to the legislation.[129] In a replay of their objections to the stamp tax, Americans had instituted nonimportation agreements against British manufactures. General Thomas Gage, commander of the British army in America, reported his view of the strategy behind such actions. Writing to Hillsborough, secretary of state for America, the general explained how the boycott's organizers hoped to affect political opinion in the mother country:

The Chief Dependence of the Americans, is upon those in Great Britain, who either thro' an opposition to all Measures of Government, or for their private Interests, they flatter themselves will betray the Interests of Great Britain to serve the Purposes and Designs of America. They rely greatly upon the Influence of the Merchants trading to America, and very much upon the Manufacturers, whom they hope will commit Riots and Tumults in their favor. Those views gave Birth to the Project not to import Goods, and they have their Emissary in England, who put various paragraphs in the News Papers concerning the people of Birmingham and other Manufacturing Towns, that they are starving for want of Employment, thro' the Resolutions taken in America not to import their Manufactures.[130]

In 1768 and 1769 the Americans' tactics proved less effective than during the stamp tax controversy. This was not a result of metropolitan confusion about imperial objectives. As in 1766, British statesmen remained centrally concerned with managing the empire toward commercial ends. The importance of colonial markets to domestic prosperity permeated government debates about American reaction to the Townshend duties as politicians from various factions claimed commercially

128. Commons debate, 8 February 1769, Cavendish Diary, Egerton MSS 217, fols. 267–68.

129. On such reactions, see Gipson, 138–51, 166–90, and Thomas, *Townshend Duties*, 76–93, 122–23, 135–37, 156–57, 173–78.

130. Thomas Gage to Lord Hillsborough, 26 September 1768, in *The Correspondence of General Thomas Gage with the Secretaries of State and with the War Office and the Treasury, 1763–1775*, ed. C. E. Carter, 2 vols. (New Haven, Conn., 1931–33), 1:197.

expedient positions. Beckford emphasized the perceived incompatibility between raising revenues and selling goods in the colonies. Not only did taxes on British exports to America encourage the development of manufacturing there, but such levies represented money colonists could not spend on purchasing British goods. As Beckford said, "The Americans contribute more by living in America, and taking our manufactures, than if they lived here."[131] Thomas Pownall upheld Parliament's right to tax the colonies but called for a repeal of the levies:

Will anyone say that duties, thus laid on your own merchandise and manufactures, exported to *America,* do not operate to a certain degree, as a prohibition against your own produce and labour, and as a premium and encouragement to that of the colonies? . . . [This Act] is unjust in its purport, inefficient as a measure of finance, and operates in direct opposition to every principle of the laws of commerce, as they stand related to the mother country.[132]

Lord North disagreed with Pownall's recommendation. If the legislature revoked the Townshend Revenue Act, it relinquished all authority to manage imperial commerce:

If there is a set of gentlemen in the House, who after having repealed the Stamp Act, are not for supporting the declaratory law they proposed, they will introduce disorder . . . There has been no proof of any real return of [American] friendship. In America they will give you no credit for affection, no credit for commercial interest. Taxation, and regulation. If America is to be the judge, you may tax in no instance, you may regulate in no instance.[133]

In 1769 British officials were not uncertain about policy ends. But for most of the year they were more concerned with the issues surrounding the Middlesex election than with America. Metropolitan priorities discouraged the kind of swift response to colonial protest that had followed the Stamp Act boycotts. As important, in 1768 and 1769 the embargoes

131. Commons debate, 15 November 1768, Cavendish Diary, Egerton MSS 215, fols. 152–53. See also Edmund Burke's speech before the House on 8 November 1768, in Simmons and Thomas, 3:6–7.

132. Commons debate, 19 April 1769, *Gentleman's Magazine* 39 (1769): 572.

133. Commons debate, 8 November 1768, Cavendish Diary, Egerton MSS 215, fols. 126–27.

took much longer to implement, with numerous colonial merchants reluctant to adhere to nonimportation agreements.[134] During 1768 certain aspects of British trade with America had appeared to be thriving, and this mitigated the power of colonial protest. In August Rockingham had written to Dowdeswell from Yorkshire, "The demand for goods to go to America from the manufacturing parts of this country have been I am told the greatest ever known."[135] In this economic climate, there was little organized outcry from British merchants and manufacturers against the Townshend duties.

During 1768 and 1769 colonial boycotts had not produced a dramatic metropolitan response. In early 1770, however, the North administration and Parliament took up American issues in earnest. Argument in the Commons centered on a petition from London merchants emphasizing the recent decline in imperial trade as well as its international importance. As a consequence of the Townshend duties, the petition alleged, Britain's economic preeminence was now threatened:

> The petitioners have been accustomed to carry on a very considerable branch of trade to, and from his Majesty's colonies in North America, the former consisting greating in exporting thither the manufactures of this country, and the latter in importing from thence raw materials of various kinds necessary to the support of several of our most important manufacturies . . . [T]his commerce, so necessary to afford employment and subsistence to the manufacturers of these kingdoms, to augment the public revenue, to serve as a nursery for seamen, and to support and increase our navigation and maritime strength, is at present in an alarming state of suspension.[136]

Customs figures confirmed the discouraged state of trade. Between 1768 and 1769 the value of British exports to the thirteen colonies had declined by 38 percent, from £2.1 million to £1.3 million.[137] Presenting the government's position on America to Parliament, the new prime minister, Lord North, cited the decline in British trade. He called for a

134. On the implementation of colonial boycotts in various ports, see Thomas, *Townshend Duties*, 85, 150–52.

135. Rockingham to William Dowdeswell, 11 August 1768, WWM, R1/1083.

136. Commons debate, 5 March 1770, Cavendish Diary, Egerton MSS 221, fols. 7–8. See also William Bollan's petition before the House, Commons Proceedings, 5 March 1770, *Journals of the House of Commons*, 32:749–51.

137. U.S. Bureau of the Census, *Historical Statistics of the United States: Colonial Times to 1970*, 2 vols. (Washington, D.C., 1975), 2:1176.

repeal of the Townshend levies, except for the tax on tea. Concerned to avoid charges that the ministry was yielding to American pressure, North belittled the boycotts and attributed the recent decline in British exports to colonial hoarding in 1768. He championed the administration's plan for partial repeal as promoting British manufactures. Parliament should move swiftly, North said, to remove the duties "upon glass, etc., which are laid universally upon those commodities when exported from Britain, and which answer to duties upon British manufactures. As far as those duties go, I confess I cannot see why the House should not do, what I feel myself inclined to do, give way to the Petition of the merchants."[138] But, the prime minister continued, he opposed revoking the duty on tea:

Upon what ground can we now propose to repeal [the tea tax]? Sir, it is not the manufacture of British commodities. It is an object of luxury. It is of all commodities the most proper for taxation . . . [I]t is one of the best [supplies] to the revenue of the port duties. It is, if not quite equal, yet certainly when the revenue is well established, it probably will go a great way towards effecting the purpose for which it was laid, which was towards supporting, or giving an additional support to our government, to our judicatures in America.[139]

Looking back over the preceding seven years, North bemoaned the vacillations in imperial governance: "Our conduct has already varied greatly with regard to America. Those variations have been the greatest cause of difficulty." In a more stable domestic political order and a less flammable American climate, he added, relations between the mother country and its prosperous offspring would have been much more peaceful and profitable. The Stamp Act, North concluded, "would have been [an enduring] Act. Other events happened. A change of ministry. A change of measures. The Act was repealed. I think, by what we see now, it produced a fallacious kind of calm . . . Another duty was laid when America was calm. We repealed the Act when America was in a fire. It is easy to say, what opinion that must give of the wisdom, of the authority of this country."[140]

Grenville echoed North's assessment of imperial relations and casti-

138. Commons debate, 5 March, 1770, Cavendish Diary, Egerton MSS 221, fols. 11–16.

139. Ibid.

140. Ibid., fols. 13–14.

gated the government for lacking a comprehensive program of imperial management. "In this situation, Sir, having given way from one step to another, from one idea to another, till we know not upon what ground we stand. Without any plan formed, without any other idea stated. [There is] no government there."[141] The former minister opposed revoking any of the Townshend taxes, since this involved concessions to defiant colonists and undermined parliamentary sovereignty. Harking back to Charles II's dealings with Ireland, he also warned of entrusting imperial management to the monarch. This, he contended, was a favorite doctrine of those "who are desirous to see the power of the Crown extended beyond the true bounds."[142]

Taking issue with both Grenville and the North ministry, the Rockinghams favored complete repeal of the Townshend duties. According to William Meredith, MP for Liverpool and a lord of the Admiralty in the first Rockingham ministry, the Declaratory Act legislated Parliament's taxing authority; to exercise this right by retaining the tea tax was destructive to the domestic economy. The taxation of America was not sufficiently important, Meredith argued, to risk £500,000 in forgone colonial orders for British goods.[143] He closed his speech with an appeal similar to the one the Rockingham Whigs used in 1766: "Can commerce with America be effected by force or good will?"[144]

It was a compelling question without simple solution. Most independent legislators agreed with their colleague Alexander Wedderburn that partial repeal of the Townshend levies represented a "step further in that repeated contradiction which has obtained with America."[145] But the reduction in imperial trade and the larger threat posed by colonial boycotts demanded an official British response. Revoking all but the tea tax offered the possibility of defusing American embargoes while preserving legislative evidence of parliamentary authority. It was in many respects a significant gamble.[146]

141. Ibid., fol. 36.
142. Ibid., fols. 37–38.
143. Thomas, *Townshend Duties*, 175–76; Commons debate, 5 March 1770, Cavendish Diary, Egerton MSS 221, fol. 47–48.
144. Commons debate, 5 March, 1770, Cavendish Diary, Egerton MSS 221, fol. 48. See also Isaac Barré's speech on the same day, fols. 49–53.
145. Ibid., fol. 45.
146. For a colonial agent's perspective on British motivations behind partial repeal, see W. S. Johnson to Governor J. Trumbull of Connecticut, 14 April 1770; *Trumbull Papers*, Collections of the Massachusetts Historical Society, 5th ser., 9 (1855): 432. As Johnson wrote, "Thus the matter is fairly brought to this issue, whether the Americans have or have not the resolution, or the ability, to continue and conform to their agreements to

Yet the political configurations of metropolitan governance afforded little choice. Parliament's authority to regulate imperial trade and raise revenues—the legislature's power to manage the foundations of Britain's geopolitical strength—had to be upheld. Continuing to enforce all the Townshend duties, as Grenville advocated, risked the nation's commercial well-being to assert Parliament's power, while repealing all the duties sacrificed legislative sovereignty for considerations of trade. Confronted by these alternatives, MPs voted in March to support the government's plan for partial repeal.

This decision was a result of political objectives and exigencies. The partial repeal of the Townshend duties was not, as many historians have contended, a product of ministerial incompetence. The men who made imperial policy knew what they were doing. Their overwhelming concern was with promoting Britain's commercial health, either by raising revenues or securing colonial markets. For ministers and MPs, the Seven Years War had demonstrated the significance of understanding and exploiting the connection between wealth and international authority.

The proposals elite politicians put forward to manage the power of commerce were conditioned by political and economic factors. Elites used imperial issues to help stake out ideological and legislative identities, appealing to specific commercial groups as important new constituencies and sources of information and championing commercial objectives with a novel urgency and consistency. The state of the British economy also shaped policy outcomes by altering the balance of political power and giving manufacturers and their priorities greater significance in imperial governance. Economic conditions also influenced the way officials perceived imperial problems. In the postwar recession of 1766 the threat colonial embargoes posed to domestic employment and social order appeared more formidable than during the trade cycle boom of 1770. The state's claim on East India Company revenues seemed justified in the

---

decline the trade of this country. Many here [in London] think is impossible, and the Ministry are of the opinion that it is now a happy time for them to make the experiment, while their trade to other parts of the world is so flourishing. Not that they have any idea of parting with the trade of the Colonies; they imagine it will return of its own accord, and that they shall then forever have done with the embarrassment in their management of the Colonies; as the combinations, once dissolved, will never be renewed again, or if renewed will give the people of this country no apprehensions. No man therefore can be at a loss at what the Colonies ought to do upon this occasion; and as they determine and conduct, such will be their fate. All depends upon it; the game (if I may be allowed the expression) is in their own hands, and whether they play it well or ill depends upon themselves; but without union and firmness they can do nothing."

fiscal exigency and speculative frenzy of 1767; five years later, a series of Company financial crises compelled government intervention on a larger scale.

Burke and other statesmen knew that Britain's economic and geopolitical transformations had important consequences. These men realized that the forces of politics were changing. With such "fluctuations of administration,"[147] as General Henry Conway termed the political instability, officials could not help but wonder whether imperial superintendence had arrived, as one MP commented, "at the brink of a precipice" from which statesmen "look[ed] down in horror."[148]

What policymakers could not resolve was their collective ambivalence toward empire. In the aftermath of the Seven Years War, anticipation comingled with anxiety about the empire's new strength. This ambivalence fed the ideological fires of partisan argument and thus affected parliamentary politics. The new world of imperial commerce promised unparalleled wealth and power. But such riches also heralded the potential moral enervation of the British people and their government.[149] Politicians' collective ambivalence colored their understanding of specific problems, restricted their policy options, and created powerful incentives to eliminate the uncertainty.

Beneath the ambiguities tearing at the body politic, however, an underlying consensus was forming about the fundamental source of imperial authority. By 1773 ministers and legislators generally agreed with Grenville that in controlling the power of commerce, "the Parliament of England [was] in all cases supreme."[150] Imperial trade was of the "highest importance," Lord North explained in 1770. "There is scarce any branch of commerce, there is no branch of equal consequence to this country, and that deserves so much the constant inspection and consideration of Parliament."[151] The importance of parliamentary superintendence in taxing colonists, in regulating the East India Company, and as North commented, in "secur[ing] to the Public the continuation of those advantages which [British] manufactures and industry drew"[152] from its domin-

---

147. Commons debate, 5 March 1770, Cavendish Diary, Egerton MSS 221, fol. 41.
148. Commons debate, 7 December, 1768, Cavendish Diary, Egerton MSS 215, fols. 316–17.
149. Brewer, *Party Ideology*, 250.
150. Commons debate, 5 March 1770, Cavendish Diary, Egerton MSS 221, fol. 38.
151. Ibid., fol. 9.
152. Commons debate, 27 February 1769, Cavendish Diary, Egerton MSS 218, fol. 106.

ions became progressively clearer in the tumultuous imperial experience of the 1760s.

This experience unfolded in an ongoing dynamic between ministerial objectives, metropolitan action, and the reaction occasioned by such policies. In the aftermath of the war, British statesmen attempted to manage the commercial and fiscal imperatives of global power. In trying to implement a number of the policies, officials encountered significant resistance and unexpected consequences. As the postwar decade wore on and the challenges to imperial governance mounted, British politicians increasingly construed these challenges as threatening the authority of Parliament. This threat and the pressing need to accommodate the management of the empire's economic potential within the British political tradition forced statesmen to come to terms with a fundamental dilemma of constitutional theory: Who ultimately controlled the intricate trading interest that defined the empire? That the Crown, executive bureaucracies, or colonial governors maintained final authority over the extensive fiscal and commercial resources of Britain's dominion was ideologically unacceptable to politicians from various factions. Adherence to the principles of the Glorious Revolution demanded that the supremacy of the legislature and thus of the king-in-Parliament be upheld.[153] By 1773 most Britons agreed that parliamentary superintendence was sovereign.

Geopolitical transformation helped shape the consensus. In the century after the Glorious Revolution, the British state underwent an important transformation. During this time, the government acquired the principal features of a fiscal-military state: high taxes, an organized civil administration, a standing army, the determination to act as a major European state,[154] *and* the imperial commerce necessary to preserve the country's international stature. The sinews of this power were economic, and after 1688 they rested squarely in legislative hands.

By 1773 British officials concurred with William Knox that Parliament's jurisdiction extended to "the property and person of every inhabitant of a British colony."[155] But metropolitan statesmen continued to argue, as they had for the preceding decade, over how and to what extent that authority was to be exercised. On the foundations of parliamentary sovereignty, the imperial debates of the later eighteenth century unfolded, conditioned in form and substance by the experience of the 1760s.

153. Langford, "Old Whigs, Old Tories."

154. Brewer, *Sinews of Power*, 137.

155. William Knox, *The Claim of the Colonies to an Exemption from Internal Taxes Imposed by Authority of Parliament, Examined: In a Letter from a Gentleman in London* (London, 1765), 2.

 FIVE

The Ambivalence of Empire

SIGNED in February 1763 by British, French and Spanish plenipotentiaries, the Peace of Paris marked the official end of the Seven Years War. As the diplomatic conclusion of a sprawling, expensive conflict, the treaty was an anomalous settlement. Overwhelmingly victorious in war, Britain in peace relinquished without compensation a large number of the territories it had won. It restored its West Indian spoils of Martinique, Guadeloupe, and St. Lucia to France. In Canada, Britain granted its Gallic enemy fishing rights in the waters of Newfoundland and in the Gulf of St. Lawrence as well, and it returned Belle Île, off the coast of Britanny, to France. With Spain the triumphant nation exchanged its important conquest of Havana for Florida, a sparsely populated and undeveloped land.

In and outside government, Britons argued over the treaty. George III applauded the agreement, saying the country had never before concluded such a peace.[1] Meanwhile a war of words raged in London and the provinces as pamphleteers debated a variety of settlement possibilities.[2] In Whitehall the peace was no less controversial. The earl of Bute, first lord of Treasury and chief architect of the final agreement, said

---

1. Quoted in Zena Rashed, *The Peace of Paris, 1763* (Liverpool, 1951), 201.
2. The two most comprehensive sources to the pamphlet literature surrounding the peace are George Louis Beer, *British Colonial Policy, 1754–1765* (New York, 1907), and C. W. Alvord, *The Mississippi Valley in British Politics* (Cleveland, 1917). See also Marie Peters, *Pitt and Popularity: The Patriot Minister and London Opinion during the Seven Years War* (Oxford, 1980).

Britain had obtained "the highest conditions that could be got."[3] The earl of Shelburne praised the removal of the French from Canada and the Spanish from Florida, contending that these arrangements would increase British navigation and naval strength while improving commerce. Speaking before the House of Lords in late 1762, he said, that the treaty "ensures to G[reat] B[ritain] the pleasing hopes of a Solid and lasting Peace."[4]

Many statesmen were less sanguine about the settlement. The duke of Devonshire, lord chamberlain, opposed the peace on the grounds that it gave away too much and devalued Britain's war effort. George Grenville, first sea lord, criticized the Havana-Florida exchange. Most opponents of the treaty shared some version of William Pitt's sentiments: "The peace was insecure, because it restored the enemy to her former greatness. The peace was inadequate, because the places gained were no equivalent for the places surrendered."[5]

Why did British ministers agree to a peace that left France a viable military and economic rival? After all, the Seven Years War had been fought in the name of commercial empire, and Britain had won decisively. The fruits of that victory had not been insubstantial—Canada, Dominica, Florida, and India—but they did not satisfy a large number of Britons. Why, in the almost three years of negotiations that preceded the treaty—years stuffed with British victories—didn't officials demand additional advantages from France and later Spain?

More than fifteen decades of intermittent scholarly attention has not resolved these questions. Since Macaulay, historians have debated the diplomatic and strategic merits of the treaty.[6] Scholars working in the first

---

3. Bute to Henry Fox, 30 November 1762, Add. MSS 51,379, fol. 118.

4. Quoted in R. B. Morris, ed., *The American Revolution, 1763–1783: A Bicentennial Collection* (Columbia, S.C., 1971), 14.

5. "Speech of William Pitt before the House of Commons on the Articles of Peace," reprinted in F. Thackeray, *The History of the Right Honourable William Pitt, Earl of Chatham*, 2 vols. (London, 1827), 2:23.

6. John Bullion, "Securing the Peace: Lord Bute, the Plan for the Army, and the Origins of the American Revolution," in *Lord Bute: Essays in Re-interpretation*, ed. Karl W. Schweizer (Leicester, 1988), 17–39; Julian S. Corbett, *England in the Seven Years War: A Study in Combined Strategy*, 2 vols. (New York, 1907), 2:327–65; Walter Dorn, *Competition for Empire, 1740–1763* (New York, 1940), 370–84; Lawrence Henry Gipson, *The British Empire before the American Revolution*, 15 vols. (New York, 1936–70), 8:207–27; Kate Hotblack, "The Peace of Paris, 1763," *Transactions of the Royal Historical Society*, 3d ser., 2 (1908): 235–67; Ronald Hyam, "Imperial Interests and the Peace of Paris," in *Reappraisals in British Imperial History*, ed. Ronald Hyam and Ged Martin (London, 1975), 21–43; Rashed; Karl W. Schweizer, "Lord Bute, William Pitt and the Peace Negotiations with France," in Schweizer, 41–55.

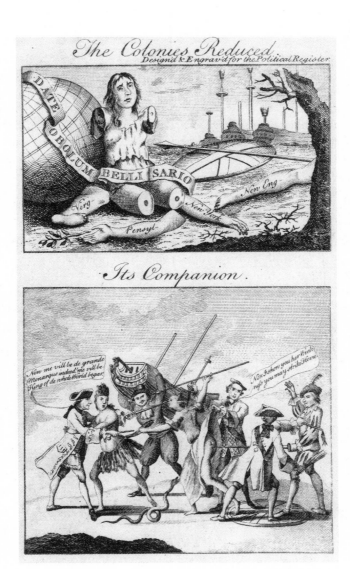

The Colonies Reduced and *Its Companion*. British Museum Catalogue 4183. Printed 1767. In words and images, the postwar empire was often represented in corporeal terms. Here mounting problems with the American colonies feed British fears of imperial dismemberment. The ships in the background of the upper engraving are dismantled. The brooms on their masts indicate they are for sale, an allusion to the commercial significance of the American colonies. The British oak at the right is leafless. The lower image depicts the geopolitical repercussions of Britain's imperial difficulties. On the left, America rushes into the arms of the French king, who proclaims Bourbon preeminence. Lord Bute, standing behind Britannia, lifts her petticoats while Spain stabs her. Meanwhile a Dutchman carries off a large British ship.

half of this century generally criticized the agreement as an unnecessary surrender of imperial security. Recent historiography has judged the peace more positively, emphasizing the extent of Britain's prizes and Bute's skill in negotiating these conquests from a French-Spanish alliance. Both groups of historians have tried to explain why, in the face of overwhelming military success, Britain relinquished so much to its geopolitical competitors.

As it was in 1762, this remains a compelling question. The purpose in reopening the problem here is not to evaluate the treaty within specific historiographic categories. Rather, it is to analyze the peace and the eighteenth-century dispute it provoked in order to broaden our understanding of official and more popular perspectives toward empire. Piqued by the experience of victorious conflict and economic transformation, these collective attitudes influenced the making of imperial policy.

In the closing years of the Seven Years War, statesmen and other Britons experienced significant ambivalence toward their enlarged empire. Victory portended new wealth and power for Britain, and its citizens welcomed their nation's novel strength with heady anticipation. But the prospect of international authority and prosperity also provoked general angst about the country's ability to manage its territorial and economic abundance. These conflicting perspectives coexisted, often turbulently, throughout the postwar decade, shaping the society's responses to imperial problems.

In its contrasting but simultaneously sustained attitudes toward empire, the eighteenth-century British polity was afflicted with a kind of collective bulimia. Bulimia is a term of our time connoting a habitual disturbance in eating behavior, but its schizophrenic symptoms—gorging followed by self-induced vomiting—preceded medical recognition of the disorder by some fifteen centuries.[7] For those affected by bulimia, these symptoms represent an overwhelming ambivalence toward eating: the pervasive interest in acquiring and consuming food—in assuring its abundance—commingles with an intense fear of the corrupting effects of such plenty.

In their political manifestations, Britons' attitudes toward the eighteenth-century empire were not dissimilar. At times imperial ambivalence motivated government officials to secure the nation's fill of wealth and

---

7. As psychiatrist Hilde Bruch has noted, cultural concern with slimness in the face of abundant food is not new. Imperial Romans scorned obesity in women, and young girls were deprived of nourishment in an effort to "make them slim as reeds." Hilde Bruch, *Eating Disorders: Obesity, Anorexia Nervosa, and the Person Within* (New York, 1973), 17.

power with all the policy tools at their disposal; at other times it restrained statesmen from active involvement in colonial governance and caused them to reverse interventionist policies. Within the dynamic created by these divergent attitudes, they debated what kind of dominion Britain was to have and how she was to control it.

Ministers and MPs agreed that the British empire was to be managed as a commercial system. The objectives of its governance were open, controllable colonial markets and reliable public revenues. How were these ends to be pursued? How much intervention should the mother country exert? Where and when should specific imperial policies be executed? The resolution of these questions owed much to the ambivalence Britons experienced. This collective uncertainty penetrated statesmen's perceptions, shaping their views of various problems and their policy choices.

Where did the ambivalence come from? To answer this, it is necessary to look closely at the Peace of Paris, the culmination of a costly, exhausting war and, as such, the focus of official and popular expectations regarding national prosperity and power. As the war's diplomatic testament, the final treaty left Britain a mixed legacy. In 1766 Thomas Pownall elaborated:

> The several changes of territories which at the last Peace took place in the Colonies of the European world, have given rise to a new system of interests, have opened a new channel of business, and brought into operation a new concatenation of powers, both commerical and political. This system of things ought, at this crisis, to be activated by a system of politics, adequate and proportionate to its powers and operations . . . The great question at this crisis is, and the great struggle will be, which of the states of Europe shall be in those circumstances, and will have the vigour and wisdom so to profit of those circumstances, as to take this interest under its dominions and to unite it to its government.[8]

Britain and France had begun transmitting terms of peace as early as March 1761. But the discussions that led directly to the final treaty did not start in earnest until the spring of 1762.[9] By this time, Britain and

8. Thomas Pownall, *The Administration of the Colonies* (London, 1766), 1, 9.

9. Rashed devotes extensive space to the diplomatic negotiations surrounding the final settlement. Unfortunately, she pays less attention to the political, economic, and social issues that accompanied the coming of peace in both countries. D. A. Winstanley, *Personal and Party Government: A Chapter in the Political History of the Early Years of the Reign of George III, 1760–1766* (Cambridge, 1910), is an older but analytically more insightful

Prussia were fighting two Bourbon powers—France and Spain—as well as Austria. The Anglo-Prussian alliance was showing the strain of a long, costly war and a change in British ministries. Bute, the effective leader of the government since Pitt's resignation in October 1761, was eager for peace. Bute wanted to abandon the German war and withdraw British troops from the Continent,[10] leaving Frederick the Great without the resources to continue fighting. In early 1762 Bute bowed to political pressure from other cabinet members and agreed to grant Prussia the same financial assistance it had received in previous years.

But the British minister altered the conditions of the subsidy in January, when the Russian empress Elizabeth died. The new czar, Peter III, was known to be a fanatical admirer of Frederick the Great. Peter's accession provided Prussia with the probability of a valuable new ally. As Bute understood, Frederick now had the option of prolonging the war with Russian assistance or using the alliance to pursue peace with his enemies on favorable terms.[11] The British leader hoped to make additional financial aid to Prussia contingent on Frederick's seeking an end to the conflict. In April it became clear that the Prussian monarch intended to continue fighting. In a reversal of his predecessor's policies, Bute decided to refuse the subsidy and lower other state expenditures on the German conflict.[12]

But elsewhere Bute, the king's favorite minister, continued Pitt's two-pronged approach to conflict—coupling a marine strategy with continental commitments. Throughout the winter of 1762 these tactics, in combination with France and Austria's fiscal exhaustion, proved successful.[13] In March the British navy captured the prosperous sugar island of Martinique. In Europe, British troops contained the Spanish invasion of Portugal, and plans continued to attack the island of Havana. When, in April, Bute opened the peace discussions to the cabinet, there were these and other territorial prizes to talk over.

The tide of war had begun to turn in 1759, a year of uninterrupted British victories. In August Frederick the Great had recaptured Minden,

reconstruction of the political underpinnings of the peace in England. See also Hotblack and Peters. On the closing years of the war in Britain, see Richard Middleton, *The Bells of Victory: The Pitt-Newcastle Ministry and the Conduct of the Seven Years War* (Cambridge, 1985).

10. Add. MSS 32,933, fol. 33.
11. Winstanley, 103.
12. Add. MSS 32,937, fol. 85.
13. For a balanced assessment of Pitt's military strategy, see Middleton.

and the British admiral Edward Boscawen had led a successful attack on the French fleet in the Mediterranean, incapacitating five enemy ships. Meanwhile in North America, three French forts—Niagara, Ticonderoga, and Crown Point—had fallen. These victories consolidated British control of the Great Lakes and promised an early western advance that would seal the fate of the French on the St. Lawrence.[14] General James Wolfe's strategic gamble in Canada had paid off miraculously. In September British armies had taken Quebec, though at the cost of Wolfe's life. Two months later, at Quiberon Bay, south of Brest, British naval vessels had dealt the French fleet a significant blow, ending Britons' long-standing fears of an enemy invasion.

By late 1761 Bute's ministers needed more than two hands to number the nation's territorial conquests. In addition to Quebec, British forces had also captured Belle Île, Goree, and Senegal off the coast of western Africa, and the West Indian islands of Guadeloupe, St. Lucia, and Marie Galante. In India, naval and land artillery under the command of the East India Company's Robert Clive had tilted the balance of power definitively toward Britain.

Which of these lands would Britain keep and make part of its empire, and which would it restore to its competitors? How were ministers to negotiate a settlement that justified the war's costs and ensured British security? Throughout the spring of 1762, Bute and his cabinet tried to iron out a treaty that would vindicate the nation's war efforts without disgracing the Bourbon powers so significantly that they immediately began planning a war of retribution.[15]

The starting point of ministerial debate was the current state of deliberations with France. Working in secret during much of 1761, Bute had reached an agreement with Louis XV's chief minister, the duc de Choiseul, by which Britain would keep most of Canada at the war's close. In exchange, France was permitted to hold the islands of St. Pierre and Miquelon south of Newfoundland and was granted fishing rights off its coasts and in the Gulf of St. Lawrence. Additionally, France was to regain control of Goree. British ministers generally agreed with these terms as the basis for a new round of discussions.[16]

14. Middleton, 132.

15. Officially, Bute was not head of the ministry until May, when Newcastle, first lord of Treasury, resigned over Bute's refusal to continue the German subsidy. He then assumed the duke's former position. But since Pitt's resignation five months earlier, the Favorite's predominant power within the ministry had been unchallenged.

16. Out of office but in command of significant popular support, Pitt strongly opposed relinquishing Canadian fishing rights to the Bourbon power. As nurseries for the French navy, these fisheries were crucial strategic interests, according to the Great Commoner.

In late April 1762, when Choiseul demanded that Britain cede to France, its recently captured prize, Martinique, the consensus among cabinet members crumbled. These men understood that agreeing to Choiseul's exaction made the ministry vulnerable to charges of leniency and to further dictates from the French government. Secretary of State Egremont, Grenville, and others favored restoring Martinique only if Britain retained Guadeloupe or Louisiana, North American territory with significant agricultural potential. Newcastle and Bedford argued that French ministers would never agree to these terms.[17]

After consideration, Bute abandoned these proposals. On 21 April, over the protests of several ministers, the Favorite dispatched a letter to Choiseul suggesting a new exchange. Britain would relinquish Martinique in return for the neutral West Indian islands of Tobago, Dominica, St. Lucia, and St. Vincent, smaller territories of less commercial and strategic value than Louisiana or the two larger Caribbean islands. Even Bedford, who strongly advocated a swift peace, thought Bute had been too generous. As Bedford told the head of the cabinet: "My doubt is, whether with such a chicaning power as France, we ought at the first opening to go to the utmost extent of the cessions we intended to make, least France, by our going such lengths at first, should think us to be so driven to the wall, as to buy peace at any terms."[18]

Choiseul's reply to Bute's offer further divided the British cabinet. In early June the French minister accepted most of the British terms, but he refused to surrender St. Lucia, one of the neutral islands. Bute recommended agreeing to this. Most of the cabinet disagreed; many were angered by Choiseul's latest demand. Egremont and Lord Mansfield thought the French response was unreasonable. Saying that he "might be beaten into a peace but would not be kicked into it," Lord Melcombe contended that the limit of concession had been reached when it had been agreed to surrender Martinique and Guadeloupe to France.[19]

After almost six weeks of discussions between Choiseul, Bute, and other spokesmen, Britain consented to return St. Lucia without compensation, on condition that the French minister persuade Spain to stop

---

To "break beyond hope of resuscitation the naval power of France" and to secure British supremacy on the seas, the fisheries must be maintained, Pitt argued (quoted in Thackeray, 2:22).

17. Add MSS 32397, fols. 341, 324. See also duke of Bedford to Lord Bute, 4 May 1762, in *The Correspondence of John, Fourth Duke of Bedford*, ed. Lord John Russell, 3 vols. (London, 1842–46), 3:77; Winstanley, 117.

18. The duke of Bedford to Lord Bute, 4 May 1762, *Bedford Correspondence*, 3:77–78.

19. Add. MSS 34,713, fol. 106.

fighting and make peace. Choiseul accepted this offer; by late August most details of a definitive settlement had been worked out.

A month later the British naval capture of Havana demonstrated the fragility of Bute's ministerial support. The first lord advocated returning outright the Spanish island, with its ten surrendered battleships and £3 million in plunder.[20] But both his secretaries of state, Grenville and Egremont, refused to sign a peace that did not stipulate some equivalent for Havana.[21] Although Bute called both ministers before the king, neither Egremont nor Grenville would alter his position. Other cabinet members would not consent to relinquishing the valuable conquest without compensation.[22] Bute now stood quite alone. Realizing he would have to demand some territory in return for Havana, Bute settled on Florida.[23] But first he reorganized the administration, demoting his most frequent opponent, Grenville, and appointing in his place Halifax, a trusted ally of the Favorite. From this point, few obstacles stood in the way of Bute's peace. In late October the end of conflict that he and George III had sought was achieved. Spain agreed to the Havana-Florida exchange, and on 3 November the preliminaries of peace between Britain, France, and Spain were signed.

Why had the first lord been so eager to make peace on French terms? Historian John Bullion has argued that Bute had initially favored a more Carthaginian settlement, one that denied France any access to the Canadian fisheries and retained Guadeloupe.[24] According to Bullion, Bute's strategic volte-face to a much more conciliatory position in the summer of 1761 was a product of the Favorite's financial anxiety. Bute believed Britain could not afford to fight any longer; the nation must have a swift end to the conflict.

Within the broader fiscal context of the Seven Years War, Bullion's thesis is problematic. Why, in late August 1761, did Bute become gripped

20. The duke of Newcastle to the earl of Hardwicke, 30 September 1762, in *Memoirs of the Marquis of Rockingham and His Contemporaries*, ed. George Thomas, earl of Albemarle, 2 vols. (London, 1852), 1:122.

21. Henry Fox to the duke of Cumberland, 29 September 1762, in *Rockingham Memoirs*, 1, 130.

22. Henry Fox to the duke of Bedford, 13 October 1762, in *Bedford Correspondence*, 3:133.

23. Egremont and Grenville thought the exchange insufficient. They favored restoring Havana for Florida *and* Puerto Rico. See *The Devonshire Diary: William Cavendish, Fourth Duke of Devonshire: Memoranda on [the] State of Affairs, 1759–1762*, ed. Peter D. Brown and Karl W. Schweizer (London, 1982), 179.

24. Bullion, 25–26.

with fear about the national finances? At this moment, why did these worries become important enough to reverse his diplomatic stance? The markets for government debt were calm throughout the summer. Since the war's outbreak, Treasury ministers such as Newcastle had been nervous about the state's finances. But throughout the conflict, Britain continued to raise unprecedented sums. Indeed, it had been relatively easy to find subscribers for the £14 million loan required for 1761, and Bute knew this.

His motives in embracing a conciliatory peace at this time were primarily political rather than financial. Once Pitt had resigned, there was no longer any reason for Bute to support a Carthaginian settlement. Instead, it was in his interest to encourage a rapid end to a conflict that had made Pitt, Newcastle, and their coalition indispensable. From August 1761 Bute pursued this objective vigorously, destroying the unity behind the war ministry, securing the resignations of the Great Commoner, Newcastle, and others, and concluding a treaty that solidified the Favorite's ministerial power.[25]

As during its diplomatic evolution, the completed treaty occasioned significant controversy when it was presented to the British public in December 1762. Bute affirmed that "this country has not made so great, so safe and so permanent a peace (for so it promises) as this for some hundred years past."[26] The king strongly agreed:

The Conditions of [this Treaty] are such that there is not only an immense Territory added to the Empire of Great Britain, but a solid Foundation laid for the Increase of Trade and Commerce, and the utmost

25. This is not to deny that George III and Bute were genuinely concerned about state finances. As John Bullion has argued, these men shared an interest in fiscal issues and a long-standing commitment to reducing the national debt; see " 'To Know This Is the True Essential Business of a King': The Prince of Wales and the Study of Public Finance, 1755–1760," *Albion* 18 (1986): 429–54. But by 1760 the attitudes of both the future monarch and Bute toward government indebtedness had become more positive (436–37). Bullion writes, "They sensibly decided in favor of continuing the [government's war-induced] borrowing to preserve and, if possible, increase the fruits of victory. Since the other choice would have been political disaster for a new king, no doubt their decision was easy to make" (437). Clearly, the young monarch and the Favorite understood the substance and politics of debt finance. In the summer of 1761 they knew Britain could raise additional loans, however much they disliked the prospect. More disturbing than the nation's debts were the political repercussions of extending the war: Pitt and Newcastle would stay in power, reducing the control George III and Bute could exercise in Whitehall and Westminster. The king and Bute pursued a primarily political, rather than fiscal, course of action.

26. Bute to the marquis of Granby, 5 November 1762. Add. MSS 38,200, fol. 93.

Care has been taken to remove all Occasions of future Disputes between My Subjects, and those of *France* and *Spain*, and thereby to add Security and Permanency to the Blessings of Peace.[27]

The duke of Bedford was more cautious in his praise:

I am convinced that nothing can give his Majesty more real pleasure than seeing his parliament and people thoroughly convinced of the happiness they enjoy under his auspicious government, and sensible of the advantages that will accrue to the nation through his Majesty's moderation in giving peace to his enemies in the midst of victories, and his paternal affection to his people in putting an end to a bloody and expensive war.[28]

Other officials were less enthusiastic. The duke of Devonshire resigned his office rather than support the peace treaty. Grenville continued to criticize the Havana-Florida exchange. The earl of Hardwicke contended that the settlement was deficient and that incomplete advantage had been taken of the British victories.[29]

Outside the cabinet, reaction to the preliminaries was similarly equivocal. Battling an attack of gout and sustained by frequent cordials, Pitt spoke for three hours on the settlement before the Commons.[30] He objected to conceding Canadian fishing rights to France on the grounds that this "would enable her to recover her marine." The Great Commoner thought Florida was "no compensation for Havana . . . From the moment Havana was taken all the Spanish treasures and riches in America lay at our mercy. Spain had purchased the security of all this and the restoration of Cuba also, with the cession of Florida only." The treaty was problematic, Pitt continued, in its West Indian provisions. Although he had wished to retain the prosperous island of Guadeloupe, the current administration had returned it:

But to Guadeloupe these persons had added the cession of Martinique. Why did they permit the forces to conquer Martinique if they were re-

---

27. Commons debate, 25 November 1762, *Journals of the House of Commons*, 29:354.

28. Duke of Bedford to the earl of Egremont, 14 December 1762, in *Bedford Correspondence*, 3:172.

29. Beer, 154. See also Hardwicke's speech in the House of Lords on the Preliminaries, 9 December 1762, in *The Parliamentary History of England from the Earliest Period to the Year 1803*, ed. William Cobbett, 36 vols. (London, 1806–20), 15:1251–58.

30. Horace Walpole, *Memoirs of the Reign of King George III*, 4 vols. (London, 1894), 1:177.

solved to restore it? . . . And to the cession of the islands of Cuba, Guadeloupe, and Martinique, there is added the island of St. Lucia, the only valuable one of the neutral islands. It is impossible . . . to form any
judgement of the motives which can have influenced his Majesty's servants to make these important sacrifices. They seem to have lost sight of
the great fundamental principle, that France is chiefly, if not solely, to be
dreaded by us in the light of a maritime and commercial power. We
[have] given to her the means of recovering her prodigious losses, and of
becoming once more formidable to us at sea.[31]

Despite Pitt's opposition in the Commons and that of Grafton, Newcastle, Temple, and Hardwicke in the Lords, the preliminaries passed both
houses of Parliament in early December. That the controversial treaty
was ratified with a significant majority in Parliament owed as much to
the absence of a tightly organized opposition as it did to Bute and the
king's carefully orchestrated campaign for parliamentary approval.
When Pitt, the most powerful enemy of the settlement, refused to ally
himself with any of the other leaders of the opposition factions, the
formal political battle on the peace was over. Bute's ministry had won a
substantial victory.[32]

Beyond Westminster and Whitehall, however, the controversy continued to swirl.[33] As Marie Peters has pointed out, public awareness and
discussion of the Seven Years War were greater than for previous conflicts.[34] Stimulated in part by a proliferation of newspapers and by the
almost serial nature of Britain's military successes, the political nation
closely followed the course of the war.[35] Britons were no less interested
in the resolution of this contest for commercial and international predominance.[36] In 1762 journalists and others knew that their country had

31. "Pitt's Speech on the Articles of the Peace," in Thackeray, 2:16–17. William Beckford,
lord mayor of the city and a West Indian merchant, also spoke against the treaty before
the Commons (Richard Rigby to the duke of Bedford, 26 November 1762, in *Bedford
Correspondence*, 3:161).

32. Peters analyzes the elite divisions surrounding the peace within the context of press
opinion, 244–61.

33. The most concise analysis of British reaction to the peace is that of Peters, 247–61.

34. Peters, 244.

35. On the empire and eighteenth-century press, see Kathleen Wilson, "Imperial Culture, Imperialist Ideologies: Empire and the British Political Nation, 1720–1785" (unpublished paper, Davis Center Colloquium, Princeton University, October 1989).

36. Undoubtedly Britain's continental commmitments played a role in the political debate over the war and what kind of peace Britain would have. But as Wilson demonstrates,
much of the printed discussion of the conflict and its closure was conducted along explicitly
imperial lines. This discussion had important implications for the way many thought about

defeated France overwhelmingly. But Englishmen disagreed about the geopolitical, economic, and social repercussions of the triumph. On the pages of newspapers and pamphlets, in pubs and coffeehouses, they argued over what kind of postwar empire Britain should have. As articulated in the press, the debate over the peace reflected the nation's bifurcated attitudes toward its newfound potential. One body of opinion was eager for the commercial and military influence of an unrivaled power. According to the *Monitor*, Britain deserved just compensation for an unprecedented victory:

At the time the Rt. Hon. Mr. Pitt was driven from the helm, the whole land was full of joy and mirth: our armies were victorious; no enemy could stand before them: our fleets maintained the dominion of the seas, and covered our conquests, colonies and islands; there was no danger of surprise from the shattered remains of a hostile navy: there was no complaint of money to continue a just and necessary war; the revenue or sources to pay our fleets and armies were reaped in the harvest of the great ocean: the trade of the whole world centered in this island; she was the mart of all nations: the merchants engrossed the riches of the universe, and lived like princes; and the manufacturers were enabled to live in credit and reputation, being supplied with many things necessary for their use from our conquests, at an easy rate for which they had been obliged to pay dear before.[37]

Where did this audacious confidence come from? It was not born anew in the circumstances of the Seven Years War. According to historian Kathleen Wilson, the War of Austrian Succession (1739–48) had been a conflict popularized in terms of a "strident imperialism that trumpeted the centrality of trade and empire in the national interest."[38] In 1739 the *Gentleman's Magazine* had proclaimed, "We are a trading nation; and whatever affects our Trade is our nearest Concern . . . Of all the Branches of our Commerce that to our own Colonies is the most valuable upon many Accounts . . . It is by that alone we are enabled to carry on the rest."[39]

---

the peace settlement. On the relation between print capitalism and perceptions of national identity, see Benedict Anderson, *Imagined Communities: Reflections on the Origin and Spread of Nationalism* (London, 1983), 37–49.

37. *Monitor*, 11 September 1762, 2250.

38. Kathleen Wilson, "Empire, Trade and Popular Politics in Mid-Hanoverian Britain: The Case of Admiral Vernon," *Past and Present* 121 (1988): 98.

39. *Gentleman's Magazine* 9 (1739): 32.

Admiral Vernon's victory at Porto Bello in 1739 had been portrayed, as were Wolfe's conquest and heroic death at Quebec two decades later, as an imperial triumph—one that extended British military and commercial power abroad. In 1740 a writer for the *Norwich Gazette* had glorified Vernon's success in the Caribbean:

> Free Born Briton, truly Brave!
> Born to revenge our wrongs, and Glory Save;
> To Teach the World Britannia Rules the Main.[40]

Almost three decades later, Wolfe's achievement at the Heights of Abraham above Quebec was also applauded as a vindication of British preeminence. Spontaneously and more formally, Britons celebrated the fall of Quebec throughout the country. The ministry announced a public funeral for the fallen warrior at Westminster Abbey. At Kensington Palace, an epithet to Wolfe was illuminated across six windows. It read:

Praise . . . General JAMES WOLFE, who Dauntless, but Deliberate, Under numerous Difficulties, September 2, 1759, Engaged to employ his little army For the Honour and Interest of his Country; and In a few Days after, Gloriously fulfilled his Promise, by the Conquest of Quebec, At the Expence of his Life.[41]

Wolfe's success was one of a score of dramatic British victories during the Seven Years War. These triumphs clarified older, previously amorphous ambitions of British power, validating imperial aspirations and imbuing them with a broadly recognized relevancy. In 1739 Vernon's success at Porto Bello had been notable as a sporadic but welcome intimation of the nation's potential. A cross section of British society had joined the chorus of patriotic self-congratulation that accompanied the admiral's victory.[42]

By the end of the Seven Years War, Britain's army had taken Canada and much of India. The navy had routed its French and Spanish competitors in Europe, Africa, and the West Indies. As it had throughout the conflict, the country's international trade continued to flourish. In heroic terms, newspapers and pamphlets brought these successes home to those concerned with the business of empire. Britons in 1762 understood that

40. *Norwich Gazette*, 22 November 1740.
41. *Gentleman's Magazine* 29 (1759): 495.
42. Wilson, "Empire, Trade and Popular Politics," 101–2.

their nation had at last achieved the military and economic predominance for which it had struggled since the reign of William III. The victory was the just, ordained culmination of almost four decades of war. The author of *A Political Analysis of the War* contended:

In the year 1758 commenced an Era resplendent with the return of British valour and success, under the auspices of a settled administration, wherein the ability of Mr. Pitt's genius had full room to display itself. Here his high and vigorous energy, seconded by divine providence, molded party into concord, and rais'd that tide of victory, conquest and national felicity, which carried the arms and character of Great Britain to the brightest summit of glory, moving her on, crowned with honour, in a rapid and unintermitting series of success[es] to the first and highest seat of dignity and fame.[43]

The victories of war, contended the *Monitor*, augured well for the empire's fortunes in peace:

The nature of our successes is adapted to a maritime and commercial nation. Acquisitions gained by our fleets, and not to be taken from us, but by a superior force at sea; which does not appear, could ever be the felicity of our enemies, are in their own nature, not ruinous, but most advantageous to England; whose natural strength and great superiority over her enemies lies on the seas. And conquests, whose situation either adds security, or improves our trade and navigation, can never be stigmatized with that hand of infamy as to bring ruin upon the conquerors; whose power, riches and glory arise upon the decay of their enemy's strength, and from the increase of their commercial establishments.[44]

The breadth of the Seven Years War made Britons increasingly aware of their extended empire. The conflict had broken out initially over disputed regions of the Ohio, the Great Lakes, and Nova Scotia, where throughout the early 1750s, France had been fortifying its position. To British officials in 1754 this had represented a significant threat to imperial interests, economic as well as strategic. The mainland colonies were the mother country's fastest-growing markets; by the war's outbreak

43. *A Political Analysis of the War* (London, 1762), 11–12.
44. *Monitor*, 11 December 1762, 2316.

Britain was selling more exports in North America than in the West Indies, once deemed its most valuable dominions.[45]

In 1755 it had appeared that America was to be the site of most hostilities.[46] Although the war had spread quickly to Europe and Africa, Britain's most dramatic victories occurred in colonial regions: Canada, the Caribbean, and India. All these areas, and most significantly North America, attracted popular attention back home. When in 1759 the city of Nottingham congratulated George II on the conquest of Quebec, its signers did so "upon the defeat of the French army in Canada, and the taking of Quebec; an acquisition not less honourable to your majesty's forces, than destructive of the trade and commerce and power of France in North America."[47]

In America and India, military success nourished national commerce. With its navy in control of the seas, Britain's trade in exports, imports, and reexports rose markedly over the conflict. In the context of eighteenth-century warfare this was unprecedented, and it stimulated the country's imperial ambitions. Britons had done the previously impossible: they had managed to simultaneously fight and trade profitably. According to Thomas Pownall, this achievement heralded Britain's commercial preeminence: "This lead [in commerce] seemed at the beginning of the late war to oscillate between the English and the French, and it was in this war that the dominion also ha[s] been disputed. The lead is now in our hands, we have such connection in its influence, that, whenever [this lead] becomes the foundation of a dominion, that dominion must be ours."[48]

Inexorably coupled with this bold confidence, however, was a collective insecurity about the nation's accomplishments. In 1763 British citizens worried about the cost, size, and future of their vast new empire. Some of these anxieties were of long standing. In the aftermath of preceding wars, Treasury officials had confronted large fiscal problems. The British state and citizenry had grappled with the social and economic effects of demobilization following the Nine Years War (1689–97), the War of Spanish Succession (1702–13), and the War of Austrian Succession

45. R. P. Thomas and D. N. McCloskey, "Overseas Trade and Empire, 1700–1860," in *The Economic History of Britain since 1700*, vol. 1, *1700–1860*, ed. Roderick Floud and Donald McCloskey (Cambridge, 1981), 90–91.

46. Middleton, 2.

47. *London Gazette*, 24–27 November 1759, quoted in Philip Lawson, "The Irishman's Prize: Views of Canada from the British Press, 1760–1774," *Historical Journal* 28 (1985): 575.

48. Pownall, 9.

(1739–48). But Britain's experience during the Seven Years War, including the scale and scope of its victory, heightened the importance of these older worries and added novel fears to the collective consciousness.

From its onset the Seven Years War had been a costly conflict, the most expensive in the country's history. By the close of 1762, the state had spent approximately £160 million fighting on two oceans and three continents. Most of these expenditures were financed through additions to the national debt, which grew almost 75 percent over the course of the conflict, to the unprecedented level of £132 million.[49] Interest charges on state indebtedness climbed in tandem, rising from £2.7 million in 1756 to £4.6 million in 1763 and fueling fears of peacetime tax increases.[50] Throughout the war and after, officials, journalists, and others worried about the nation's capacity to finance its debt without damaging Britain's geopolitical position. At the close of the hostilities, the author of a *Letter to a Gentleman in the City* bemoaned the costs of the country's liabilities:

What will be the condition of this country if the present enormous expence continues? *France* already feels its full distress; ours is not yet come: if the war continues, our distress is near at hand.

France supports the expence of this war by an immediate and cruel taxation; we borrow immense sums, the burden of which we shall feel hereafter. Already the want of men and money is complained of in every county of kingdom.[51]

Related to these general financial anxieties were persistent apprehensions about the country's military involvement in Germany. Opponents of the German war argued that Britain's large annual expenditures there, which ranged between £2 million and £4 million over the war, were

49. B. R. Mitchell and Phyllis Deane, *Abstract of British Historical Statistics* (Cambridge, 1962), 402. Military expenditures for the Seven Years War represented a larger percentage of national income than those for any other of the five eighteenth-century wars; John Brewer, *Sinews of Power: War, Money and the English State, 1688–1783* (New York, 1989), 41.
50. Mitchell and Deane, 390.
51. *A Letter to a Gentleman in the City with regard to the Contemplated Peace with France* (London, 1762), reprinted in *Gentleman's Magazine* 32 (1762): 406. See also Edmund Burke, "History of the Present War," *Annual Register* 5 (1762): 45–46. Such fiscal worries were generally unfounded. As I argued in chapter 1, the supply of loanable funds available for military expenditures was greater and more elastic than contemporaries believed. But economic hindsight did not affect the debate over the peace; contemporary perceptions did.

incredible, unparalleled expenses.[52] According to Israel Mauduit, author of the best-selling pamphlet *Considerations on the Present German War*, British commitments to Prussia were "ruinous and impracticable"[53] because they diverted the nation's funds and energies from maritime and colonial conquests, the primary objects of the war. Britain, Mauduit wrote, had made a comparable mistake during the War of Austrian Succession: "We at last forgot both the Spanish war and the French, and spent our money in Germany against the King of Prussia, for fear he should get, what we are now spending still more millions to prevent his losing."[54] In the three months following its original November 1760 publication, *Considerations on the German War* went through five editions, selling almost six thousand copies.[55] Many agreed with Mauduit that the Prussian alliance was costly and unprofitable for Britain.

The controversy about the nation's military obligations on the Continent dated back to the later seventeenth century. Since the reign of Charles II, statesmen had argued over the merits and disadvantages of naval and continental strategies.[56] What distinguished this debate during the Seven Years War from earlier dialogues was the scale of Britain's involvement. The country had never before committed such enormous resources to a secondary theater of conflict. As Mauduit commented, "Thus are Britain's treasures to be lavished away in millions, and more money spent on the German war alone, than the whole sea and land service cost in the Duke of Marlborough's campaigns."[57]

Also new in 1760 was the accession of a king hostile to Britain's German commitments and the prosecution of a multicontinent war.[58] George III's accession in November 1760 coincided closely with the publication of Mauduit's pamphlet. Under his predecessors, the young king declared

52. *Letter to a Gentleman in the City*, 405. In 1762 Britain spent £4.1 million on its German commitments. Of this sum, almost £700,000 was provided as a subsidy to Frederick the Great; the remaining £3.3 million was used for military expenses.

53. Israel Mauduit, *Considerations on the Present German War* (London, 1760), 61. On the more popular political impact of this pamphlet, see Peters, 182–90.

54. Mauduit, 47.

55. John Brewer, *Party Ideology and Popular Politics at the Accession of George III* (Cambridge, 1976), 146.

56. Brewer, *Sinews of Power*, 59–60, 140, 168–69, 170–71, 173–75, 178; Paul Kennedy, *The Rise and Fall of British Naval Mastery* (London, 1976), 66–122; Richard Pares, "American versus Continental Warfare, 1739–63," *English Historical Review* 51 (1936): 429–65.

57. Mauduit, 51. Mauduit estimated that the Germany subsidy in 1760 was five times greater than that paid to German princes during the War of Spanish Succession (68).

58. Prince of Wales to Bute, 2 July 1758, in *Letters from George III to Lord Bute, 1756–1766*, ed. Romney Sedgewick (London, 1939), 11; Winstanley, 92–93, 96–99, 101–8.

in his first address, adequate measures had not been "taken to keep advantage of our insular situation, nor effectual bars put to continental influence."[59] The monarch's opposition to the German war helped fuel growing apprehension about the extent of the nation's military and financial obligations and added credence to Mauduit's pessimistic projections:[60]

We may talk as we please of a French bankruptcy; but can any man prove, that our enemies may not go on seven years longer? Will any man avow the running his country a hundred millions farther in debt? Dare we imagine that our credit can extend so far; or our manufactures and exports bear the load of such an interest? I will leave the reader to picture for himself, what must happen long before we have gone such a length. Shall we then, when all the neighbouring nations have been drawing their money out of our hands, and quarreling with us for their principal; with all the confusions of bankruptcy; in that general state of distrust, which every individual must have of his neighbour; with our swords possibly aimed at each other's throats; shall we then be able to raise 10 millions within the year to protect the Electorate [of Hanover] or to defend ourselves?[61]

To many, Britain's involvement in Germany anticipated imperial overstretch. The nation's huge wartime responsibilities far exceeded its capacity to manage these commitments, according to Mauduit. "Should it therefore be said, that a nation may overconquer itself: and by being fed with more conquests than it can digest, may have the overplus turn to surfeit and disease instead of nourishment?"[62] History had answered this question unequivocally, opponents of the German war contended. Remember the ancient Sicilians, Mauduit cautioned, who "when their riches and naval power were at their greatest height . . . neglected their own war, to go upon a distant land-war in support of a little remote state, scarce heard of before, and made important only by that alliance." The pamphleteer hoped Britain would see the mistake of persisting in "such impracticable attempts" in Germany.[63]

59. RA Add. 32/1292, quoted in John Brooke, *King George III* (New York, 1972), 58.
60. See Peters, 180–81; Robert W. Tucker and David C. Hendrickson, *The Fall of the First British Empire: Origins of the War of American Independence* (Baltimore, 1982), 33–37.
61. Mauduit, 139–40. See also *A Political Analysis of the War*, 13–21, and *The Plain Reasoner, or Farther Considerations on the German War* (London, 1761), 18–19.
62. Israel Mauduit, *Occasional Thoughts on the Present German War* (London, 1761), 1.
63. Mauduit, *Considerations on the Present German War*, 141. See also *Plain Reasoner*, 36–37, and Mauduit, *Occasional Thoughts on the Present German War*, 1–2.

On the Continent, in North America, in India, and elsewhere, the nation's experience during the Seven Years War sharpened collective attitudes toward power and prosperity. Previous conflicts had elicited occasional outpourings of imperial ambition and insecurity from Britons. But the war at midcentury gave new form and urgency to older aspirations and fears, validating their significance in the national consciousness. On the one hand, the country's military and economic performance throughout the Seven Years War surpassed even the most optimistic projections and expanded popular conceptions of national potential. On the other hand, however, the unprecedented magnitude of Britain's obligations during and after the conflict threatened its imperial, commercial, and moral future. In 1763 the political nation could not avoid confronting both these irreconcilable possibilities.

These contrasting views formed the perceptual backdrop against which the public debate over the peace treaty played itself out. As framed by the press, the controversy surrounding the settlement was one of territorial and commercial justification. Did the negotiated end to a long, expensive war vindicate its costs—human and financial? Did the treaty adequately reflect the strength of the victory? Britons disagreed vehemently over the answers to these questions. Taken together, their discordant responses reflected a fundamental ambivalence regarding the fate of the empire.

Opponents of the settlement argued that the proposed peace was dishonorable because it devalued the nation's war effort. According to George Heathcote, a former London alderman and lord mayor, the treaty did not compensate the nation sufficiently for "the Effusion of Oceans of *British* Blood, and the Expence of upwards of £100,000,000 of Treasure."[64] The peace was deficient, Heathcote continued, because it re-

---

64. [George Heathcote,] *A Letter to the Right Honourable the Lord Mayor, the Worshipful Aldermen, and Common-Council; the Merchants, Citizens and Inhabitants, of the City of London: From an Old Servant* (London, 1762), 5. See also John Douglas, *A Letter Addressed to Two Great Men* (London, 1760), 4. The author of *A Detection of the False Reasons and Facts Contained in Five Letters, Entitled Reasons for keeping Guadeloupe at a Peace, preferable to Canada; in which the Advantages of both Conquests are fairly and impartially stated and compared. By a member of Parliament* (London, 1761) argued that only the retention of Canada could vindicate the cost of Britain's North American victories: "It is true that the *French* are conquered, but it was such a Conquest as covered *Britain* with Mourning. The Tears of the Fatherless and of the Widow, and the bleeding Hearts of Parents for the Loss of their Sons, such as a *Howe* and a *Wolfe*, have confirmed, beyond Contradiction, That *North America* was not able to defend itself against the *French* in Possession of Canada; and that

stored too many valuable prizes to France. For although Britain gained Canada, an important foothold in India, and several West Indian islands, it relinquished Guadeloupe, Martinique, Goree, and the Newfoundland fisheries to France. The Bourbon enemy, Heathcote insisted, could not be allowed to control the imperial abundance Britain had so recently conquered:

If any Credit is to be given to the publick Reports, all the Blessings, this Nation flattered itself with Enjoyment of, from the Ruin of the *French* Commerce and naval Power, are in Danger of being lost, by the Restitution of *Goree* and *Guadeloupe*; if not of far the greatest Part of our late Conquests, to our perfidious and inveterate Enemy; and by leaving the *Newfoundland* Fishery, upon the Footing it stood before the War; which is not a Whit better, than giving them up that very profitable Branch of Trade and great Nursery of Seamen: The Profits annually arising from the Fish Trade, together with those arising from *Guadeloupe* and *Goree*, being sufficient, with such a Nursery, to turn the Balance of Trade in favour of *France*; and revive their now expiring naval Force to an Height, that will enable her, in a few Years to cope again with *Great Britain*, for the Dominion of the Sea; and to insult, annoy and injure *us*, and all her Neighbours.[65]

Supporters of the administration's settlement argued against a grander peace. Britain could not possibly keep all its conquests, contended many statesmen and journalists. Two years before the war's end, the author of *Remarks on the Letter Addressed to Two Great Men* cautioned against making a Carthaginian treaty, alleging this would be strategic suicide for Britain. Attempting to maintain all that it had won might

indeed mortify the Enemy, but it would add nothing to our real Strength; whilst it would alarm every Nation near us, and assist *France* in exciting that Jealousy of the *British* Naval Power, which she [France] has for a long Time been labouring with great Industry, and some Success to

---

it was with the utmost Difficulty and Hazard the whole Force by Sea and Land, which *Great Britain* was able to spare for that Service, has at last disarmed and reduced them to the *British* Government" (34–35).

65. Heathcote, 3–4; See also *The Proper Object of the Present War with France and Spain Considered* (London, 1762), 20–30; *Monitor*, 19–26 June, 10–17 July, 14–21 August, 2 October, 4–11 December 1762; *London Evening Post*, 24–26 August, 23 September 1762; *Gazetteer*, 18 October 1762.

infuse into all the Nations of *Europe* and particularly into the Maritime states. You have very well observed upon the Terror which was excited by the Power of Lewis XIV and upon the general Confederacy against him, which was the Consequence of this Power: but you have forgot[ten] to add, that the insolent use he made of his Greatness alarmed as much, and provoked much more, than that enormous Power itself: it was indeed the true Cause of his Fall.[66]

Proponents of Bute's settlement also contested the commercial feasibility of controlling more territory. It was unproductive and impracticable for Britain to keep additional prizes. How could the nation successfully manage Guadeloupe or Martinique, one pamphleteer asked, when the British sugar trade was already overextended? "Nothing being more certain, than that we have more Sugar-Lands than there are People to cultivate them, and that all Measures tending to divide and disperse our Sugar-Colonies will be injurious to *Great Britain*, and to the Sugar Trade of the Nation."[67] With its vast unsettled tracts and 70,000 French Catholic inhabitants, Canada alone would be very difficult to integrate into the empire; the mother country had more than enough to manage without accessing other lands. The author of *Remarks on the Letter Addressed to Two Great Men* elaborated: "By eagerly grasping at extensive Territory, we may run the risque, and that perhaps in no very distant Period, of losing what we now possess. The Possession of *Canada*, far from being necessary to our Safety, may in Consequence be even dangerous."[68]

The controversy over the preliminaries was thus portrayed by the press and conceptualized by officials as a dispute over which lands Britain should control. Much of the printed debate over the peace, as historian Philip Lawson has pointed out, was framed as a choice between Guadeloupe and Canada.[69] In such stark form, this particular decision was not directly relevant to ministerial negotiations, according to Lawson. But, he continues, "the pamphlet literature contains all the doubts and anxieties about what should be done at the peace table experienced by politicians . . . Most of the work written in the years 1760–3 appeared anonymously, but a great deal of it would be written either by the politicians or by hacks

66. *Remarks on the Letter Addressed to Two Great Men* (London, 1761), 15–16. See also Edward Richardson, *A Letter to a Gentleman in the City*, reprinted in the *Monitor*, 18 September 1762.

67. *Remarks on the Letter Addressed to Two Great Men*, 17.

68. Ibid., 51.

69. Lawson, 575–77.

in their employ. The political world was simply not that disinterested; to produce over sixty pamphlets took a great deal of official encouragement."[70]

Why was the printed controversy structured in territorial terms? How does this structure inform our understanding of imperial attitudes during the closing years of the war? The pamphlet debate of the early 1760s represented the ambivalence most Britons felt toward their postwar dominion. Officials and journalists wanted a prosperous empire of impressive dimensions, but at the same time they feared the political and economic degeneration that seemed to accompany this abundance. This perceptual conflict was articulated along territorial lines and rationalized with reference to commercial success.[71]

Those who advocated retaining Canada did so with exhilarating anticipation. The great expanse of North America symbolized Britain's possibilities for unprecedented wealth and power. As the author of *A Detection of the False Reasons and Facts* (1761) noted, "The Advantages, which might be expected from such a vast extent of Territory, if it be judged of from the great Access of Power, Trade, and Riches gradually received by *England* from that Continent, in proportion to the Extension of its Cultivation, are beyond all Conception."[72] William Shirley, former governor of Massachusetts, outlined specific benefits from driving the French out of Canada:

The growing advantages, w[hich] would accrue to the Nation must be immense; the State of Security, which the Settlers in North America would be put into, by the Removal of the French; The extensive Trade with the Indians, the Increase of the Fishery, the Rich vacant Country for new Settlements, and the quick Growth of their Estates would make the Inhabitants increase if not in a Duplicate proportion to what they have hitherto done, yet in a much greater degree.[73]

But this North American acquisition also presented significant challenges for imperial governance. How was the mother country to manage

70. Ibid., 577–78.
71. See especially *Court Magazine*, September 1762, 602, and October 1762, 652–53; *Imperial Magazine*, January 1760, 3.
72. *Detection of the False Reasons and Facts*, 23.
73. William Shirley to Thomas Robinson, 15 August 1755, Colonial Office Papers. See also Benjamin Franklin, *The Interest of Great Britain Considered with regard to Her Colonies* (London, 1760); Douglas, *Letter Addressed to Two Great Men*; and *The Comparative Importance of Our Acquisitions from France in America* (London, 1762).

the distant lands? Perhaps it could not. Those who opposed keeping Canada rather than Guadeloupe expressed diffidence about Britain's ability to control new, alien territories and peoples. The West Indian island with its established sugar trade demanded fewer government resources to manage than Canada while still promising commercial rewards.[74] As the author of *Reasons for Keeping Guadeloupe at a Peace, Preferable to Canada,* wrote in 1761;

The having all North America to ourselves by acquiring Canada, dazzles the eyes and blinds the understanding of the giddy and unthinking people, as it is natural for the human mind to grasp at any appearance of wealth and grandeur. Yet it is easy to discover that such a peace might soon ruin Britain . . . Such a country as North America, ten times larger in extent than Britain, richer in soil in most places, all the different climates you can fancy . . . such a country at such a distance could never remain long subject to Britain.[75]

Even if Britain could manage its Canadian colonies, James Marriott wrote, this would ultimately prove destructive to the country's geopolitical and moral stature:

It is with whole nations as it is with private men; an accumulation of possessions only serves to increase a violent desire for still greater acquisitions. Every conquest opens new views; and the imagination already grasps the mines of Chile, Peru, and Mexico. What subjects for declamation! Every voice and every pen is employed to increase the national rage of perpetuating war: and by a thirst of military glory we seem to have entirely forgot[ten] that moderation and equity which always gave this nation the greatest weight in Europe . . . With respect to the conquests which we have already made with such unparalleled success, are we not embarrassed how to preserve them?[76]

Too much land, like too much commercial wealth, according to Marriott, was destructive to the country's health. A surfeit of riches created a

74. *Reasons for Keeping Guadeloupe at a Peace, Preferable to Canada, Explained in Five Letters from a Gentleman in Guadeloupe to His Friend in London* (London, 1761); *An Examination of the Commercial Principles of the Late Negotiation* (London, 1762); *Remarks on a Letter Addressed to Two Great Men.*

75. *Reasons for Keeping Guadeloupe at a Peace,* 29.

76. James Marriott, *Political Considerations, being a few Thoughts of a Candid Man at the Present Crisis* (London, 1762), 55–57.

situation in which "the world's victors would be subdued very soon by their own vices. Luxury, profusion, and the want of every principle of good government and subordination in all orders of men would bring on effeminacy, indolence, depopulation, and all the wretched train of misery that accompanies the degeneracy of every great nation."[77] Look at Spain, the pamphleteer continued. Before the discovery of the Indies, the Iberian country "was full of people, brave and free. What she is now, our success has shown us, weak, contemptible, and vulnerable in every part."[78]

Modern scholars have closely scrutinized the printed debate about the peace. Many historians have contended that the controversy reflected a fundamental disagreement about the relative importance of trade and dominion in the postwar empire.[79] According to several scholars, supporters of Bute's treaty generally wanted an empire based firmly on trade rather than territorial expansion. Not surprisingly, these "little Englanders," as they came to be called in the academic literature, opposed the accession of Canada in favor of retaining Guadeloupe. The expansionists, of whom Pitt was an extreme example, viewed the assimilation of Canada as the culmination of a fifty-year struggle to vanquish the French in North America. Expansionists generally opposed the ministry's settlement as inadequate.[80]

Undoubtedly, a debate occurred in the early 1760s about Canada's fate and that of the larger empire. But in reconstructing this dialogue as a product of clear conceptual divisions, historians have underestimated the complexity of imperial attitudes after the Seven Years War. British perspectives did not fit neatly into either the dominion or the trade classification. Both supporters and opponents of the preliminaries based their arguments on economic criteria. Expansionists backed territorial aggrandizement for primarily commercial reasons. The "little Englanders," who worried about the geographic extent of Britain's empire, wanted to ensure that the mother country maintained control of its most prosperous colonies. No group could afford to ignore the power of commerce in justifying its position.

The arguments over the treaty did not anticipate a consistent division over imperial management in the postwar period, as some scholars have

77. Ibid., 59.
78. Ibid.
79. Beer, 160–227; Vincent T. Harlow, *The Founding of the Second British Empire, 1763–1793*, 2 vols. (London, 1952–64), 1:162–6; Lawson, 575–81.
80. Lawson, 578.

alleged.[81] Policymaking toward the empire was conditioned by economic change, political economy, the configurations of elite politics, and collective perceptions. These perceptions were bifurcated: bold, expansionist impulses coexisted with those of an insecure isolationism.

But one should not assume that this coexistence translated directly into political alignments, with expansionists and "little Englanders" trying to outshout each other. Throughout the decade, the factions that affected imperial governance and the influence they commanded fluctuated significantly. These alliances were affected by several factors, including a pervasive ambivalence toward Britain's prospects.

Given this ambivalence, how did literate Britons react to the peace treaty? Opinions varied. The City had been generally hostile to Bute and his negotiations since mid-1762. In October the *London Gazette* had joined the *Monitor*, the *London Evening Post*, and other City newspapers in demanding a settlement "adequate to our glorious successes."[82] Released publicly in early December, the preliminaries did not generally satisfy these priorities.[83] As the journalist John Almon remarked, "The restoration of the West India islands, and other matters relative to America . . . instantly spread such an alarm throughout the kingdom, that the people rose up like one man, in detestation and abhorrence of such conditions. The trading part of the Kingdom was most sensibly affected."[84]

Some observers believed the City's opposition to the treaty reflected opinion across the country. Earl Temple thought most Britons were against the proposed settlement.[85] Edmund Burke noted that provincial merchants understood the "danger they were in of losing so vast a Trade" to the conquered Caribbean islands.[86] In an address to one of the secretar-

81. Harlow, 1:161–65; Lawson, 580–81.

82. *London Gazette*, 2–5 October 1762. On City animosity to Lord Bute, see John Brewer, "The Misfortunes of Lord Bute: A Case Study in Eighteenth Century Argument and Political Opinion," *Historical Journal* 16 (1973): 6.

83. Lord Bute to the duke of Bedford, 10 November 1762, in *Bedford Correspondence*, 3:152. On the politics of the City's opposition to Bute, see Peters, 248–51.

84. [John Almon], *A Review of Lord Bute's Administration* (London, 1763), 88. Not all London merchants opposed the Peace of Paris. Many sugar traders supported the restoration of Guadeloupe and Martinique to France. In an already glutted sugar market, they did not want additional competition. In defining this position, their criteria were primarily commercial.

85. Earl Temple to John Wilkes, 11 September 1762, in *The Grenville Papers*, ed. William James Smith, 4 vols. (London, 1852–53), 1:469. See also Robert D. Spector, *English Literary Periodicals and the Climate of Opinion during the Seven Years War* (The Hague, 1966), 88–129.

86. Edmund Burke to Charles O'Hara, 30 October 1762, in *The Correspondence of Edmund Burke*, vol. 1, *April 1744–June 1768*, ed. Thomas W. Copeland (Cambridge, 1958), 152.

ies of state, Liverpool traders protested the relinquishment of Guadeloupe to France:

Your memorialists . . . beg leave to represent to your lordship, that
though they possessed [West Indian and African] commerce in a very
great and extensive manner before the reduction of Guadeloupe and its
dependencies, yet the possession of that island has increased their trade
beyond all comparison with its former state in the demand of British manufactures . . . And your memorialists have all possible reason to believe
and be assured, that in succeeding years this demand will be prodigiously
increased . . . [We] entreat your lordship to lay before his majesty their
humble but earnest hopes, that the possession of Guadeloupe, and its dependencies, so valuable at present, and so constantly and greatly increasing, may, if not incompatible with the general scheme of affairs, be
deemed an object worthy of his Majesty's attention in the negotiation of a
peace.[87]

Others protested more violently against the administration's peace. At
the November opening of Parliament, Bute was "very much insulted,
hissed in every gross manner, and a little pelted," according to one official
witness.[88] Although the first lord tried to conceal himself when he left
Parliament, he was discovered and chased by the mob, who "by threats
and menaces, put him very reasonably in great fear . . . [for] if they had
once overturned [his hackney] chair, he might very soon have been
demolished."[89] In the West End, theater audiences applauded assaults
on favorites and Scots.[90] Some of this discontent, as John Brewer has
noted, was a product of Bute's perceived place in the political ideology
of the 1760s.[91] To many Britons, the Favorite represented an overmighty
subject who had made an irresponsible peace.[92]

Not all Britons thought the ministry's settlement unreasonable. The
earl of Bath thought the terms of peace gave general "satisfaction to

87. "The Memorial of the Merchants of Liverpool Trading to and in Africa and the
West Indies, to the Right Honourable, the Earl of Egremont, One of His Majesty's Principal
Secretaries of State," reprinted in Almon, 88–89.
88. Richard Rigby to the duke of Bedford, 26 November 1762, in *Bedford Correspondence*,
3:160.
89. Ibid.
90. Peters, 251.
91. Brewer, "Misfortunes of Lord Bute," 40–43.
92. See *The Peace-Botchers: A New, Satyrical, Political Medley* (London, 1762).

most people."[93] The same month, the *London Chronicle* challenged the assertion that the nation was united against peace.[94] By October the *Critical Review* assessed the works it was reviewing and declared that "the popular tide seems to have taken a turn favourable to the pacific measures of the present administration."[95] Several of the literary publications, such as the *Imperial Magazine*, assumed a balanced position toward the treaty, endorsing neither the administration nor the opponents' position.[96]

On balance, what was public reaction to the Peace of Paris? The proposed treaty seems to have fallen short of most expectations regarding the settlement that Britain's victory merited. It had been a long, expensive conflict, and most Britons were glad to see it end. But they did not want peace on any terms. The war's length and cost and the nation's ability to endure both nurtured popular hopes surrounding the peace. As one political observer commented after the conquest of Havana, "The nation in general will expect something very advantageous in the future treaty with Spain, in exchange for such a [victory], and it is well, if the old cry of *Take and Hold*, is not revived on the occasion. The uninterrupted course of prosperity which has attended our arms, in enterprises the most difficult and important, is scarce to be paralleled in history, and will make this era in our annals a most splendid one."[97] In late 1762 this anticipation was transmogrified into territorial ambitions. Most Britons wanted a treaty that would justify the costs of war, the strength of the country's success, and their expectations of power and profit.[98] From this perspective, Bute's preliminaries did not satisfy public appetites.[99]

In reconstructing opposition to the Peace of Paris, it is important to recognize the diffidence that simultaneously characterized imperial perceptions at the war's end. British citizens favored a commercial empire with unchallenged international supremacy, but at the same time they worried about the financial, administrative, and moral viability of this dominion. These anxieties grew out of the interaction between older

---

93. Bath to Lord Lyttleton, 26 August 1762, in *The Memoirs and Correspondence of George, Lord Lyttleton from 1734 to 1773*, ed. Robert J. Phillimore, 2 vols. (London, 1845), 2:636–37.

94. *London Chronicle*, 4–7 September 1762. See also Karl Schweizer, "Lord Bute and the Press: The Origins of the Press War of 1762 Reconsidered," in Schweizer, *Lord Bute*, 91.

95. *Critical Review*, October 1762, 316.

96. *Imperial Magazine*, 3 (1762): 217–22.

97. Viscount Royston to Dr. Birch, 30 September 1762, in *Rockingham Memoirs*, 1:124.

98. See especially *Imperial Magazine*, June 1762, 305, 307–8.

99. For contrasting analyses of public opinion toward the peace, see Peters, 251, and Schweizer, "Lord Bute and the Press," 91.

conceptions of dominion and the specific circumstances of the recent conflict.

This angst, in more subtle form, had preceded the war. In Holland and Britain, seventeenth-century observers had worried about the repercussions and caprice of sudden prosperity.[100] Writing about Dutch culture in the golden age, Simon Schama has described these collective misgivings:

[Holland] had become a world empire in two generations . . . All that power and stupendous wealth was, in the end, sucked into the cramped space between the Schedlt and the Ems . . . The prodigious quality of their success went to their heads, but it also made them a bit queasy. Even their most uninhibited documents of self-congratulation are haunted by the threat of *overloed*, the surfeit that rose like a cresting flood—a word heavy with warning as well as euphoria.[101]

Working at the end of the seventeenth century, British political economists had expressed similar nervousness toward an overlarge empire.[102]

England's experience during the Seven Years War transformed older imperial perceptions into collective bulimia. How did the political nation conceptualize these contrasting sensibilities? How did officials, manufacturers, and others take in and come to harbor the ambitions and insecurities of empire? Several factors were significant in transmitting these shared perceptions.[103] Perhaps most important was the midcentury proliferation of metropolitan and provincial newspapers. In 1750 more than 7 million newspaper stamps were issued; by 1760, this figure had climbed

100. Joyce Appleby, *The Economic Thought and Ideology in Seventeenth Century England* (Princeton, N.J., 1978), and James W. Johnston, "The Meaning of Augustan," *Journal of the History of Ideas* 19 (1958): 501–22.

101. Simon Schama, *The Embarrassment of Riches: An Interpretation of Dutch Culture in the Golden Age* (Berkeley, Calif., 1988), 8. Thomas Pownall, *Principles of Polity, Being the Grounds and Reasons of Civil Empire* (London, 1752), compares Britain's imperial situation in the mid-eighteenth century with that of Holland one hundred years earlier (65).

102. See, for example, Charles Davenant, *Discourses on the Publick Revenues and the Trade of England*, 2 vols. (London, 1698), 2:204; Carew Reynell, *The True English Interest* (London, 1679), 88. Few historians have analyzed the anxieties of empire, but a small, growing number of historians, such as Kathleen Wilson; Linda Colley, "The Apotheosis of George III: Loyalty, Royalty and the British Nation, 1760–1820," *Past and Present* 102 (1984): 94–129; idem, "Whose Nation? Class and National Consciousness," *Past and Present* 113 (1986): 97–117; and Marie Peters, have begun to examine the interrelationship between imperial confidence, popular politics, and emerging conceptions of national identity.

103. I am indebted to Benedict Anderson's analysis of the spread of eighteenth-century nationalism (*Imagined Communities*, 11–79).

to 9.4 million, and fifteen years later, some 12.6 million stamps were issued—almost 35,000 a day.[104] The aggregate number of papers increased, as did the quantity of individual newspapers, journals, and advertisers. By 1760 London had four dailies as well as five papers published three times a week; in sum, there were eighty-nine newspapers paying advertising revenues in the city. The number of papers in the provinces grew similarly, from thirty-two in 1753 to fifty in 1782.[105] Not surprisingly, the areas experiencing the most rapid economic development, such as the Midlands and the north, witnessed the most rapid proliferation of publications. In the postwar decade Newcastle had three newspapers and its own magazine, the *Newcastle General*. The *Northampton Mercury*, *Aris's Birmingham Gazette*, and *Jopson's Coventry Mercury* served the Midlands.[106]

Many newspapers, magazines, and journals had sections on the "British Plantations." These sections included information on the histories and settlement patterns of specific colonies as well as news on trade and politics. Some of the publications covered the "etiquette" of colonization.[107] Press coverage of the empire was largely a function of the Seven Years War. Like all military conflicts, it had promised an abundant supply of what Defoe had termed those "dear Things call'd Blood and Battle," and press attention toward Britain's dominions had expanded tremendously over the course of the conflict.[108]

Published for two years beginning in 1760, the *Imperial Magazine* was illustrative of the press's growing interest. This monthly publication included regular surveys on foreign and military affairs as well as an ongoing discussion of postwar settlement possibilities. In mid-1762 the magazine commented proudly on the country's emergence as an international power, contending that Britain should dominate global trade without heed to the opinions of other nations.[109] In this way, as Benedict Anderson has written, newspapers, magazines, and other publications refracted "world events into a specific imagined world of vernacular

---

104. *Journals of the House of Commons*, 27:769.

105. Brewer, *Party Ideology*, 142–43. See also G. A. Cranfield, *The Development of the Provincial Newspaper, 1700–1760* (Oxford, 1962); A. Aspinall, "Statistical Accounts of London Newspapers during the Eighteenth Century," *English Historical Review* 63 (1948): 220–23.

106. G. A. Cranfield, *The Press and Society: From Caxton to Northcliffe* (London, 1978), 179; Brewer, *Party Ideology*, 143.

107. Wilson, "Imperial Culture," 7–8.

108. Quoted in Cranfield, *Press and Society*, 58.

109. *Imperial Magazine*, 3 (June 1762): 305, 307–8.

readers."[110] For Britons in 1762 this imagined community revolved around their empire, powered by its new territorial and commercial strength.

Economic change affected imperial perceptions. In the three decades after 1740, both agricultural and manufacturing output in Britain grew significantly. Domestic and international commerce expanded. This growth was inexorably connected to the penetration of print. Trade, as Linda Colley has noted, nourished print, making it indispensable. Shopkeepers, peddlers, and others had to deal with bills, orders, credit instruments, advertising copy, and invoices. To help them master the printed tools of trade, businessmen bought dictionaries, grammar books, and primers, the autodidactic literature that rolled off eighteenth-century presses.[111] The burgeoning economy fed the market for print and was in turn nourished by the widening exchange of words.

Economic development also accelerated national integration and the spread of imperial attitudes. Increased economic activity at midcentury, T. S. Ashton has told us, was related to the simultaneous expansion in turnpike and canal construction.[112] Improved mobility and communication between town, village, and countryside helped shape Britons' sense of collective identity in a commercial society, according to other historians.[113] Scholars have devoted less attention to how these perceptions were related to official and popular attitudes toward empire.

In the aftermath of the Seven Years War, the British Empire became a repository for a set of collective ambitions and fears surrounding prosperity and international authority. Statesmen and others understood that their country's victory was entwined with Britain's commercial ascendancy. Thomas Whatley, a Treasury official under George Grenville, explained: "That the Wealth and Power of Great Britain depend upon its Trade, is a Proposition, which it would be equally absurd in these times to dispute or to prove: it was not indeed apprehended that they

110. Anderson, 63.

111. Linda Colley, "Britannia's Children: Images and Identities" (unpublished paper, Davis Center Colloquium, Princeton University, October 1989), 14. For a distinct perspective on the relation between capitalism and the proliferation of print, see Anderson, 38–40.

112. T. S. Ashton, *An Economic History of England: The Eighteenth Century* (London, 1966), 63–90. See also G. R. Hawke and J. P. P. Higgins, "Transport and Social Overhead Capital," in Floud and McCloskey, 227–51.

113. See Colley, "Britannia's Children"; John Brewer, "Commercialization and Politics," in *The Birth of a Consumer Society: The Commercialization of Eighteenth-Century England*, ed. Neil McKendrick, John Brewer, and J. H. Plumb (Bloomington, Ind., 1982).

were so great as they have been found to be, we did not ourselves know our own Strength, till the Vigour of the Last War applied the Resources of that Wealth, and exerted the Efforts of that Power."[114] The debate over the peace reflected this emerging commercial nationalism. "What part soever we cede or restore out of our conquests," one writer warned in 1763, "we diminish our trade and strength in proportion and give so much trade and strength to our enemies."[115]

But the nation's new power also posed darker possibilities. In 1763 the author of *Propositions for Improving the Manufactures, Agriculture and Commerce of Great Britain* sketched out the crossroads at which a victorious Britain had arrived:

As it has pleased Almighty God to put an end to this very expensive and bloody war, and to furnish us with the means of putting every part of this vast empire in a state of security, we should think no more of victory and conquest, but use our utmost endeavors to outdo each other in promoting the arts of peace; especially as the era is approaching, and near at hand, which will doom this mighty empire to future glory, or inevitable destruction.[116]

Along the less fortuitous path, overexpansion as well as fiscal and commercial destruction beckoned. Moral degeneration followed. Without strong public measures, William Knox predicted, Britain's citizens would become "a people luxurious and licentious, impatient of rule and despising all authority!" The resulting government would be "relaxed in every sinew [with] a corrupt selfish spirit prevading the whole!"[117]

Nervousness and confidence coexisted in Britons' attitudes toward their nation's future, their economy, and their own positions in a changing global order. The concept of empire embraced all these issues. The

114. Thomas Whately, *Considerations on the Trade and Finances of This Kingdom and on the Measures of Administration with respect to These Great National Objects since the Conclusion of the Peace* (London, 1769), 3; John Wilkes, ed., *Political Controversy* (London, 1763), 1:359; Spector, 88–129.

115. *Political Controversy*, 1:359. See also *Political Controversy*, 1:18, 2:134, and Edmund Burke, "Speech on the East Indian Settlement," 27 February 1769, in *The Writings and Speeches of Edmund Burke*, vol. 2, *Party, Parliament and the American Crisis, 1766–1774*, ed. Paul Langford (Oxford, 1981), 220.

116. *Propositions for Improving the Manufactures, Agriculture and Commerce of Great Britain* (London, 1763), 3–4.

117. William Knox, *The Present State of the Nation: Particularly with respect to Its Trade, Finances etc.* (London, 1768), 65–66.

discussions surrounding Britain's dominion mirrored a polity trying to come to terms with newfound international strength and unprecedented commercial success.

It is now possible to understand how imperial attitudes shaped the debate about the peace. George III, Bute, and several cabinet members sought more moderate settlement terms than many citizens demanded. Undoubtedly there were political reasons for Bute's conciliatory posture toward the French government: he wanted to end the war quickly. This would reduce Pitt's influence and consolidate the Favorite's ministerial and parliamentary power.[118] Why was the Great Commoner seemingly so indispensable? In 1761 and 1762 Pitt's following rested primarily on his role as chief architect of Britain's successful war effort. Politicians knew Pitt had intended to pursue a peace that retained most of Britain's conquests and severely weakened France. If in 1762 the former war minister represented the nation's keen imperial appetite, Bute's stance toward the peace appeared fastidious. That each of these men saw political benefits in such divergent positions was indicative of the cleavages in Britons' imperial attitudes.

Equally important from the perspective of historical hindsight were the terms in which Bute's cabinet members justified the treaty. By ending a costly and overextended conflict, these men argued, the Peace of Paris ensured Britain's lasting commercial glory. The territorial rewards secured by the settlement were extensive but manageable. The treaty enabled the nation to avoid the pitfalls that had snared Greece, Rome, and Spain. The Iberian nation, commented one observer, had "grasped conquests in a foreign country in the New World, so far above the Extent and Ability of the Mother Country, that she depeopled herself, and gradually declined from being the Dread of Europe and the first Naval Power to the State she is now in."[119] Those who supported the treaty argued that the country could not stomach a more ambitious peace. Britain could not afford to wage a longer war; it could not countenance extra taxes; it could not manage additional lands and commerce.

Opponents of the Peace of Paris argued strongly against this diffidence. The speeches, pamphlets, and demonstrations of protest attacking the administration's settlement disclose an almost intoxicating collective anticipation. For its unprecedented victory, Britain deserved numerous

118. Winstanley, 77–155; On George III's interest in ridding the cabinet of Pitt, see Bullion, "Prince of Wales," 450.

119. *Reasons for Keeping Guadeloupe*, 31.

commercial prizes: Canada, India, Martinique, Guadeloupe, Havana, Senegal, and more. Like its accomplishments, the country's rewards and empire were to be unparalleled.

These attitudes were fluid. Many of those, such as Grenville, who supported Bute's peace in early 1762 opposed it by the year's end. Other statesmen favoring a moderate peace in 1763 backed aggressive govern-ment intervention in India four years later. As Britons grappled with new imperial dilemmas and prospects, the contrasting inclinations of collective bulimia shaped official outlooks, discussion, and action.

In an era steeped in the value of history, some tried to articulate their ambivalence by referring to classical models. Eighteenth-century Englishmen understood politics as a science not unlike mathematics. They also held that human nature was unchanged across societies and centuries. From this perspective, history was regarded as a cache of political examples that ministers were obliged to study as a guide to their present conduct.[120] The *London Magazine* noted that history had positive and negative lessons to impart:

The rise and fall of kingdoms and states, the establishment of liberty and laws, or the encroachments of slavery and despotism, the flourishing of arts and sciences, or the prevalence of ignorance and barbarity; the ener-vating effects of luxury and vice, or the happy influence of temperance and virtue: These . . . are the contents of the historick page, and in these men of quality and fortune are deeply interested, as their conduct must necessarily have great influence in promoting the grandeur and happi-ness, or preventing the fall and misery of their country.[121]

The history of ancient Greece and the Roman Empire provided the most useful comparisons for eighteenth-century commentators.[122] A year after the Peace of Paris, Edward Gibbon decided to recount Rome's rise and fall.[123] Several years later Gibbon explained the success of his mag-num opus:

120. Brewer, *Party Ideology,* 257–58. See also Johnston, 516.
121. "Letters to a Young Nobleman," *London Magazine* 31 (1762), 76.
122. *Universal Magazine,* 45 (1769), 198. See also Richard Koebner, *Empire* (Cambridge, 1961), 193; David Hume, *On the Balance of Trade* (London, 1787), 71–72; Knox, 22; Adam Smith, *Inquiry into the Nature and Causes of the Wealth of Nations,* ed. Edwin Cannan, 2 vols. (Chicago, 1976), 2:106–7, 132.
123. Patricia Craddock, *Young Edward Gibbon: Gentleman of Letters* (Baltimore, 1982), 198.

History is the most popular species of writing, since it can adapt itself to the highest or the lowest capacity. I had chosen an illustrious subject. Rome is familiar to the schoolboy and the statesman . . . I am at a loss how to describe the success of the work without betraying the vanity of the writer. The first impression was exhausted in a few days; a second and third edition were scarcely adequate to the demand . . . My book was on every table, and almost on every toilette; the historian was crowned by the taste or fashion of the day.[124]

The resemblances between the ancient empire and Britain in the 1760s were clear. Both had been enormously successful in war and earned large, commercially prosperous empires. The citizens of each nation had perceived their economic and political power as supreme. The author of *The Present State of the British Empire* commented, "[Our] empire is more extensive and perhaps more powerful than any that had hitherto existed, even the great Roman Empire not excepted."[125]

In tandem with these heady identifications, less auspicious analogies persisted. Eighteenth-century Britons knew their wealth and power might well prove ephemeral. The earl of Shaftesbury dryly noted, "Once the summit is reached, the only direction is down."[126] If the fate of the classical empires was exemplary, political commentators reasoned, the very presence of wealth and international ascendancy subjected the body politic to a host of morally debilitating diseases. The riches of empire, as they had done in ancient Rome, would make men grow venal and surrender inescapably to the "Wantonness of Luxury."[127] The corruption of government followed inevitably from this collective loss of virtue.[128]

---

124. Edward Gibbon, *The Autobiography of Edward Gibbon, as Originally Edited by Lord Sheffield* (London, 1972), 179–80. Gibbon begins his preface to *The Decline and Fall* by justifying his choice of epochs for study, "The first of these periods may be traced from the age of Trajan and the Antonines, when the Roman monarchy, having attained its full strength and maturity, began to verge toward decline." *A History of the Decline and Fall of the Roman Empire*, ed. J. B. Bury, 7 vols. (London, 1909), 1:xxxix.

125. *The Present State of the British Empire in Europe, America, Africa and Asia* (London, 1768), 486.

126. Quoted in Johnston, 511. Contemporary French observers of British wealth had a similar prognosis for their national rival. See François Crouzet, "The Sources of English Wealth: Some French Views in the Eighteenth Century," in *Shipping, Trade and Commerce: Essays in Memory of Ralph Davis*, ed. P. L. Cottrell and D. H. Aldcroft (Leicester, 1981), 63.

127. William Strahan to David Hall, 7 October 1769, in "Some Further Letters of William Strahan, Printer," ed. J. E. Pomfret, *Pennsylvania Magazine of History and Biography* 60 (1936): 473.

128. Brewer, *Party Ideology*, 246; *Reflections on the Domestic Policy Proper to Be Observed on the Conclusion of the Peace* (London, 1763), 2–3.

In this immoral economy of manners and men, Britain's success was as precarious as that of the Roman Empire.[129] Even the eighteenth-century state's control over its colonies was subject to the snares of imperial supremacy: "That Corruption, Luxury and a general Decay of Religion, Piety, Industry, and Love for our Country may in Time, weaken the Strength, and reduce *Great Britain* to a State of Slavery; and that there may hereafter rise up a vast Empire of our Brethren in *North America* with Power to give Laws to all the World, are Events that I won't pretend to affirm or Deny."[130]

The risks and possibilities of empire had never seemed as great as they did to Britons in 1763. At this juncture, ministers looked back to former leading nations for guidance. In ancient Rome, the Ottoman Empire and sixteenth-century Spain, they saw what must have appeared to be an inexorable link between the rise and fall of the great powers. In this sense history sustained Britons' collective ambitions and fears. Not before in the eighteenth century had these contrasting inclinations toward imperial authority been so clearly articulated in public discourse.

Within a complicated political order, ministers and MPs debated what kind of empire Britain would have. At a variety of levels, this discussion was affected by statesmen's conflicted views of empire. Even the debates about parliamentary sovereignty mirrored a fundamental ambivalence about the mother country's power. The deeper statesmen dug into questions of legislative authority, the more uncertain they grew about the implications of their findings. On the one hand, metropolitan officials hoped that the political relationship between Britain and the North American colonies would be resolved on terms satisfactory to all parties. On the other hand, they strongly feared that continued examination of that relationship would yield results destructive to the very structure of the empire.[131]

The Seven Years War and the peace that concluded it piqued citizens' expectations regarding prosperity and global preeminence. In the war's aftermath, Britons faced both the pride and the anxiety of place. In Britain as in other nations, these contrasting attitudes would influence national strategy and economic performance down to our own time.

---

129. Knox, 65–66. See also *Detection of the False Reasons and Facts*, 50; Owen Ruffhead, *Considerations on the Present Dangerous Crisis* (London, 1763), 37; *Parliamentary History*, 17:671–72; *An Application of Political Rules to Great Britain, Ireland and America* (London, 1766), 17–20.

130. *A Detection of the False Reasons and Facts*, 50.

131. See Jack P. Greene, *Peripheries and the Center: Constitutional Development in the Extended Politics of the British Empire and the United States, 1607–1788* (Athens, Ga., 1986), 105.

 SIX

Extending Commerce and Improving Revenue

Repeal of the Stamp Act

IN AUTUMN 1765 the Rockingham administration took up consideration of the recently enacted Stamp Act and North American reaction to this legislation. First Lord of Treasury Rockingham and his ministers were alarmed by colonial resistance to the revenue-raising measure.[1] Riots had broken out in New England, with the Massachusetts stamp distributor hung in effigy. Various colonial assemblies had voted resolves against the Stamp Act, and most of the colonies had organized boycotts of British imports to protest the tax measure. These efforts at disrupting commerce seemed to be successful: by November British trade to North America had fallen off significantly. Observers on both sides of the Atlantic attributed this decline to the repercussions of the stamp tax.

Through the autumn, British manufacturers and merchants involved in North American trade had become increasingly nervous about their business. In November they began making their upset known to various government officials. George Savile, a Yorkshire MP and a friend of Rockingham, summarized British commercial opinion about the Stamp Act's economic consequences: "[These men of commerce] speak as igno-

---

1. On British reaction to the crisis in America and its representation in the London press, see P. D. G. Thomas, *British Politics and the Stamp Act Crisis: The First Phase of the American Revolution, 1763–1767* (Oxford, 1975), 131–53.

rant men. Our trade is hurt, what the devil have you been a doing? For our part, we don't pretend to understand your politics and American matters, but our trade is hurt; pray remedy it, and a plague of you if you wont."[2]

For economic and political reasons, the prime minister and his supporters could not ignore these commercial distress signals. Rockingham, his chief financial minister, William Dowdeswell, and Edmund Burke were certain that colonial reactions to the Stamp Act accounted for the recent decline in British trade to North America. In 1765 British exports to America had fallen by 15 percent.[3] These same men were also sure they could capitalize on the political opportunities the stamp tax crisis presented. One prospect involved cultivating extraparliamentary support. In the chaotic political landscape of the 1760s, Burke and other Rockingham Whigs knew that any government or opposition "[was] crippled if it [could] obtain no kind of support out of doors."[4] Administration officials realized that this support could come from the men of movable property, especially manufacturers in provincial cities, who were most concerned about the stamp tax crisis. Representatives of London commercial and financial institutions, such as the Bank of England or the East India Company, with whom government officials had long consulted and dealt, had not registered significant interest. The economic consequences of the Stamp Act brought the ministry into close contact with new, potentially significant constituencies.

The problems surrounding the stamp levy also presented the Rockinghams with the chance to increase their parliamentary strength. By emphasizing the role of the Grenville administration in enacting what proved to be a commercially disastrous measure, the first lord and his followers hoped to discredit their predecessors. In addition, the Rockinghams wanted to distinguish themselves politically from other factions and gain the backing of independent MPs. Through November and December of 1765, administration officials worked to establish a causal chain between Grenville's legislation, colonial disorder, and British commercial distress.[5]

2. George Savile to Lord Rockingham, 1 November 1765, quoted in *Memoirs of the Marquis of Rockingham*, ed. George Thomas, earl of Albemarle, 2 vols. (London, 1852), 1:253.

3. Wentworth-Woodhouse Muniments (hereafter WWM), Sheffield City Library, R61/9.

4. Quoted in Lucy Sutherland, "Edmund Burke and the First Rockingham Ministry," *English Historical Review* 47 (1932): 47.

5. Paul Langford, *The First Rockingham Administration, 1765–1766* (Oxford, 1973), 110–11.

The Rockingham Whigs intended to fashion a political strategy and a policy response to the Stamp Act crisis based on this perceived sequence of events.

To do this, they knew they would need extensive extraparliamentary support. They soon found it. Several months earlier Barlow Trecothick, a London merchant and MP, and other manufacturers and merchants from around the country had organized a general commercial response to the Stamp Act. In protest against the tax and the American Mutiny Act, the British businessmen had formed the London North American Merchants Committee. Under the direction of Trecothick, committee members had gathered information about the state of North American trade. In early November Trecothick wrote to Rockingham, forecasting commercial disaster in Britain if swift action was not taken by the government. Because the colonists seemingly were determined not to accept the stamp tax, the lobbyist reasoned, all colonial business requiring stamps would cease, the British export market in North America would collapse under the weight of colonial nonimportation agreements, and economic havoc would reign in London, Bristol, Birmingham, and other cities dependent on this imperial commerce:

These accumulated disappointments must prov[e] fatal to many British merchants trading to America, who will be disabled from paying their Engagements here . . . Even those of them that can stand the present shock, will be under the necessity of declining further exports, so that a total stop must be put to all purchases of Manufactures for a Country whence no returns can be expected. From this State it naturally and unavoidably follows that an exceedingly great number of manufacturers are soon to be without Employ and of course without Bread! . . .

[H]ere I must stop, not daring to pursue any further the dreadful Chain of Consequences . . . My great fear is that too great Delay and Caution in administering the Remedy may render the Disasters of this embarrassed nation incurable; and even an instant administration may therefore be deemed accountable for Effects proceding from the Error of their Predecessors.[6]

As a political appeal, this letter was extremely effective. Almost immediately, Rockingham was convinced of the need for ministerial action.[7] He

6. Barlow Trecothick to Lord Rockingham, 7 November 1765, WWM, R43/8.
7. Langford, 111.

agreed to meet with Trecothick. The prime minister also began to search for evidence to substantiate the case against the Stamp Act.

The North American Merchants Committee had already begun putting this evidence together. In December committee members dispatched a circular letter to the chief magistrates of thirty outports and manufacturing towns, urging local manufacturers and merchants to pressure their MPs for repeal of the North American stamp levy. In terms that demonstrate their emerging political confidence, committee members wrote:

As the gentlemen of your city and almost every other maritime and manufacturing part of these Kingdoms must be affected by the distresses of North American commerce we have thought it our duty to acquaint you . . . with our proceedings, as well as to ask your concurrence and assistance in support of a regular application to Parliament or otherwise by a petition from your body and by all the interest you can make with your own Members and with the Members in your neighbourhood, who with all other land owners we think greatly interested in the prosperity of trade and manufactures from which so great an additional value is derived to their property.[8]

Response to the letter was swift. In Birmingham, amid significant anxiety about unemployment, manufacturers met and produced a petition to Parliament as well as letters to all regional MPs and peers.[9] Southwest of the Midlands in Bristol, men like William Reeve, head of the Society of Merchant Adventurers, requested that the legislature revoke the Stamp Act. Petitions poured into Parliament from over twenty cities, including Liverpool, Manchester, Halifax, Leeds, Sheffield, Nottingham, Glasgow, Lancaster, Bradford, and other key industrial areas. These appeals outlined the importance of North American trade to local employment and chronicled the current economic malaise, attributing this affliction to the Stamp Act. All the petitions underscored the urgent necessity for government action. As John Milnes, a Yorkshire woolen maker, wrote to Rockingham, "Steps need to be taken to retrieve the trade and export of our Manufactures to those parts. [T]he want thereof is pretty severely felt in the most principal manufacturing places through the Kingdom."[10]

8. Add. MSS 22,358, fol. 52.
9. Langford, 120.
10. John Milnes to Lord Rockingham, 24 November 1765, WWM, R24/37.

Petitions for repeal of the stamp tax, 1766. *Journals of the House of Commons.*

During December and January, Rockingham and his ministers closely followed the commercial campaign for repeal of the stamp tax and debated what action to take. After almost eight weeks of discussion with Trecothick, Samuel Garbett—a Birmingham industrialist—and other business representatives, the first lord and his colleagues decided on a two-pronged strategy.[11] They would couple repeal of the stamp tax with a declaration that affirmed Parliament's right to tax the colonies. These twin policy resolutions reflected the political assessments of the prime minister, Dowdeswell, and other supporters. The Rockingham Whigs realized the upcoming legislative discussion of the Stamp Act crisis was important. They knew a recommendation to repeal would be highly controversial. "There are wonderful materials of combustion at hand; and surely, since this monarchy, a more material point never came under the consideration of Parliament," was Burke's evaluation.[12]

Making repeal acceptable to a public and a legislature angered and horrified by the violence of colonial protests against British laws would not be easy. Most British politicians and observers understood that the legislature's authority to tax the colonies was an important constitutional principle, one that critically affected imperial governance. The intemperance with which the colonies had repudiated this principle necessitated its assertion.[13] The proposed Declaratory Act was a response to Britons' consensus on legislative authority, mirroring the ubiquitous, hitherto unstated faith of the political nation in the sovereignty of Parliament. As one minor official said, "The only thing I am clear in, and that I have been from the beginning, is, that the Right of the British Legislature to tax the Colonies is clear and uncontestable, and that it must not, cannot be given up, without annihilating the British Constitution in British America."[14]

Articulating this right and enforcing it, however, were, as the Rockingham Whigs realized, two very different objectives. The Declaratory Act defended the mother country's legislative supremacy over the colonies. Repeal of the Stamp Act attempted to avoid the violence and economic adversity involved in the practical application of this sovereignty. Politi-

11. On ministerial discord over repeal and the evolution of the administration's posture toward the Stamp Act, see Langford, 125–26; Thomas, 154–84.

12. Edmund Burke to Charles O'Hara, 31 December 1765, in *The Correspondence of Edmund Burke*, vol. 1, *April 1744–June 1768*, ed. Thomas W. Copeland (Chicago, 1958), 229.

13. Langford, 149.

14. Historical Manuscript Commission, 24 December 1765, Westwood Underwood MSS, series 10, 399, quoted in Langford, 150.

cally, the ministers knew they could not hope to revoke the Stamp Act without avowing parliamentary authority. A colonial observer explained the dynamics of legislative opinion: "Mr. Conway [one of two secretaries of state] told me there were 3 parties in the House, one was severe method, the other for a Repeal but for previous resolves to assert the right and Power of Parliament, the third which includes the ministry for a Repeal without any previous resolutions at all but in Order to secure the repeal they were obliged to agree to the resolves in order to secure a majority for the Repeal."[15]

On the last day of January 1766, Parliament approved the resolution that was to become the Declaratory Act. The legislature was now ready to consider repealing the Stamp Act. Having affirmed the legislature's right to tax the colonies, administration efforts now focused on demonstrating the commercial consequences of enforcing that power.[16] Organized by the North American Merchants Committee, other lobbying groups, and the Rockingham ministry, an immense flood of propaganda supporting repeal poured out from London and other cities. Cartoons, newspaper articles, pamphlets, and other polemics highlighted the disastrous economic repercussions of the Stamp Act. By mid-February it seemed to Bristol merchant Henry Cruger that previously uncommitted MPs and others were moving behind the administration: "The Vox Populi now begins to gain ground, and I think since the Legality of Taxation is allowed, the Act will be repeal'd upon the Grounds of *Expediency*."[17]

The administration concentrated on persuading members of Parliament of the importance of repeal. In a carefully orchestrated campaign, Rockingham and his ministers worked closely with various lobbyists. Together, the government and the business representatives brought forward numerous witnesses and two dozen petitions from manufacturers and merchants in provincial cities. The witnesses and written appeals

15. "Letters of Dennys De Berdt, 1757–1770," *Publications of the Colonial Society of Massachusetts* 13 (1910–11): 312.

16. Undoubtedly the Rockinghams had political reasons for supporting Parliament's authority to tax the colonies. But as Paul Langford has pointed out, Rockingham and his followers agreed in principle as well that the British legislature's right to tax the colonies was supreme. In this respect they differed significantly from William Pitt and his allies. See Paul Langford, "The Rockingham Whigs and America, 1767–1773," in *Statesmen, Scholars and Merchants: Essays in Eighteenth Century History Presented to Dame Lucy Sutherland*, ed. Anne Whiteman, J. S. Bromley, and P. G. M. Dickson (Oxford, 1973), 135–52.

17. Henry Cruger Jr. to Henry Cruger Sr., 14 February 1766, in *Commerce of Rhode Island, 1726–1800*, vol. 1, *1726–1774*, Collections of the Massachusetts Historical Society, 7th ser., 9 (1914): 142.

were chosen to focus legislative attention on the commercial harms of the stamp tax and the unanimity of mercantile opposition to it. On 12 February 1766 Robert Dawson, a worsted manufacturer from Leeds, testified before the Commons that he had dismissed nearly a thousand hands. He was forced to fire these workers, he explained, because since August 1765 he had "not experienced a single order from America."[18] A merchant from Liverpool, William Halliday, said that almost all the spring orders of an export trade worth £240,000 annually had been withdrawn because of colonial opposition to the Stamp Act.[19] In Manchester, according to Robert Hamilton, a resident merchant, as many as 2,400 people were out of work as a result of the sluggish North American exchange.[20]

Nineteen well-rehearsed witnesses came before the House. Much of this testimony centered on the employment effects of the stamp tax. As contemporary observers understood, there were political reasons for this particular point of emphasis. The Rockinghams were eager to appeal to independent MPs as well as to the men of movable property. One commentator noted the political significance of attributing unemployment in London and provincial cities to the Stamp Act:

A Manufacturer from Leeds was order'd to the Barr, who said, since the Stagnation of the American Trade he has been constrained to turn off 300 Families of 600 he constantly employ'd. [T]his fact will have great weight when added to many more evidences of the like kind. The Country Members are somewhat alarmed at so many People losing Employ, if anything repeals the Act, it must be this. [T]he present Ministry see and have declared the *Expediency* of repealing on *this ground*. [I]f the late Ministers come in again, and enforce the Act, they will have 20,000 unemployed Poor in a suppliant manner petitioning a Repeal of the S[tamp] Act, otherwise they must starve.[21]

As a corollary to the concerns about rising unemployment, administration officials and lobbyists also raised the issue of colonial manufacturing capabilities. Several witnesses, including Benjamin Franklin, contended that if Americans consistently refused to buy British manufactures, colonists would have no choice but to make similar goods themselves. This

18. Commons debate, 12 February 1766, Add. MSS 33,030, fols. 141–142.
19. Commons debate, 13 February 1766, Add. MSS 30,030 fol. 146.
20. Ibid., fol. 154.
21. Cruger, 140.

would cause permanent damage to British manufacturing and mercantile concerns.[22] To many MPs, including the country gentlemen, the implications of the evidence presented to Parliament were clear: Britain's current economic troubles, including significant unemployment in the nation's manufacturing trades, were directly attributable to colonial disturbances caused by the Stamp Act. As important, legislators understood that these disturbances threatened the long-term commercial health of the mother country.

George Grenville, leader of the legislative opposition to repeal, could not muster a convincing refutation to the administration's evidence. On 4 March the Commons voted 250 to 122 to revoke the Stamp Act. The repeal received the royal assent in late March, its preamble demonstrating the statute's political justification: "The Continuance of the said Act would be attended with many Inconveniencies, and may be productive of Consequences greatly detrimental to the Commercial Interests of these Kingdoms."[23] Horace Walpole, a chronicler of eighteenth-century politics, was more colloquial in explaining Parliament's decision. "It was the clamour of trade, of the merchants, and of the manufacturing towns, that had borne down all opposition."[24]

Building on the success of the repeal, government ministers and lobbyists now extended their parliamentary campaign to further ease the burdens imposed on American commerce by the Grenville administration.[25] Lobbyists hoped to relax the regulations governing colonial trade with foreign islands, which the Grenville ministry had strengthened in 1764 and early 1765. After a series of negotiations, Trecothick and other British merchants involved in North American trade joined forces with a group of traders with West Indian interests.[26] For several weeks representatives of the North American Merchants and West India Committees hammered out a revision of Grenville's commercial legislation palatable to both groups. Although the Rockingham ministry supported revision of Grenville's program, Treasury and Board of Trade officials played virtually no role in the businessmen's discussions. As historian Paul Langford has noted, "In the dying months of the Rockingham Ministry, the

22. Benjamin Franklin, Commons debate, 13 February 1766, Add. MSS 33,030, fol. 148.

23. *Statutes at Large*, 7, 6 George III, c. 11.

24. Horace Walpole, *Memoirs of the Reign of George III*, 4 vols. (London, 1894), 2:211–12.

25. Jack Sosin, *Agents and Merchants: British Colonial Policy and the Origins of the American Revolution, 1763–1775* (Lincoln, Neb., 1965), 81.

26. On these negotiations, see Langford, *First Rockingham Administration*, 203–5.

The Repeal, or The Funeral of Miss Ame-Stamp. British Museum Catalogue 4140. Printed 1766. This print depicts the commercial rationale behind Parliament's decision to repeal the American stamp tax. Along the banks of the Thames, British warehouses, named for the nation's manufacturing towns, pile up with goods that cannot be sold in the colonies because of the embargo. In the background three ships, the *Rockingham, Grafton,* and *Conway,* stand ready to carry British goods to America when the stamp tax has been repealed and properly buried. The mourners for the levy cluster around Mr. Stamper, who carries the now-repealed act toward a tomb already inhabited by failed legislation. The small numbers on the flags and the rowboats in the background are the Lords (105 and 71) and Commons (250 to 122) vote totals on repeal.

direction of colonial policy passed largely into the hands of the mercantile pressure groups; at no time in the eighteenth century were Administration and Parliament more at the command of commercial interests than in the spring of 1766."[27]

In May the North American and West Indian Committees made their legislative recommendations. The centerpiece of the lobbyists' joint initiative was the opening of free ports in Jamaica and Dominica. The proposed legislation ran directly counter to the principles of the Navigation Acts, which since their enactment in the later seventeenth century, had served as the overarching regulatory framework for imperial trade policy. The legislation put forward by the two lobbying groups legalized Spanish American trade with Jamaica, an important source of raw materials and bullion as well as a key market for British manufactures. Provision of a free port in Dominica effectively allowed the formerly illicit trade between the New England colonies and the French West Indian islands. These islands bought American produce in return for cheap molasses and sugar, crucial elements in the fishery and slave trades.[28] Cruger described parliamentary perspectives on these novel proposals: "[MPs'] Eyes are at last open'd and they seem convinc'd what vast Benefit will accrue to this Kingdom by giving [North American colonists] almost an unlimited trade, so farr as doth not interfere with British Manufactures."[29]

Initially West Indian traders were strongly opposed to freer trade between British colonies and foreign islands in the Caribbean. Opening commercial relations between Massachusetts and the French colony of Martinique threatened West Indian interests in maintaining high prices for British-grown sugars. West Indian traders countenanced free ports in exchange for a reduction in the duty on English sugar imported to North America. They also obtained a provision requiring that all sugar traveling to England via Dominica or North America be treated as foreign and taxed accordingly. The provision effectively lowered the relative price of the commodity grown by British planters in the West Indies and shipped directly to Britain.

In late May the Rockingham administration presented this program of commercial reforms to Parliament. Before a thinly attended House Grenville could marshal little opposition to the measures. They passed

27. Ibid., 200.
28. Ibid., 201.
29. Cruger, 143.

both houses easily, receiving the royal assent in early June. For the men of movable property, represented by Trecothick, Garbett, and others, it was a significant victory. The London North American Merchants Committee noted the significance of the free ports legislation:

We consider [them] as the basis of an extensive system of Trade between Great Britain and her Colonies framed on liberal principles of reciprocal Advantage, relieving the Colonies from injudicious restrictions and severe Duties, enlarging old, and opening to them, new Channels of Commerce, and by securing to Great Britain an increasing consumption of her Manufactures, and of consequence an extension of her Navigation and Revenue.[30]

Other contemporary observers recognized the novelty of this experiment in free trade. As John Yorke, lord of the admiralty, said to another MP, "I see they are oversetting every American idea that ever was established."[31] According to Burke, the Rockingham ministry and organized business interests had succeeded in "demolishing the whole Grenvillian Fabrick" of commercial policy.[32]

What were the short- and longer-term political implications of the administration's strategy? In the months after the Stamp Act's repeal and passage of the free ports legislation, Rockingham received scores of grateful letters from British manufacturers and merchants. From all over Britain, "Sons of Traders and Liberty" thanked the prime minister and

acknowledge[d] the uncommon zeal of Attention shown by his Lordship to the Commercial Interest of this Nation. [T]hey hope[d] and trust[ed] that under the reviving Showers of his Lordship's paternal care and Oversight, the seeds now intended to be sown may another year spring up and open to Great Britain (and her Colonies) a *new* and Beneficial Branch of Commerce whereby her Manufactures and her Navigation may be increased and extended and Her children shout for Joy.[33]

30. 13 June 1766, "London Merchants on the Stamp Act Repeal," *Proceedings of the Massachusetts Historical Society* 55 (1921–22): 220.

31. John Yorke to the earl of Hardwicke, 19 May 1766, Add. MSS 35,374, fol. 291.

32. Edmund Burke to Charles O'Hara, 23, 24 April 1766, in *Correspondence of Edmund Burke*, 1:252.

33. 30 April 1766, WWM, R58/6.

These letters continued to reach the Yorkshire politician even after his administration fell from power in midsummer. Out of office, Rockingham, Dowdeswell, and Burke recognized the longer-standing political benefits of their new commercial associations. Most of these affiliations were originally initiated by lobbyists such as Trecothick and Reeve. But this does not diminish the Rockinghams' political savvy. Late in 1765 a unique political opportunity presented itself to the Rockingham Whigs. They grabbed it, claiming the trading classes as their natural constituencies and promising that "as it ever will be [our] Desire so shall it be [our] constant attention . . . to promote the commercial Interests" of the country.[34] For the next ten years the championship of commerce was to become an important tool and policy guide in the Rockingham Whigs' struggle for parliamentary influence. In the autumn of 1766, Burke himself intimated as much. Celebrating the late ministry, he wrote:

Scarcely had [the Rockinghams] entered into office, when letters arrived from all parts of America, making loud complaints, backed by strong reasons, against several of the principal regulations of the [Grenville] ministry, as threatening destruction to many valuable branches of commerce. These were attended with representations from many merchants and capital manufacturers at home, who had all their interests involved in the support of lawful trade . . . If the opinion and wish of the landed interest is a motive, and it is a fair and just one, for taking away a real and large revenue, the desire of the trading interest of England ought to be just ground for taking away a tax.[35]

As he understood, there was more to the repeal of the Stamp Act and the enactment of free ports in the West Indies than a reversal of imperial trade policy. Convinced of the power of commerce in maintaining the nation's international stature and well versed in the doctrines of political economy, government officials were interested in securing colonial markets and revenues. The relative importance of these two often conflicting policy objectives depended on political factors and on the particular macroeconomic context in which imperial events unfolded. Political and

34. Lord Rockingham to Lancaster manufacturers and merchants, September 1766, WWM, R59/1.

35. Edmund Burke, "Observations on a Late State of the Nation," in *The Writings and Speeches of Edmund Burke*, vol. 2, *Party, Parliament and the American Crisis, 1766–1774*, ed. Paul Langford (Oxford, 1981), 189–91. See also Burke's "Short Account of a Late Administration," in *Writings and Speeches of Edmund Burke*, ed. Langford, 2:55.

economic considerations also affected the amount of government regulation administered to achieve policy goals. In 1764 and 1765 most MPs
had approved the Stamp Act and other commercial legislation directed
toward increasing and improving revenue collection from the colonies.
In 1766 an economic recession piqued imperial anxieties in Britain.
Worries about commercial hardship, unemployment, and social unrest
proliferated: ministers, MPs, and the larger political nation agreed that
the government had to do something.

Political, economic, and perceptual factors influenced the choice of
government action. During the debates surrounding the repeal of the
Stamp Act, new commercial forces pushed onto the stage of national
politics. In London, Wakefield, Liverpool, and elsewhere, these men of
movable property had been gaining organizational cohesion throughout
the 1740s and 1750s. The urgency of imperial issues in the 1760s, in
tandem with novel arrangements in the sphere of elite politics, provided
these men with new opportunities to use their political skills. At the same
time, macroeconomic transition expanded their numbers, sharpened
their political focus, and strengthened their importance in the eyes of
established politicians. In 1765 and 1766 the Rockingham Whigs capital-
ized on this emerging influence; the prime minister and his supporters
were eager for new constituencies as well as for a means of discrediting
their most viable political opponents. Administration officials seized on
the arguments of various commercial interests, especially provincial manufacturers, using these arguments to formulate a policy response to the
Stamp Act as well as to secure their parliamentary position in a fractious
environment. By supporting repeal of the stamp tax, the Rockingham
Whigs committed themselves to securing colonial markets and forgoing
colonial revenues. In doing so, they mapped out a political strategy they
were to use with varying success over the ensuing decade.

Before Parliament in 1766, this tactic paid off handsomely. Uncertain
about the stability of the imperial economy, MPs were quick to believe the
administration's assertions and manufacturers' testimony that Britain's
commerce with North America was on the verge of collapse. These
apprehensions were undoubtedly confirmed, and perhaps exacerbated,
by legislators' knowledge of regional grain riots, rising unemployment,
and a nationwide financial crisis. Well on the road to economic growth,
in 1766 Britain suffered a minor puncture. Unemployment rose; exports
declined; output and real incomes grew less rapidly. This distress was
not caused, as economic historians now know, by colonial boycotts or a

slump in North American trade as a result of the Stamp Act, but rather by a far-reaching European financial crisis and a domestic recession.

But from the vantage point of MPs in 1766, trepidation about dominion appeared economically valid. The presence of such perceptions helps explain the success of the administration's campaign for repeal of the Stamp Act. Focused on the importance of imperial trade and its relation to domestic employment issues, this campaign was conducted along economic lines that seemed at times surprisingly modern. Unemployment was rising; transatlantic commerce was failing. The government would have to do something, and nothing short of a complete reversal of imperial policy would rescue the capricious economy of empire.

The political corollary to the repeal of the Stamp Act was the enactment of free ports in the Caribbean. Here too imperial politics, political economy, and the larger macroeconomic context interacted to condition government decisions. When Parliament decided, on the recommendation of two commercial lobbies, to sanction economic interchange between the North American colonies and French and Spanish islands in the West Indies, it was not just dismantling the policy edifice that it and the Grenville ministry had so recently constructed. The legislature was also embarking on a limited experiment in free trade. Some ten years before Adam Smith would take the doctrines of mercantilism to task and half a century before David Ricardo would articulate the theory of comparative advantage, MPs decided that the prosperity of the imperial economy was best promoted by *not* regulating all aspects of colonial exchange. In reaching this conclusion, legislators were undoubtedly influenced by the same economic factors that governed their decision to reverse the Stamp Act. Evidence of rising domestic unemployment, local social unrest, and regional commercial adversity convinced a majority of MPs that past policies were to blame. Revenues and specific trade regulation were sacrificed on the political altar of markets and the health of the imperial economy.

In deciding to reverse the stamp levy and dismantle much of Grenville's Sugar Act, Parliament and the political nation faced explicitly for the first time an issue they were to wrestle with until 1776: Who ultimately controlled the governance of this newly enlarged imperium, and how was this authority to be exercised? In the wake of an expensive victory, the commercial and fiscal imperatives of political economy gave birth to a new species of concerns about parliamentary sovereignty. In 1766 government officials, MPs, and the political nation decided that if Parliament was to be the supreme court in adjudicating the power of commerce, how and to what extent that sovereignty was to be executed were less easily resolved. With reference to North America and India, Britons were to debate these issues—often with portentous results—for the rest of the century and beyond.

The East India Company Regulating Act of 1773

Until the Seven Years War, Britain's dealings in India had centered on the trading operations of the East India Company. Since the early seventeenth century, the Company had functioned as a commercial monopoly, controlling goods and specie exchange between Britain and India. By the outbreak of war in 1756, the chartered concern had trading bases at Madras, Calcutta, and Bombay, a posting station in Sumatra, and a significant interest at Canton in the China tea trade.[36] From these eastern locations, Company servants purchased tea, textiles, saltpeter, and other goods for import into Britain. Export cargoes to India comprised principally woolen goods, copper, lead, tin, iron, steel, and bullion.[37]

Under Company control, British trade with the East Indies had grown continuously throughout the first part of the eighteenth century. Imports from the subcontinent had risen almost 300 percent from 1700 to 1750. Exports had climbed even faster, increasing sevenfold during the same period.[38] This commercial expansion was part of a longer-term shift in Britain's trading patterns. Since the first decades of the eighteenth century, British colonial interchange had steadily supplanted trade with Europe.[39] For most of the period, the mother country's commerce with America outpaced that with the Far East.[40] But by the middle decades of

36. On the extension of the East India Company's activities in the eighteenth century, see P. J. Marshall, "British Expansion in India in the Eighteenth Century: A Historical Revision," *History* 60 (1975): 28–43, and idem, *Bengal: The British Bridgehead: Eastern India, 1740–1818* (Cambridge, 1987).

37. Townshend Papers, Clements Library, 8/38/62; H. V. Bowen, *Revenue and Reform: The Indian Problem in British Politics, 1757–1773* (Cambridge, 1991), 110.

38. B. R. Mitchell and Phyllis Deane, *Abstract of Historical Statistics* (Cambridge, 1962), 312. Trade figures for the East Indies include Asia.

39. R. P. Thomas and D. N. McCloskey, "Overseas Trade and Empire, 1700–1860," in *The Economic History of Britain since 1700*, vol. 1, *1700–1860*, ed. Roderick Floud and Donald McCloskey (Cambridge, 1981), 87–102; Ralph Davis, "English Foreign Trade, 1700–1774," *Economic History Review* 15 (1962–63): 285–303.

40. Both the volume and growth rate of Britain's trade with North America and the West Indies exceeded those with India; see Mitchell and Deane, 312; Thomas and McCloskey, 91.

the century, political economists and politicians recognized the important role East Indian trade played in the imperial economy.[41]

The Seven Years War and its aftermath radically altered the Company's fortunes in India. Between the battle of Plassey in 1757 and Robert Clive's assumption of the *diwani* in 1765, a series of military victories had gained the concern enormous territorial, political, and economic authority on the subcontinent. By the mid-1760s, not only had the French presence in India been ousted, but specific local rulers had been over-thrown and replaced with dependent viceroys. As a consequence, the East India Company controlled the provinces of Bengal, Bihar, and Orissa, emerging as the preeminent force in the lower Ganges valley. In southeastern India the British company exercised significant influence through its relationship with the ruler of the Carnatic. To protect these positions, the East India Company maintained a large, costly army on the subcontinent. Over the course of eight years, the trading concern had become a near sovereign power in key regions of India.

The transformation in the Company's status did not go unnoticed in Britain. By 1766, when news of Clive's assumption of the *diwani* reached London, many government officials recognized the significance of the trading concern's achievements. As Thomas Pownall, an MP and imperial commentator, noted:

The exercise of the sovereignty of populous and extensive dominions in the East Indies, have come into the hands of the East India company; the revenues of these dominions are actually in the possession of this company; and in consequence of power arising from this exercise of sovereignty, and of influence from this possession of the revenues, the same company have, as merchants, while they acted as sovereigns, carried on an absolute monopoly of the commerce of one of the richest manufacturing countries in the world. The profits of this trade have been so great that difficulty and embarrassment have arisen how to invest, or bring home the balance of it.[42]

41. See, for example, *The Importance of the British Dominions in India Stated, and Compared with That in America* (London, 1770); Thomas Mortimer, *The Elements of Commerce, Politics and Finances in Three Treatises on Those Important Subjects* (London, 1772), 130–31; "Thoughts on the Present State of the East India Company," Shelburne Papers, Clements Library, 90/243; Liverpool Papers, Add. MSS 38,397, fols. 82–91; Commons debate, 27 February 1769, Cavendish Diary, Egerton MSS 218, fols. 105–7.

42. Thomas Pownall, *The Right, Interest, and Duty, of the State, as Concerned in the Affairs of the East Indies* (London, 1773), 5–6.

Statesmen concerned with imperial governance realized that the Company's sovereignty had important implications. Some of these were financial: its assumption of territorial and customs revenues in the provinces of Bengal, Bihar, and Orissa was valued at over £1.6 million a year.[43] Many Britons viewed these revenues as a national resource.[44] The earl of Chatham and others were certain these funds should be used to relieve the state's postwar fiscal burdens—to help finance the huge national debt and the costs of governing Britain's expanded dominions. Totaling almost £6 million annually, these expenses equaled over 60 percent of government income.[45]

Concerned in 1767 to secure an external revenue source, MPs had supported a state agreement with the Company. Under the act's terms, the East India Company had paid the Treasury £400,000 annually for two years and consented to limit dividends to 10 percent of the concern's nominal trading capital.[46] In 1769 the government's agreement with the Company had been renewed under terms generally similar to the original act. The charter was extended five years, and the annual £400,000 payment to the Treasury was continued. The Company was also required to lend any surplus cash, net of business debts, to the state at 2 percent interest. Fearful that officials at India House would neglect the concern's trading functions in favor of revenue collection, administration officials required the Company to adhere to an annual export floor.[47] Under the terms of the settlement, the state allowed it to raise its stock dividend to

43. Robert Clive to the Court of Directors, 30 September 1765, *Fort William-India House Correspondence*, vol. 4, *1764–1766*, ed. C. S. Srinivasachari (Delhi, 1962), 337.

44. See, for example, William Beckford's parliamentary speech of 9 December 1766. According to the MP, the East India Company acquisitions were "a source of riches that ought to be converted to national advantage;" quoted in H. V. Bowen, "British Politics and the East India Company, 1766–1773" (Ph.D. diss., University of Wales, 1986), 307.

45. In 1767 annual service charges on the national debt (£131 million) totaled £4.6 million (Mitchell and Deane, 390). Estimates of military expenses in North America and India varied between £1.3 million and £2.5 million. *Parliamentary Diaries of Nathaniel Ryder, 1764–1767*, ed. P. D. G. Thomas (London, 1969), 235; Bowen, *Revenue and Reform*, 12; Alexander Dow to the earl of Shelburne, 6 October 1768, Shelburne Papers, Clements Library, 99/114. Government income figures are from Mitchell and Deane, 388.

46. Dividend payments were made biannually and represented a conversion by Company directors of a portion of the Company's trading profits into a specific percentage of its nominal trading capital. H. V. Bowen, "Investment and Empire in the Later Eighteenth Century: East India Stockholding, 1756–1791," *Economic History Review*, 2d ser., 42 (1989): 190.

47. On revenue collection supplanting the Company's export trade, see North's remarks in Commons debate, 27 February 1769, Cavendish Diary, Egerton MSS 218, fol. 106. The Company agreed to export British goods equal to the average annual export value of the past five years (Bowen, *Revenue and Reform*, 111–12).

a maximum of 12.5 percent.[48] The legislation of 1769, like that of two years earlier, committed the British government to a growing stake in the operations of the East India Company, both at home and abroad.[49]

In addition to the fiscal implications of the East India Company's new authority, there were other indirect financial consequences. East India Company stock was a critical part of the London market: in 1769 it was worth approximately £11 million and constituted a significant pool of investment capital.[50] This stock was not held primarily by the landed aristocracy, as historian H. V. Bowen has demonstrated.[51] Bankers, merchants, retailers, and other members of the mercantile and professional classes owned East India assets and were thus concerned with its fluctuations. Anything that affected the price of East India stock had potentially larger political and economic ramifications. As George Grenville said before Parliament,

What condition will you be in, when a war [in India] breaks out! [Some] have seen East India stock fall before, but never from such a height to nothing. This [stock] is an object of 11 millions of money. If, in the commencement of that war, the whole 11 millions should be blown into the air at once—if that misfortune should befall you—do you believe that the City of London would lose 11 million without threatening the [entire stock market] at once. This is, perhaps the last stake of our finances.[52]

The former prime minister knew that British businessmen, including the men of movable property, investors, and the state needed access to smoothly functioning asset and debt markets: Britain's economic well-being and geopolitical stature depended on their stability. After 1766 the speculative booms surrounding East India stock threatened the equilibrium of London's capital markets.[53]

48. Bowen, "British Politics and the East India Company," 437–48.

49. Ian R. Christie, *Wars and Revolutions: Britain, 1760–1812* (Cambridge, Mass., 1982), 82.

50. Commons debate, 28 February 1768, Cavendish Diary, Egerton MSS 218, fols. 175–76.

51. Bowen, "Investment and Empire," 195–96.

52. Commons debate, 28 February 1769, Cavendish Diary, Egerton MSS 218, fols. 175–76.

53. The day after news of the Company's assumption of the *diwani* reached London in April 1766, East India stock jumped from 164 to 172 and then to 190. By 1767 the price stood at 273. In 1769, when London investors learned that French forces were gathering at Mauritius off the eastern coast of Africa for a possible invasion of India, Company stock fell quickly from 273 to 250 and continued to fall to 239 a month later. As Lucy Sutherland

As important as the financial repercussions of the Company's new power were the economic issues confronting statesmen and Company servants. During the Seven Years War, exports from England to Asia, as well as those to North America and Europe, had climbed to record levels, stimulated primarily by military demand. Beginning in 1763, British exports to India began to slacken, a cyclical response to the end of major hostilities there. In 1767, however, British exports rose 62 percent, from £784,000 in 1766 to almost £1.3 million. The value of goods sent to the eastern subcontinent remained high through 1771.[54]

During the later 1760s, most MPs were more concerned with the financial issues surrounding British involvement in India than with trade questions. But statesmen who were interested in imperial governance, such as Lord North and Shelburne, remained absorbed by the economic problems and possibilities raised by the Company's de facto sovereignty. They were anxious to exploit India's potential as a market for British goods—a role that became increasingly significant as North American markets appeared more precarious.[55] Speaking before the Commons in 1769, North voiced his economic ambitions for Britain's eastern dominions: "We have reason to hope that the consequences of these great [Indian] acquisitions will be an endeavor to extend our trade, to find out new countries, to discover sources of commerce hitherto unexplored."[56]

By the early 1770s North, Edmund Burke, and others understood that the commercial and financial implications of East India Company

has written, East India stock "gained a new and unfavourable reputation as a 'very fluctuating and gaming Stock' and there can be no doubt from 1766 onwards it became the chief subject of speculative dealings on world markets and that by contemporary standards the volume of these speculative dealings was very large." *The East India Company in Eighteenth Century Politics* (Westport, Conn., 1979), 141.

54. Mitchell and Deane, 310.

55. Lord North, Commons debate, 27 February 1769, Cavendish Diary, Egerton MSS 218, fols. 105–7; *Importance of British Dominions*, 10–11; Alexander Dow, *The History of Hindostan*, 2 vols. (London, 1768), vol. 2, appendix, 94; See also Peter Marshall, *Problems of Empire: Britain and India, 1757–1813* (London, 1968), 91; M. E. Yapp, " 'The Brightest Jewel': Origins of a Phrase," in *East India Company Studies: Papers Presented to Professor Sir Cyril Philips*, ed. Kenneth Ballhatchet and John Harrison (Hong Kong, 1986), 35, 44. Vincent Harlow has noted that the "British empire of trade in Asia" did not develop fully until the late 1780s and early 1790s (*The Founding of the Second British Empire, 1763–1793*, 2 vols. [New York, 1952–64], 2:486). But significant government and commercial concern with eastern outlets for British manufactures emerged in the 1760s.

56. Commons debate, 27 February 1769, Cavendish Diary, Egerton MSS 218, fols. 105–7. See also William Bolts, *Considerations on Indian Affairs* (London, 1772), 227; *Importance of the British Dominions*.

activity were closely linked to the fate of the empire. In 1773 Pownall commented on this mutual dependency:

People now at last begin to view those Indian affairs, not simply as beneficial appendages connected to the empire; but from the participation of their revenues being brought into the very composition and frame of our finances; from the commerce of that country being indissolubly interwoven with our whole system of commerce; from the intercommunion of funded property between the Company and the state—people in general from these views begin to see such a union of interest, such a co-existence between the two, that they tremble with horror even at the imagination of the downfall of this Indian part of our system; knowing that it must necessarily involve with its fall, the ruin of the whole edifice of the British empire.[57]

Before the Commons, Burke was even more emphatic about the challenges India posed to imperial management. In reference to Clive's recent parliamentary speech on India's economic and financial possibilities, he said:

We are bound by the Noble Lord's arguments. He has laid open such a world of commerce, he has laid open so valuable an Empire both from our present possessions and future operations, and revenue as I believe never was laid before any Committee in so short words. The orient sun never laid more glorious expectations before us . . . You are plunged into Empire in the east. You have formed a great body of power, you must abide by the consequence.[58]

In the late 1760s, few officials were certain how to "abide by the consequence" of Britain's empire in the east. How, and to what extent, was the state to manage these new dominions? Clive, Pownall, and others thought that India should be fully integrated into the imperial system. According to this reasoning, the mother country would benefit from considering all its colonies as constituent parts of an ordered economy. If British exports to America were threatened, more goods would be sent to India. If revenues could not be raised in Boston, they would be obtained in Bengal. If Indian subjects could not afford British metal-

57. Pownall, 10.
58. Commons debate, 27 February 1769, Cavendish Diary, Egerton MSS 218, fol. 161.

wares, these manufactures would be shipped to New York. Losses, fore-
seen or actual, in one part of the empire would be offset by gains in
another.[59] As one commentator noted, "The East India] Company's dominions in the East are part of the British Empire, and that unless the
state views the transactions of that country as that of the great body of
the nation, there is wanting that harmony and universal bond of interest
which secures the prosperity of national affairs."[60] George Colebrooke,
an MP and East India Company director, called for regulated economic
relations between India and America. In Parliament, he said: "Let us
try to give permanency to these [eastern] acquisitions, and by doing so
secure the prosperity of Great Britain. Let us open a connection between
the East Indies and our American colonies—[between William Beckford's
West Indian] sugars and my sugars. You cannot be sovereigns in one
part and merchants in another. India should be combined into one
system."[61]

Throughout the postwar decade, statesmen, political economists, and
others became more aware of the connections—intended and unfore-
seen—between the empire's western and eastern parts. The state's 1767
agreement with the East India Company had included tax concessions
on the tea exported to North America. In 1768 and 1769 American
colonists had staged boycotts of British goods, including tea, to protest
the Townshend duties. The campaign against tea proved very successful,
and Company shipments of the commodity fell from over 868,000
pounds in 1767 to 108,000 in 1770.[62] By the late 1760s most government
officials recognized that the Indian and American economies could not
be governed as discrete units.[63]

This not to argue that most statesmen in 1770 thought India was as
commercially significant to Britain as America. Ministers, legislators, and
colonial experts firmly believed that politically and economically America
was the most important of the dominions. As Lord North said in 1768,
"Great as the [East] Indies may be in point of revenue and navigation,

59. Bowen, *Revenue and Reform*, 25.

60. *An Address to the Proprietors of India Stock, Showing from the Political State of Indostan the Necessity of Sending Commissioners to Regulate Their Affairs Abroad* (London, 1769), 30, quoted in Bowen, *Revenue and Reform*, 25.

61. Commons debate, 27 February 1769, Cavendish Diary, Egerton MSS 218, fols. 134–35.

62. Benjamin W. Labaree, *The Boston Tea Party* (Oxford, 1964), 331.

63. See, for example, Commons debate, 7 December 1768, Cavendish Diary, Egerton MSS 215, fols. 289–303; Commons debate, 5 March 1770, Cavendish Diary, Egerton MSS 221, fols. 27–28.

it can't be put in competition with America."[64] But British officials learned that affirming the preeminence of the western dominions did not ensure efficient governance there. As American challenges to metropolitan authority increased, legislators, and Company servants realized that East Indian commerce and revenues could be used for imperial ends.

This collective realization did not constitute a cohesive vision of an integrated global empire. Bowen contends that the policies connecting East India Company fortunes to North American commerce were short-term expedients and were "not intended as the development of a larger system of trade." He points out that only a handful of men in the 1760s were prepared to sanction and articulate proposals for India's incorporation into the empire on the same terms as America.[65] But the absence of such plans does not invalidate contemporaries' interest—explicit and implicit—in managing Britain's eastern territories toward the same broad objectives as those that guided the governance of America. In and outside government, imperial authorities understood that India and America were to be ruled to ensure Britain access to the markets and revenues on which its international power depended. If one part of the empire could not provide these economic sinews, then they must be obtained elsewhere. For metropolitan policymakers, geopolitical exigency drew the western and eastern dominions into closer commercial relations. The demands of England's preeminence also forced the British state to play a much larger role in India.

As prime minister in the early 1770s, North was not eager to involve the state more actively in the government of India. He and other politicians understood that additional state responsibility on the subcontinent presented a host of practical and political obstacles. The practical problems centered on personnel and administrative issues. Only a small group of government officials had expert knowledge of or significant experience with Indian commerce or politics.[66] In 1770 the administrative structure of the state was not particularly well suited to collecting and coordinating

64. Commons debate, 7 December 1768, Cavendish Diary, Egerton MSS 218, fol. 297. See Bowen's analysis of contemporary comparisons of India and America, *Revenue and Reform*, 26–27.

65. Bowen, *Revenue and Reform*, 25–26.

66. On contemporary knowledge of India, see Marshall, *Problems of Empire*, 24, 53, and Bowen, *Revenue and Reform*, 30–32. There was a core group of MPs and ministers who had experience with Indian issues. Bowen notes that many of the MPs who spoke on Indian affairs in the House of Commons between 1768 and 1774 were "simply making available much-needed expert advice which had been acquired during periods of Company or military service on the subcontinent" (ibid., 32).

information relevant to India. East India Company matters were the Treasury's responsibility; Indian issues were handled by the secretary of state for the southern department.

The political problems surrounding state responsibility in India were equally formidable. Any attempt by the government to increase its involvement on the subcontinent risked political conflict with those MPs who had East India Company interests.[67] An expanded state role in India also upset those legislators who feared the growth of ministerial and royal power. Finally, some statesmen worried that British power was overextended. According to this line of reasoning, additional responsibilities would prove the administrative and commercial undoing of the empire.

For eighteen months beginning in 1770, the North ministry had avoided state action on Indian issues, allowing Company servants to settle their own affairs.[68] But in mid-1772 financial and economic events overwhelmed the government's reluctance to air East India issues in Parliament. During the summer, a Europeanwide credit crisis resulted in the closing of numerous London and provincial banks.[69] The effects of the crisis spread quickly: "Like a company connected by an electrical wire, the people in every corner of the country have almost instantaneously received the same shock,"[70] commented James Boswell. David Hume described the repercussions of the national specie shortage to Adam Smith: "We are here in a very melancholy Situation: Continual Bankruptcies, universal Loss of Credit and endless Suspicions."[71] In Yorkshire, Lancashire, London, and elsewhere, various businesses, especially textile concerns, closed their doors. As Shelburne wrote to Chatham, "The distress for money is inconceivable. The manufacturers throughout the kingdom feel it most materially."[72]

67. On the complexities of Company politics, see ibid., 30–47, and Sutherland, 138–268.

68. P. D. G. Thomas, *Lord North* (London, 1976), 62. Lord North, as Bowen notes, was by no means ignorant of Indian affairs or unprepared to deal with the political and practical challenges to state intervention (*Revenue and Reform*, 98–99). The prime minister had known as early as the autumn of 1771 that parliamentary discussion of Indian issues could not be postponed indefinitely. At that time he had begun formulating a substantive, politically acceptable response to the Indian problem.

69. On the origins of this crisis, see Julian Hoppit, "Financial Crises in Eighteenth-Century England," *Economic History Review* 39 (1986): 50–54.

70. James Boswell, *Reflections on the Late Alarming Bankruptcies in Scotland* (Edinburgh, 1772), 1.

71. David Hume to Adam Smith, 27 June 1772, in *The Correspondence of Adam Smith*, ed. Ernest Campbell Mossner and Ian Simpson Ross (Oxford, 1977), 162.

72. Shelburne to the earl of Chatham, 25 April 1773, in *Correspondence of William Pitt, Earl of Chatham*, ed. William Stanhope Taylor and John Henry Pringle, 4 vols. (London, 1838–40), 4:262.

So did the East India Company. By autumn the concern was unable to declare a dividend, pay customs duties, or negotiate a large loan from the Bank of England. Some of the Company's liquidity problems were attributable to the credit crisis, some revolved around its cash-management techniques,[73] and others were a result of declining tea sales in America. Still others were a function of the Company's falling revenue collections in Bengal and Bihar.[74] Regardless of their origins, the Company's financial troubles threatened its annual payment to the Treasury. These problems also jeopardized the value of Company stock: by September its price had fallen below 200, the lowest level in fifteen months. Public indignation and fear mounted, nourished by rumors of financial and administrative mismanagement at India House.

The administration could no longer stand aside. Parliament was called to a special session to consider the Company's operations. When the legislature convened in November, the economic and political pressures for state intervention in Indian affairs were running high. Burke, who had vociferously opposed the first East India Company inquiry, commented glumly, "By an unhappy and rare conjuncture of circumstances, the designs of the Court coincide exactly with the phrensy of the people."[75] Before the Commons in December 1772, North announced the ministry's aim in opening a legislative inquiry: "It is the wish of parliament, and particularly of [the] administration, to make the East India Company a great and glorious Company, and settle it upon a permanent foundation. They are going into an expensive commission, at a time when they are considerably in arrears to government, at an expence . . . of £120,000. Surely . . . it is the duty of parliament to preserve [the Company] from ruin."[76]

The prime minister was determined to proceed cautiously. On his

---

73. Burke believed the Company's finances were basically sound. He attributed their "present embarrassment" to a "difficulty with regard to Cash: Into this difficulty they could never have fallen by the mismanagements of their servants abroad, though these have been, I make no Doubt, very considerable and very culpable; It is the rapine of Parliament . . . that ha[s] now given theirs and publick Credit such a Shock." (Edmund Burke to Rockingham, 23 November 1772, in *Correspondence of Edmund Burke*, vol. 2, *July 1768 to June 1774*, ed. Lucy S. Sutherland [Chicago, 1960], 383–84). For a historical analysis of the East India Company's liquidity troubles in 1772, see Bowen, *Revenue and Reform*, 119–27.

74. Bowen, *Revenue and Reform*, 103–4.

75. Edmund Burke to William Dowdeswell, 6, 7 November 1772, in *Correspondence of Edmund Burke*, ed. Sutherland, 365.

76. Commons debate, 7 December 1772, in *The Parliamentary History of England from the Earliest Period to the Year 1803*, ed. William Cobbett, 36 vols. (London, 1806–20), 17:561. See also Cavendish Diary, Egerton MSS 243, fols. 82–83.

A New Scene for the Proprietors of India Stock

Leave the glory's of your deeds. But I my have Money.

Save us my Lord or we Perish.

You shall have the wealth of my Indies

Report of the Secret Comittee

India Stock no Price

Job in the Alley gone off

The Present times, or the Nabobs CL-VE and C-L-KE brought to Account.
Deel awa wi em au R-gues all alike, Bribers & Bribed

The Present Times, or the Nabobs Clive and Colebrooke Brought to Account, printed
1 May 1773. British Museum Catalogue 5111. Printed in the midst of parliamentary debate on the Regulatory Act, this plate depicts Robert Clive and George Colebrooke offering East India Company revenues to Lord North. In the foreground Colebrooke, an MP and Company director, pleads for government aid for the troubled trading concern. Behind him, Clive pledges to North a portion of his personal claim on Indian revenues. In the background in Highlander's dress, Lord Bute tries to protect the two men from the sword of justice.

initiative, a secret committee was established to "enquire into the state of the East India Company; . . . to inspect the books and accounts of the said Company; and to report to the House what they find material therein, in respect to the debts, credits, and effects of the Company, as also to the management and present situation of the Company's affairs."[77] Under the auspices of Charles Jenkinson, this committee produced nine reports over the next six months. These reports were comprehensive accounts of Company operations at India House and on the distant subcontinent. Although they made no specific policy recommendations, they represented the first significant attempt by the British state to acquire the background information it would need for active intervention in Indian governance.

Through the first half of 1773, Parliament debated the fate of the East India Company. In an early session of the assembled Commons, North justified government involvement in Company operations. He first pointed to legal arguments, saying; "Many men, far my superiors in abilities, in learning, and knowledge of the laws, have declared themselves of this opinion . . . that 'such territorial possessions as the subjects of any state shall acquire by conquest, are virtually the property of the state, and not of those individuals who acquire them.' "[78] The prime minister then turned to the fiscal implications of the government's claim. Since the Company could acquire nothing by conquest but for the state, he continued, "The public has been entitled to these conquests and, having agreed with the Company to let them remain in possession on certain conditions, was as well entitled to [the] £400,000 [annual payment the Company had been making to the state] as any gentleman to his land. The Company in that respect are farmers to the public."[79] There were also commercial reasons, according to North, for government action in East Indian affairs. With annual receipts of almost £4 million and British export sales of £400,000, the Company "is of too great a consequence, considered in a commercial light, not to call our attention to its welfare."[80] To assist the financially troubled concern, the minister proposed an immediate government loan of £1.4 million. This sum would be advanced only on condition that Company operations were reformed.

The opposition, composed chiefly of Lord Rockingham and his sup-

77. Commons debate, 26 November 1772, in *Parliamentary History*, 17:528.
78. Commons debate, 9 March 1773, in *Parliamentary History*, 17:803.
79. Commons debate, 9 March 1773, Cavendish Diary, Egerton MSS 244, fol. 288.
80. Commons debate, 9 March 1773, in *Parliamentary History*, 17:804; Cavendish Diary, Egerton MSS 244, fols. 297–98.

porters, immediately challenged the administration's plan and rationale for intervention. As they had in 1767, the Rockinghams challenged any legislative decision on the Company's right to territory and revenues. According to the political group's chief spokesmen, Burke and William Dowdeswell, eastern lands and money belonged solely to the trading concern. Any other acknowledgment constituted an assault on property rights—an attack completely inimical to the interests of commerce. Dowdeswell explained this position before the Commons:

Respecting those territorial acquisitions the English East India Company hath made in Asia, every dispute relative thereto must be settled by the Company itself, the crown of England ha[s] no right to interfere in what is allowed to be the legal and exclusive property of a body corporate belonging to the English nation . . .

I think the proposition [that the territorial acquisitions of the Company belong of right and justice to the state] utterly repugnant to truth; and in behalf of an injured Company, I here stand up to disavow such notions, as inconsistent with the chartered rights of the Company, as inconsistent with that encouragement which should ever be given in a commercial state to companies of such consequence as that trading to the East Indies.[81]

The largest chartered body in the country, the city of London, echoed Dowdeswell's views in its petition to Parliament. The mayor, aldermen, and common council of London contended that state regulation of the East India Company represented "a direct and dangerous attack on the liberties of the people." Such government interference in a chartered company carried "the most fatal consequences to the security of property in general and particularly the franchises of every corporate body in this kingdom."[82]

Although the opposition relied primarily on constitutional arguments, the Rockinghams sounded other objections to government intervention. During the first East India inquiry of 1767, Rockingham's followers had feared the growth of ministerial and royal power that accompanied state involvement in Company affairs.[83] Five years later, they returned to this

81. Commons debate, 9 March 1773, in *Parliamentary History*, 17:801, 806.
82. "The Petition of the City of London against Lord North's Regulating Act," 28 May 1773, *Journals of the House of Commons*, 34:343.
83. In 1767 the Grenvillites had also been concerned with the corrupting effects of increased royal power. Grenville's death in 1770 had robbed his supporters of their previous political effectiveness, and they played a much smaller role in the debates of 1772 and 1773.

theme: spokesmen for the group contended that state management of Indian trade and revenues would perilously increase the powers of the Crown and corrupt the body politic.[84] The more influence and wealth the government gathered, Burke contended, the more venal its objectives became:

In the year 1767, [the] administration discovered, that the East India Company were guardians to a very handsome and rich lady in Hindostan. Accordingly, they set parliament in motion: and parliament, (whether from love to her person or fortune is, I believe, no problem), parliament directly became a suitor, and took the lady into its tender, fond, grasping arms, pretending all the while that it meant nothing but what was fair and honourable; that no rape or violence was intended.[85]

Because the stakes of government action in 1773 were considerably higher, he continued, the results could only be worse. The ultimate fate of the British empire would be that of Rome:

God knows that the places and pensions and expectancies furnished by the British establishment, are too powerful for the small remains of patriotism and public spirit in our island. What, then, will become of us, if Bengal, if the Ganges pour in a new tide of corruption? Should the evil genius of British liberty so ordain it, I fear this House will be so far from removing the corruption of the East, that it will be corrupted by them. I dread more from the infection of that place, than I hope from your virtue. Was it not the sudden plunder of the East that gave the final blow to the freedom of Rome? What reason have we to expect a better fate?[86]

Legislators recognized the potential validity of the Rockinghams' objections. Many independent MPs worried that an abridgment of the Company's chartered rights threatened the sanctity of individual and corporate property rights.[87] As historian Peter Marshall has observed, "Few men seriously contended that charters could not be revised by Parliament as circumstances altered or for the greater good of the community,

---

84. Rockingham to Edmund Burke, 28 October 1772, in *Correspondence of Edmund Burke*, ed. Sutherland, 344.

85. 18 December 1772, in *Parliamentary History*, 17:671.

86. Ibid., 672–73; see also 856–58.

87. Marshall, *Problems of Empire*, 22. A considerable number of MPs temporized on the issue of state regulation in 1773, refusing to join government or opposition factions. See Sutherland, *East India Company*, 240, and Yapp, 50–51.

but this could only be done with the utmost circumspection and after exhaustive investigation."[88] Members also understood Burke's suspicions about the corrupting effects of state involvement in the Company. These were long-standing fears, with a political history almost as old as that of the Company.

But in 1773 all arguments against government intervention were overwhelmed by economic factors. By late spring these factors convinced a majority of MPs that the state had to assume a significant role in overseeing Company activities in Leadenhall Street and India. A general credit crisis threatened the trading concern and London financial markets. Without state action, the soundness of government and business debt was jeopardized. All over the country, merchants and manufacturers complained about the shortage of money and the instability of trade credit.[89] As important, the Company's precarious financial condition endangered the concern's annual payment to the Treasury and other potential Indian revenues.[90] As the prime minister said before the Commons in April, "We are on a precipice; the object of £400,000 we look down so far upon that its magnitude is diminished; and if we offer to stoop to grasp it, we shall fall headlong down to the ruin of ourselves, and the Company too. I am clearly of opinion, that the first business to be attended to, is to fix the Company on a firm and solid footing."[91] The magnitude of these liquidity problems underscored the Company's other economic responsibilities. In the face of unreliable American outlets, Far Eastern markets for British goods had to be carefully managed. To most MPs, the power of Indian commerce—both the potential revenues and the trade of the subcontinent—appeared too important to be left to a divided and financially troubled Company. As one back-bencher said:

This is an object of such magnitude, that every member of this House who thinks of its importance, and the difficulties which attend it, must tremble at entering on the discussion; yet entered on it must be, and without delay . . . [T]his is no trifling question between ministry and opposi-

88. Marshall, *Problems of Empire*, 22.

89. By September, in Leeds there was "scarce any Money to be got on personal Secur'y" (quoted in Hoppit, 52).

90. Under the terms of earlier agreements, the Company's £400,000 annual payment to the Treasury was paid in two equal six-month installments. In September 1772, financial difficulties had forced Company directors to postpone the biannual £200,000 payment due that month.

91. Commons debate, 5 April 1773, in *Parliamentary History*, 17:832; Cavendish Diary, Egerton MSS 245, fols. 253–54.

tion, whether men of this or that description shall ascend the thrones of Leadenhall-street. It is the stake of empire; and on the issue, perhaps, will be determined, whether Great Britain is to be the first nation of the world, or a ruined and undone country.[92]

Amid general anxiety about the East India Company's operations, a bill emerged from Parliament in April. The legislation had several purposes. To oversee Company relations with native states in India, the bill established a governor-general and council in Bengal. The Crown was to name the appointees to these posts. A supreme court of judicature, staffed by Crown nominees, was appointed to protect Indian subjects from exploitation by Company servants. The bill also attempted to reform India House affairs.[93] Government oversight was increased by requiring Company directors to transmit all correspondence from India to either the secretary of state or the Treasury within fourteen days of its arrival.

In return for these extensive reforms, the North ministry offered the Company significant financial and commercial assistance. The trading concern secured a £1.4 million loan from the government and an outlet for its seventeen million pounds of unsold tea.[94] The Tea Act of 1773 allowed the Company to sell its surplus stocks of the commodity directly to North America, appointing its own agents on commission. By late June the Regulating Act had passed both houses and become law.[95]

It was legislation without precedent. Laurence Sulivan, an MP and a

92. William Burrell, Commons debate, 26 November 1772, in *Parliamentary History*, 17:522–23. See also George Germain's comments in Commons debate, 18 December 1772, in *Parliamentary History*, 17:663.

93. The legislation raised voting qualifications for the General Court, the body of Company stockholders that made major policy decisions. Before the 1773 act, those holding £500 or more in Company stock were eligible to vote on Company business. This stipulation had led to the widespread practice of stock splitting. By subdividing a particular holding into £500 blocks for distribution to specific individuals, votes could be created to affect Company operations. It was widely perceived by 1773 that vote splitting had exacerbated the anarchy of the General Court and resulted in poor management of Company assets. The Regulating Act doubled the voting qualification and required that stock be held for at least twelve months before the shareholder became enfranchised.

94. Unsold tea estimates are from North's parliamentary speech in April (Commons debate, 26 April 1773, Cavendish Diary, Egerton MSS 246, fol. 2).

95. The final legislation involving the Company consisted of three acts: 13 George III, c. 63, the Regulating Act, which incorporated the ministry's reforms in Company organization and in Indian administration; 13 George III, c. 64, the Loan Act, which gave the trading concern the state loan; and 13 George III, c. 44, the Tea Act, which granted the Company concessions on the tea exported to America.

veteran of Company politics, thought that the Regulating Act would eventually vest virtual control of the concern in the state. He called North "the boldest minister the realm had been blest with since the days of Oliver Cromwell."[96] Sulivan overstated the act's intent and consequences,[97] but he understood that it represented the British government's new commitment to undertake some of the financial, administrative, and commercial responsibilities of its eastern dominions.

That commitment evolved haltingly in the imperial experience of the postwar decade. The Seven Years War victory had clarified older ideas of global authority and their relation to economic performance, giving these conceptions new urgency and importance. The country's changing economy gave them new form. After 1763 statesmen knew that to remain a world power, Britain would need to sell its manufactures in distant markets and raise substantial government revenues.

As the difficulties of levying taxes and securing markets in North America mounted, metropolitan authorities became increasingly concerned with India.[98] A host of obstacles confronted government officials considering state action toward the subcontinent. Most of these problems were political, but some were perceptual. Throughout the postwar period, legislators and others expressed significant ambivalence about the consequences of Indian dominion. Perhaps the subcontinent's potential was too rich for Britain. As William Meredith, MP for Liverpool, said, "We might also have considered whether it is at this crisis prudent, whether it is rational to make so vast an addition to the British empire, sinking already under the weight of its own greatness."[99] There were other barriers to effective state rule in India. It was six months by sea from London to Bengal. In 1773 only a handful of ministers and MPs had actually been to India;[100] a few more had substantial experience with Indian ways of life. The cultural expanse separating most Britons from the peoples and history of India may have exceeded the geographic distance.

But in 1773, geopolitical imperatives dominated the problems posed

96. Laurence Sulivan to Warren Hastings, undated, Add. MSS 29,194, fols. 84–85.

97. See Marshall, *Problems of Empire*, 34–35.

98. On the outpouring of British interest in India in the mid-1760s, see *Annual Register* 10 (1767): 41–45; Isaac Barré's speech, Commons debate, 27 February 1769, Cavendish Diary, Egerton MSS 218, fol. 114; Nancy F. Koehn, "The Power of Commerce: Political Economy in the First British Empire" (Ph.D. diss., Harvard University, 1990), 311–12.

99. Quoted in Yapp, 51.

100. Of the Parliament elected in 1768, only nineteen members had visited India (Bowen, *Revenue and Reform*, 30).

by Indian governance. To the east and west, the costs of empire had to be borne. Looking outward from London that summer, statesmen realized that the commerce of India and America was entwined with Britain's imperial future. They could not see that the prospects for regulated trade between the eastern and western dominions would quickly prove so disastrous.[101] What legislators knew with certainty was that the resources of India represented a possible solution to some of the fiscal and economic problems of empire. These problems and the policies chosen to address them in 1773 continued to shape the Anglo-Indian connection well into the nineteenth century.

101. Thirteen months after the Boston Tea Party, North said that it had been impossible in 1773 to foresee the consequences of the East Indian legislation (Commons debate, 23 January 1775, in *Parliamentary History*, 18:177–78).

Afterword

IN DECEMBER 1782, twenty years after the preliminaries to the Peace of Paris were announced, George III considered another treaty. The introspective monarch had been ebullient about the earlier settlement. But he displayed a serious countenance as he addressed Parliament on this gray winter's day some two decades into his reign. As he and others knew, the country's victory in the Seven Years War had put weight on the *corpus imperium*—territorial bulk with the potential to make Britain strong, vital, and prosperous or fat, indolent, and impotent. Within the dynamic formed by these contrasting perspectives, Britons throughout the 1760s had tried to come to terms with their new stature.

In 1782, looking back across the War for America, George III was pessimistic about the outcome of these exertions. In corporeal language, he bemoaned the loss of the thirteen colonies: "I make it my humble and earnest prayer to Almighty God, that Great Britain may not feel the evils which result from so great a dismemberment of the Empire."[1] Along with many others, the king believed that, bereft of America, Britain would degenerate into a minor power, unable to check Bourbon preponderance.[2] The collective anxieties that accompanied the country's victory

---

1. "King's Speech on Opening the Session of Parliament," 5 December 1782, in *The Parliamentary History of England from the Earliest Period to the Year 1803*, ed. William Cobbett, 36 vols. (London, 1806–20), 23:203.

2. Ian R. Christie, *Wars and Revolutions: Britain, 1760–1815* (Cambridge, Mass., 1982), 158.

in 1763 had been painfully vindicated. As Shelburne commented gloomily in 1782, "The sun of England might be said to have set."[3]

But of course the empire's fate was not nearly so dark. Powered by a growing economy, by expanding, freer trade with an independent America and the far East, and by men—such as Shelburne, Burke, Fox and the younger Pitt—who understood the interrelations between the nation's commercial strength and its global status, Britain in the coming years was to see ever more sunlight shine on its dominions. Imperial historians have credited British ascendancy between 1783 and 1813 to these economic and political factors. Scholars have paid less attention to the connections between policymaking and perceptions in the first decade of the empire and its life after the American Revolution.

Imperial problems and opportunities after the Peace of Versailles have seemed very different historiographically from those that a victorious Britain confronted after the settlement of 1763, also signed in the splendor of a French palace. But statesmen who tried during the 1780s to manage the power of commerce to national advantage in France, Madras, and Philadelphia saw no real disjuncture between the imperatives of the first and second empires. What kind of dominion was Britain to have? A commercial power, committed to selling as many of its manufactures as possible, Shelburne answered confidently in 1786 amid discussions over the Eden Treaty.

The first empire had given birth to the form and structure of imperial governance in the late eighteenth century. How was Britain to pay for and rule this trading dominion? At the close of the American War these were complicated and contingent questions, but they owed much to the political economy, configurations, and perspectives of the empire Britain earned in the Seven Years War. Within a changing economy, Britons in 1782 faced the challenges of their nation's predominance. This was the stuff of which the empire was made in 1763, injured in 1782, and reconstituted in the ensuing century.

3. Lord Shelburne, Lords Debate, 10 July 1782, *Parliamentary History* 23:217–18.

❧❧❧ Bibliography

Note to the reader. An expanded bibliography, including secondary sources, is available from the author.

Manuscript Sources

Bank of England, London
  Stock Ledger Books
Bodleian Library, Oxford
  Dashwood MSS
  North MSS
  Shelburne Papers, Bowood Muniments
British Library, London
  Bute MSS
  Egerton MSS
  Grenville MSS
  Hardwicke MSS
  Liverpool MSS
  Newcastle MSS
Clements Library, Ann Arbor, Michigan
  Dowdeswell Papers
  Shelburne Papers
  Townshend Papers
East India Company, London
  Committee of Correspondence (Memoranda, Reports)
  Court Books
John Rylands Library, Manchester
  Legge Correspondence
  Wedgwood Correspondence

Public Record Office, Kew Gardens
  Board of Trade Papers
  Chatham MSS
  State Papers, Colonial America and West Indies
  Treasury Papers
Scottish Public Record Office, Edinburgh
  Dalkeith MSS
Sheffield City Library
  Burke MSS
  Rockingham MSS
  Wentworth-Woodhouse Muniments (WWM)

Pamphlet Sources

[Almon, John], ed. *A Collection of the Most Interesting Tracts, Lately Published in England and America, on the Subjects of Taxing the American Colonies and Regulating Their Trade.* 2 vols. London, 1766.
————. *A Review of Lord Bute's Administration.* London, 1763.
————. *A Review of Mr. Pitt's Administration.* London, 1764.
Anderson, Adam. *An Historical and Chronological Deduction of the Origin of Commerce from the Earliest Accounts to the Present Time.* 2 vols. London, 1764.
An Application of Political Rules to Great Britain, Ireland, and America. London, 1766.
Bentley, Thomas. *To the Tradesmen of This Kingdom in General, Especially the Manufactures, Warehousemen, Publicans and Shopkeepers of London, Westminster and Southwork.* London, 1766.
————. *A View of the Advantages of Inland Navigation with a Plan of a Navigable Canal.* London, 1766.
Bolts, William. *Considerations on Indian Affairs.* London, 1772.
Boswell, James. *Reflections on the Late Alarming Bankruptcies in Scotland.* Edinburgh, 1772.
The Case of Great Britain and America, Addressed to the King, and Both Houses of Parliament. London, 1769.
Child, Josiah. *A Discourse about Trade.* London, 1690.
————. "The Nature of Plantations, and Their Consequences to Great Britain, Seriously Considered." Written in 1669; published in *Dissertations on Colonies.* London, 1775.
————. *A New Discourse of Trade.* London, 1718.
The Comparative Importance of Our Aquisitions from France in America. London, 1762.
Considerations on the American Stamp Act and on the Conduct of the Minister Who Planned It. London, 1766.
Considerations on the Expediency of Admitting Representatives from the American Colonies into the British House of Commons. London, 1770.
Dalrymple, Alexander. *The Rights of the East India Company.* London, 1773.
Davenant, Charles. *Discourses on the Publick Revenues and the Trade of England.* 2 vols. London, 1698.
————. *A New Discourse on Trade.* London, 1693.

————. *An Essay on the East-India Trade.* London, 1696.

Davenant, Charles, Josiah Child, and William Wood. *Select Dissertations on Colonies and Plantations.* London, 1775.

Decker, Matthew. *An Essay on the Causes of the Decline of the Foreign Trade.* London, 1744.

————. *Serious Considerations on the Several High Duties Which the Nation in General (as Well as Trade in Particular) Labours Under.* London, 1744.

Defoe, Daniel, *A Tour Through the Whole Island of Great Britain, Divided into Circuits or Journies.* 3 vols. London, 1724.

A Detection of the False Reasons and Facts, Contained in the Five Letters, Entitled, Reasons for keeping Guadeloupe at a Peace, preferable to Canada; in which the Advantages of both Conquests are fairly and impartially stated and compared. By a member of Parliament. London, 1761.

Dickinson, John. *The Late Regulations respecting the British Colonies on the Continent of America Considered, in a Letter from a Gentleman in Philadelphia to His Friend in London.* London, 1766.

————. *Letters from a Farmer in Pennsylvania, to the Inhabitants of the British Colonies.* London, 1768.

Douglas, John. *A Letter Addressed to Two Great Men.* London, 1760.

Dow, Alexander. *The History of Hinostan.* 2 vols. London, 1768.

Dulaney, Daniel. *Considerations on the Propriety of Imposing Taxes in the British Colonies: For the Purpose of Raising a Revenue by Act of Parliament.* London, 1766.

Du Pont de Nemours, Pierre Samuel, ed. *Physiocratic, ou Constitution naturelle du gouvernement le plus avantageux du genre humain.* Paris, 1768.

Essay on the Trade of the Northern Colonies. London, 1764.

An Examination of the Commercial Principles of the Late Negotiation. London, 1762.

Fauquier, Francis. *An Essay on Ways and Means for Raising Money for the Support of the Present War without Increasing the Public Debts.* London, 1756.

Fielding, Henry. *Enquiry into the Causes of the Late Increase of Robbers, with Some Proposals for Remedying This Growing Evil.* London, 1751.

Foote, Samuel. *The Nabob.* London, 1772.

Forster, Nathaniel. *An Enquiry into the Causes of the Present High Price of Provisions.* London, 1767.

[Fothergill, John]. *Considerations relative to the North American Colonies.* London, 1765.

Franklin, Benjamin. *The Interest of Great Britain Considered with regard to Her Colonies.* London, 1760.

Grellier, J. J. *The History of the National Debt, from the Revolution in 1688 to the Beginning of the Year 1800.* London, 1810.

[Hartley, David]. *The Budget, Inscribed to the Man Who Thinks Himself Minister.* London, 1764.

[Heathcote, George]. *A Letter to the Right Honourable the Lord Mayor, the Worshipful Aldermen, and Common-Council; the Merchants, Citizens and Inhabitants, of the City of London: From an Old Servant* London, 1762.

Hume, David. *An Impartial Enquiry into the Right of the French King to the Territory West of the Great River Mississippi, in North America, Not Ceded by the Preliminaries.* London, 1762.

————. *Three Essays: On the Balance of Trade; On the Jealousy of Trade; On the Balance of Power.* London, 1787.

The Importance of the British Dominions in India Stated, and Compared with That in America. London, 1770.

Knox, William. *The Claim of the Colonies to an Exemption from Internal Taxes Imposed by Authority of Parliament, Examined: In a Letter from a Gentleman in London.* London, 1765.

————. *The Controversy between Great Britain and Her Colonies Reviewed.* London, 1769.

————. *Extra-official State Papers, Addressed to the Right Honourable Lord Rawdon.* 2 vols. London, 1789.

————. *The Interest of the Merchants and Manufacturers of Great Britain in the Present Contest with the Colonies Stated and Considered.* London, 1774.

————. *The Late Occurrences in North America, and Policy of Great Britain Considered.* London, 1766.

————. *A Letter from an Independent Man to His Friend in the Country, upon a Late Pamphlet Entitled,"Observations on the Papers relative to the Rupture with Spain."* London, 1762.

————. *A Letter to G[eorge] G[renville].* London, 1767.

————. *The Present State of the Nation: Particularly with respect to Its Trade, Finances etc. Addressed to the King and Both Houses of Parliament.* London, 1768.

A Letter to a Gentleman in the City with regard to the Contemplated Peace with France. London, 1762.

A Letter to the Gentlemen of the Committee of London Merchants, Trading to North America. London, 1766.

Lindsay, Patrick. *The Interest of Scotland Considered.* London, 1733.

[Lloyd, Charles]. *The Anatomy of a Late Negotiation: Earnestly Addressed to the Serious Consideration of the People of Great Britain.* London, 1763.

————. *A Critical Review of the New Administration.* London, 1765.

————. *A True History of a Late Short Administration.* London, 1766.

Malynes, Gerard de. *Center of the Circle of Commerce.* London, 1623.

Marriott, James. *Political Considerations, being a few Thoughts of a Candid Man at the Present Crisis.* London, 1762.

Massie, Joseph. *A Representation concerning the Knowledge of Commerce as a National Concern Pointing out the Proper Means of Promoting Such Knowledge in This Kingdom.* London, 1760.

Mauduit, Israel. *Considerations on the Present German War.* London, 1760.

————. *Occasional Thoughts on the Present German War.* London, 1761.

Mildmay, William. *The Laws and Policy of England relating to Trade.* London, 1765.

Mortimer, Thomas. *The Elements of Commerce, Politics and Finances in Three Treatises on Those Important Subjects.* London, 1772.

————. *The Mutual Interest of Great Britain and the American Colonies Considered.* London, 1765.

————. *Observations on the Review of the Controversy between Great Britain and Her Colonies.* London, 1770.

Observations on Public Liberty. London, 1769.

On the Plantation Trade. London, 1698 (reprinted 1775).

The Peace-Botchers: A New, Satyrical, Political Medley. London, 1762.
Plaine Path-Way to Plantations. London, 1624.
The Plain Reasoner, or Farther Considerations on the German War. London, 1761.
A Political Analysis of the War. London, 1762.
Postlethwayt, Malachy. *Britain's Commercial Interest Explained and Improved.* 2 vols. London, 1757.
———. *Great Britain's True System.* London, 1757.
———. *The Universal Dictionary of Trade and Commerce.* 2 vols. London, 1755.
Pownall, Thomas. *The Administration of the Colonies.* London, 1766.
———. *Principles of Polity, Being the Grounds and Reason of Civil Empire.* London, 1752.
———. *The Right, Interest, and Duty, of the State as Concerned in the Affairs of the East Indies.* London, 1773.
The Present State of the British Empire in Europe, America, Africa and Asia. 4 vols. London, 1768.
The Present State of the English East India Company's Affairs. London, 1772.
The Proper Object of the Present War with France and Spain Considered. London, 1762.
Proposals for Carrying on the War with Vigour, Raising the Supplies Within the Year, and Forming a National Militia. London, 1757.
Propositions for Improving the Manufactures, Agriculture, and Commerce of Great Britain. London, 1763.
Reasons for Keeping Guadeloupe at a Peace, Preferable to Canada, Explained in Five Letters from a Gentleman in Guadeloupe to His Friend in London. London, 1761.
Reasons for Raising a Fund for the Support of a Colony at Virginia. 1607.
Reflections on the Domestic Policy Proper to Be Observed on the Conclusion of the Peace. London, 1763.
Reflections on the Present State of Our East Indian Affairs. London, 1764.
Remarks on the Letter Addressed to Two Great Men. London, 1761.
A Reply to a Letter Addressed to the Right Honourable George Grenville. London, 1763.
Reynell, Carew. *The True English Interest.* London, 1679.
Ruffhead, Owen. *Considerations on the Present Dangerous Crisis.* Edinburgh, 1763.
———. *The Sentiments of an Impartial Member of Parliament.* London, 1762.
A Short History of the Conduct of the Present Ministry with regard to the American Stamp Act. London, 1766.
Sinclair, Sir John. *The History of the Public Revenue of the British Empire.* London, 1785–89.
Thoughts on Trade in General. London, 1763.
The Tradesmen's Director, or The London and County Shopkeeper's Useful Companion. London, 1756.
The Trade with France, Italy, Spain and Portugal Considered. With Some Observations on the Treaty of Commerce between Great Britain and France. London, 1713.
The True Whig Displayed. Comprehending Cursory Remarks on the Address to the Cocoa Tree. London, 1762.
Tucker, Josiah. *A Brief Essay on the Advantages and Disadvantages Which Respectively Attend France and Great Britain with regard to Trade.* London, 1767.
———. *The Case of Going to War for the Sake of Procuring, Enlarging or Securing of Trade.* London, 1763.

———. *Four Letters on Important National Subjects Addressed to the Right Honourable Earl of Shelburne.* 2d ed. London, 1783.

———. *Four Tracts Together with Two Sermons on Political and Commercial Subjects.* Gloucester, 1774.

———. *Instructions for Travellers.* London, 1758.

———. *A Letter from a Merchant in London to His Nephew in North America relative to the Present Posture of Affairs in the Colonies.* London, 1766.

———. *The Manifold Causes of the Increase of the Poor Distinctly Set Forth.* London, 1760.

———. *The True Interest of Great Britain Set Forth in regard to the Colonies.* Philadelphia, 1776.

Vanderlint, Jacob. *Money Answers All Things.* London, 1734.

Vansittart, Henry. *A Narrative of the Transactions in Bengal, 1760–1764.* London, 1766.

Verelst, Harry. *A View of the Rise, Progress and Present State of the English Government in Bengal.* London, 1772.

A Vindication of the Present Ministry, from the Many Flagrant Calumnies, Gross Misrepresentations and Evident Falsities in a book Entitled, "The History of the late Minority." London, 1766.

Whately, Thomas. *Considerations on the Trade and Finances of This Kingdom and on the Measures of Administration with respect to These Great National Objects Since the Conclusion of the Peace.* London, 1769.

———. *The Regulations Lately Made concerning the Colonies and the Taxes Imposed upon Them, Considered.* London, 1765.

[Wheelock, Matthew]. *Reflections, Moral and Political, on Great Britain and Her Colonies.* London, 1770.

Whiston, James. *A Discourse on the Decay of Trade.* London, 1693.

Wilkes, John, ed. *Political Controversy.* London, 1763.

Young, Arthur. *Political Essays concerning the Present State of the British Empire.* London, 1772.

———. *A Six Months' Tour through the North of England.* 3 vols. London, 1770.

Printed Sources
(Organized by Subject)

Bedford

Russell, Lord John, ed. *The Correspondence of John, Fourth Duke of Bedford.* 3 vols. London, 1842–46.

Board of Trade

Journals of the Commissioners for Trade and Plantations, 1704–1782. 15 vols. London, 1920–38.

Bowdoin

The Bowdoin Temple Papers. Collections of the Massachusetts Historical Society, 6th ser., 9 (1897).

Burke

Bate, W. J., ed. *Selected Works of Edmund Burke*. New York, 1960.
Copeland, T. W., Lucy S. Sutherland, et al., eds. *The Correspondence of Edmund Burke*. 10 vols. Chicago, 1958–78.
Langford, Paul, ed. *The Writings and Speeches of Edmund Burke*. 8 vols. to date. Oxford, 1980–.
The Works of the Right Honorable Edmund Burke. 12 vols. Boston, 1865–71.

Chatham

Taylor, W. Stanhope, and J.H . Pringle, eds. *The Correspondence of William Pitt, Earl of Chatham*. 4 vols. London, 1838–40.

DeBerdt

"Letters of Dennys DeBerdt, 1757–1770." *Publications of the Colonial Society of Massachusetts* 13 (1910–11): 293–461.

Devonshire

Brown, Peter D., and Karl W. Schweizer, eds. *The Devonshire Diary: William Cavendish, Fourth Duke of Devonshire: Memoranda on [the] State of Affairs, 1759–1762*. London, 1982.

East India Company

Fort William–India House Correspondence and Other Papers relating Thereto (Public Series). Vol. 4, 1764–66, ed. C. S. Srinivasachari (New Delhi, 1962); vol. 5, 1767–69. ed. N. K. Sinha (New Delhi, 1949); *(Select and Secret)*, vol. 6, 1770–72, ed. B. Prasad (New Delhi, 1960); *(Secret and Select Committee)*, vol. 14, 1752–81, ed. A. Prasad (New Delhi, 1985).

Fitch

The Fitch Papers: Correspondence and Documents during Thomas Fitch's Governorship of the Colony of Connecticut, 1754–1766. Vol. 2, 1749–66. Collections of the Connecticut Historical Society 18 (1920).

Franklin

Labaree, Leonard W., ed. *The Papers of Benjamin Franklin*. 29 vols. to date. New Haven, Conn., 1959–.

Gage

Carter, C. E., ed. *The Correspondence of General Thomas Gage with the Secretaries of State and with the War Office and the Treasury, 1763–1775*. New Haven, Conn., 1931–33.

Garth

Barnwell, J. W., ed. "The Correspondence of Charles Garth," *South Carolina Historical and Genealogical Magazine* 29 (1928–29).

George III

Fortescue, Sir John, ed. *The Correspondence of King George III from 1760 to 1783.* 6 vols. London, 1927–28.
Sedgwick, Romney, ed. *Letters from George III to Lord Bute, 1756–1766.* London, 1939.

Gibbon

Bury, J. B., ed. *The Autobiography of Edward Gibbon, as Originally Edited by Lord Sheffield.* London, 1972.
———. *The History of the Decline and Fall of the Roman Empire.* 7 vols. London, 1909–14.

Grafton

Anson, Sir William, ed. *Autobiography and Political Correspondence of Augustus Henry, Third Duke of Grafton.* London, 1896.

Grenville

Smith, W. J., ed. *The Grenville Papers. Being the Correspondence of Richard Grenville, Earl Temple, and the Right Honourable George Grenville, Their friends and Contemporaries.* 4 vols. London, 1852–53.
Tomlinson, John R. G., ed. *Additional Grenville Papers, 1763–1765.* Manchester, 1962.

Hardwicke

Yorke, P. C., *The Life and Correspondence of Philip Yorke, Earl of Hardwicke.* 3 vols. Cambridge, 1913.

Jenkinson

Jucker, Ninetta S., ed. *The Jenkinson Papers, 1760–1766.* London, 1949.

Johnson

"Letters of William Samuel Johnson to the Governors of Connecticut." *Trumbull Papers.* Collections of the Massachusetts Historical Society, 5th ser., 9 (1855): 211–490.

London Merchants

"London Merchants on Stamp Act Repeal." *Proceedings of the Massachusetts Historical Society* 55 (1921–22).

Lyttleton

Phillimore, Robert J. *The Memoirs and Correspondence of George, Lord Lyttleton, from 1734 to 1773.* 2 vols. London, 1845.

Parliament

Almon, John. *The Debates and Proceedings of the British House of Commons from 1743 to 1774.* 11 vols. London, 1766–75.

Cobbett, William, ed. *The Parliamentary History of England from the Earliest Period to the Year 1803.* 36 vols. London, 1806–20.

Journals of the House of Commons.

Parliamentary Diary of Matthew Brickdale, 1770–1774. 11 vols. Bristol University Library.

Public Income and Expenditure, 1688–1869 (Sessional Papers, 1868–69 vol. 35).

Simmons, R. C., and P. D. G. Thomas, eds. *Proceedings and Debates of the British Parliaments respecting North America, 1754–1783.* 6 vols. to date. Millwood, N.Y., 1982–.

Wright, J., ed. *Sir Henry Cavendish's Debates of the House of Commons during the Thirteenth Parliament of Great Britain.* 2 vols. London, 1841.

Rhode Island

The Commerce of Rhode Island, 1726–1800. Vol. 1, *1726–1774.* Collections of the Massachusetts Historical Society, 7th ser., 9 (1914).

Rockingham

Thomas, George, earl of Albermarle. *Memoirs of the Marquis of Rockingham and His Contemporaries.* 2 vols. London, 1852.

Ryder

Thomas, P. D. G., ed. *The Parliamentary Diaries of Nathaniel Ryder, 1764–1767.* London, 1969.

Shelburne

Fitzmaurice, Lord, ed. *Life of William, Earl of Shelburne: Afterwards First Marquis of Lansdowne, with Extracts from His Papers and Correspondence.* 2 vols. London, 1912.

Smith

Cannan, Edwin, ed. *An Inquiry into the Nature and Causes of the Wealth of Nations.* 2 vols. Chicago, 1976.

———, ed. *Lectures on Justice, Police, Revenue and Arms.* Oxford, 1896.

Mossner, Ernest Campbell, and Ian Simpson Ross, eds. *The Correspondence of Adam Smith.* Oxford, 1977.

Steuart

Skinner, Andrew S., ed. *An Inquiry into the Principles of Political Economy.* Introduction by Andrew Skinner. 2 vols. Edinburgh, 1966.

Strahan

Pomfret, J. E., ed. "Some Further Letters of William Strahan, Printer." *Pennsylvania Magazine of History and Biography* 60 (1936).

Tucker

Schuyler, Robert L., ed. *Josiah Tucker: A Selection from His Economic and Political Writings*. New York, 1931.

Turner

Vaisey, David, ed. *The Diary of Thomas Turner, 1754–1765*. Oxford, 1984.

Walpole

Walpole, Horace. *Memoirs of the Reign of George III*. 4 vols. London, 1894.

Index